The Chilean Kitchen

The Chilean Kitchen

Authentic, Homestyle Foods,

Regional Wines, and Culinary

Traditions of Chile

Ruth Van Waerebeek-Gonzalez

HPBooks

HPBooks
Published by The Berkley Publishing Group
A division of Penguin Putnam Inc.
375 Hudson Street
New York, New York 10014

Copyright © 1999 by Ruth Van Waerebeek-Gonzalez
Book design by Richard Oriolo
Cover design by Dorothy Wachtenheim
Cover photography by Philippe Desruelles, Santiago, Chile
Back cover photographs taken at the Hacienda los Lingues, Chile

"Ode to Conger Chowder" by Pablo Neruda, pages 114–115, from *Selected Odes of Pablo Neruda,* translated/edited by Margaret Sayers Peden, printed with permission of University of California Press

First edition: August 1999

Published simultaneously in Canada.

The Penguin Putnam Inc. World Wide Web site address is
http://www.penguinputnam.com

Library of Congress Cataloging-in-Publication Data

Van Waerebeek-Gonzalez, Ruth.
The Chilean kitchen : authentic, homestyle foods, regional wines, and culinary traditions of Chile / Ruth Van Waerebeek-Gonzalez.
p.   cm.
ISBN 1-55788-307-6
1. Cookery, Chilean. I. Title.
TX716.C5V36 1999
641.5983—dc21   99-13012
CIP

Printed in the United States of America

10 9 8 7 6 5 4 3 2 1

To Sergio, for introducing me
to his fascinating homeland,
Chile

Acknowledgments

How does one thank all the people who make a book possible?

Writing a cookbook involves a great deal of hard work. But it gives great satisfaction because one gets to meet so many interesting people. I will be forever thankful to the countless Chileans who so wholeheartedly opened their homes and kitchens, and who invited me to their generous tables.

I can't begin to thank the professional cooks, bakers, farmers, food and wine aficionados, and home cooks alike, whose dedication and hard work are at the core of Chile's unique and special appeal. All have nurtured this book at every step along the way. You will meet many in these pages but there are a great number who deserve special thanks.

To begin with the women in Sergio's extended family, especially his mother, Julia Gonzalez Galvez, who adopted me immediately as a second daughter. His aunt Digna Sanchez, a great cook; his sister, Julita; his many sisters-in-law and aunts; and the countless acquaintances and friends of the house. They all shared with me a profound appreciation for the bounty of their homeland.

I want to express my gratitude to Luis Toro and his family for introducing me to the "right" people but above all for sharing many wonderful bottles of his impressive wine collection with me.

I owe special thanks to Angel Germade Barros, the general manager of the Torres wineries in Curicó for his invaluable advice about the wine chapter.

Thank you also to the family Claro Lyon at the Hacienda "Los Lingues" who so generously opened their precious home and shared many old family recipes.

A heartfelt thanks to my dear friend Maria-Theresa Mosqueira, whose inventive and sharp mind and broad view of the Chilean culture and soul has been a constant source of inspiration.

A special thanks to Marcella, our dedicated cook in the restaurant, to my friend Pilar Vera in Melipilla, who let me consult a lifetime collection of cookbooks and boxes filled with recipe clippings. I also want to express my gratitude to La Señora Chita Ponce, a wonderful cook, for sharing her favorite family recipes with me.

Thank you to Philippe Desruelles, a talented young photographer, who captured so delicately the poetry of life in images.

This book wouldn't have been the same without Angelica, my maid, nanny, gardener, companion, and mentor, whose innate wisdom and deep knowledge of Nature were a constant source of delight.

Don Juan Pablo Asenjo, pastry chef extraordinaire and poet, graced this book with his expertise, recipes, food lore, and legends.

A heartfelt thanks goes to the family Yaconi where I experienced the legendary Chilean hospitality on so many occasions.

A very special thank-you to two dear friends Joyce Patton and Hans Polleman, who helped me out more than once in very critical moments.

And I want to express my profound gratitude to my agent, Jane Dystel, who believed in this project from the start and made miracles happen to see this book published.

I would also like to thank the entire crew at Penguin Putnam Inc., especially John Duff and Jeanette Egan for their skillful editing, guidance, and patience.

Contents

The Chilean Kitchen

Introduction

Ode to Chile

*L*ife and love brought me to Chile, this narrow, strangely shaped South American country, nestled between the Pacific Ocean and the imposing Andes Mountains. Here I discovered a mysterious world of contrasts and extremes.

My venture began in the Central Valley, where the land is fertile, the people passionate and welcoming, and the sun exuberant and warm. From the first day, my adventurous nature was completely seduced; upon my first visit to the *feria*, the local country market, the foodie in me was hooked! The earthy tones, the colorful bounty of fresh vegetables and incredible fruits, the abundance of seafood and fish . . . all this can only be described as a feast for the senses.

The foods I tasted were wholesome, uncomplicated, and fully flavored.

Appetizing stews brimming with a myriad of vegetables, unique corn preparations, hearty soups, flaky turnovers, exquisite seafood, and some of the best bean dishes I've ever tasted, all washed down with glorious wines.

Strangely enough, it was also in Chile that I rediscovered forgotten flavors and images from my childhood in Belgium and from the many vacations spent in the south of France and Italy in the late 1960s (before mass tourism spoiled it for me).

In Chile, I found the charming lifestyle I had always longed for. Imagine my surprise when I heard the bell of the milkman on his daily rounds, coming by with horse and wagon, selling fresh unpasteurized milk with a thick layer of cream floating on top. I must have been nine years old when I last tasted that on a small farm in a Flemish village. The divine strawberries, juicy melons, sweet cherries, and golden apricots, sun ripened and picked fresh that morning by the local farmers, were truly as tasty as the ones my great-grandmother Marie chose for me in her small orchard.

Three times a day, the Chileans line up in tiny old-fashioned bakeries to buy their bread, crunchy and warm out of the oven, a luxury long lost in the modern world. It had been years since I had experienced these tastes and smells, a world that I thought existed only in my nostalgic memories.

I understood why Sergio, my husband, was dying to go back to his native country; and when he proposed, after spending years abroad in Europe and the United States, to start all over again in his homeland, I didn't have to think twice. No other place in the world that I had visited during my extended travels exerted such a strong attraction for me, surely an irrational feeling but nonetheless producing a deep sense of belonging.

We settled down in Sergio's birthplace, Melipilla, a small country village only an hour from the bustling capital of Santiago, and opened a restaurant, which we named Mediterraneo. There we introduced our neighbors to Mediterranean flavors while honoring the Chilean specialties, prepared by our dear cook, Marcella.

From the start, it was a fascinating collaboration, a respectful meeting of two worlds, the old and the new. Interestingly enough, with time our cooking became more and more Chilean. And thus the idea for this book was born.

The recipes came spontaneously to me. The women in Sergio's family immediately adopted me and honored me in the best way they knew, by inviting me to their table. Proud of their culinary abilities and flattered by my eagerness to learn, each one tried to outdo the other as I was served the local specialties in a seemingly endless feast. And even though I spoke only a handful of Spanish words at the time, we understood that we shared a passion: *¡Viva!* the good life and the good food!

A few years later, our little family moved even farther away from civilization, to a huge apple and kiwifruit farm in the foothills of the imposing Andes Mountains. There I completed my education in *la cocina criolla*, the rustic, soulful cooking I came to love so much.

The originality and charm of Chilean cooking is truly found in the deep countryside, the land of the *huaso,* the proud horseman and his family. Because of the country's peculiar geographic isolation—Chile is closed in by an arid desert to the north, the Pacific Ocean to the west, the Andes Mountain chain to the east, and windswept Patagonia to the south—its culture and pristine environment have been exceptionally well preserved.

Yet things are changing rapidly. Many areas of the capital, Santiago, could easily be mistaken for neighborhoods in any North American city. This invasion of the "civilized" world is also strongly felt on the culinary level. With every newly paved road, many ancestral cooking methods and heirloom recipes, as well as the vast knowledge that comes from an ongoing communication with the land, are lost.

I have tried to capture the authentic flavors of Chile's everyday dishes as faithfully as possible. Therefore, I've recorded and included stories and portraits of the people who cultivate the land and actually cook these dishes. Through the years, I've learned to live within the limitations of what the countryside supplies (there are no shops around for miles) and to appreciate its richness: the golden eggs my chickens give me every day, a succulent pot of perfectly cooked beans, freshly sliced tomatoes still warm from the sun, and a slowly roasted rack of lamb offered by my neighbor.

These are dishes you won't find on most restaurant menus; and if you do, they are mostly poor renditions. Only a few hidden local places, the *picadas,* will offer you the excellence you experience when invited to a Chilean table (and the farther away from the capital, the more authentic the food).

All these dishes, however, are easily reproduced in North American kitchens. Some combinations of flavors may seem new to your palate, although few of the ingredients are hard to find. Let's not forget that the New World staples—such as tomatoes, sweet and hot peppers, potatoes, corn, and pumpkins—form an integral part of our common American heritage.

Only in a few cases did recipes need to be adapted, mostly because of specific cooking methods, such as baking in an authentic mud oven versus a gas or electric oven. It is indeed amazing and interesting to learn how many similarities there are between the cooking of the United States and that of this "other" America.

What Is Chilean Food?

The Chilean culinary tradition represents, as does that of many South and Central American countries, an interesting mélange of different cultures and flavors. Yet, in my humble opinion, it is a mistake to consider the cuisines of South America as one whole, which is assumed in many cookbooks.

Chile has always kept a low profile on the culinary level. And, indeed, Chilean food can hardly be described as having a highly elaborate haute cuisine, based on exclusive and costly ingredients or complicated cooking methods.

Lately, however, Santiago has become a booming cosmopolitan restaurant city, infatuated by the new international food scenes. Sadly, most fine restaurants turn their back on their own rich roots, leaving us, the curious gourmets, with the typical (but often mediocre) small restaurants to get a taste of Chilean cuisine. As always there are some hard-to-find but great exceptions. Needless to say, a true taste of the country can be experienced only in the homes.

The ever-evolving new food trends will not be the focus of this book. I turned to the hidden treasures of this remarkable country: to the wonderful products offered by a generous land and ocean and to the unpretentious, full-flavored dishes prepared with them and based on age-long traditions.

Here you will find the authentic Chilean dishes. Their origin and wealth must be learned in family kitchens, in the humble *ruca* (tent) of the Mapuche Indian, and in the little *picadas*, where women and men cook the hearty, homey dishes that delight through their simplicity and honesty.

The Chilean cuisine is largely a result of the encounters between two opposing cultures: the native Indians and the Spanish conquistadores. Today, many of the Chilean specialties testify to this fusion. Just think of the popular empanada, a flaky turnover with a definite Spanish origin that has taken on a Chilean identity in its savory filling of pino, derived from the Araucana Indian word *pinu* (ground meat flavored with lots of sweet onions and spices).

The Chilean cuisine is specked with Arabic influences in the use of certain spices and herbs and in the combination of sweet and salty in national favorites; this influence is especially seen in a long list of traditional sweets. Quite logical knowing the strong effect the Moorish occupation had on the Spanish culture.

The Chilean Indians' fondness for corn, called *choclo*, led to development of unique dishes. Two examples are the beloved *pastel de choclo* (a rich meat, onion, chicken, and olive pie topped with a crispy corn mixture) and the delicate humitas (creamed corn and basil steamed in corn husks).

The central and southern valleys are known for their unique and ideal climate. Winters are mostly frost free, and the summers are long and dry. The region would be a desert, however, if a valuable source of water, Andean snowmelt, weren't so ingenuously channeled down the slopes to irrigate the lush, glowing hills and the orchards and vineyards, guaranteeing a fairly consistent crop. In these valleys, farmers produce the bulk of the fresh fruits and vegetables known in the United States as winter produce.

With the help of my Chilean friends, I rediscovered the true taste of vegetables and the simple manner in which they can be prepared. For example, freshly picked young carrots don't need more than a splash of lemon juice and some salt; yet I am fully aware that this is only possible if the vegetables are of outstanding quality. Superior-quality vegetables are a luxury that is hard to come by in our modern society; but if you seek them, you'll see they're not impossible to find. Farmers markets are sprouting up all over the country that offer local, top-quality produce. These initiatives deserve our full support.

I discovered an intriguing aquatic world of islands and canals in the southern islands of Chiloé, one of the places of origin of the humble potato and a true paradise for the seafood lover. I also came across a wealth of inspiring recipes based on the humble peasant staple of legumes. There is nothing like a heartwarming, full-flavored pot of perfectly cooked beans, chickpeas, or lentils, unless it's a pot of *porotos granados*, fresh shelled beans cooked with sweet corn.

Chileans are avid meat lovers, and their favorite social events are the *asados,* or cook-out feasts. Skillful masters confided in me, revealing their secret methods, their favorite adobos (marinades), and their family recipe for the best salsa and making sure I understood that grilling is a man's business.

In this thin, long-bodied country, the ocean is never far away. The cold Humboldt current guarantees a wide variety of fish and seafood of impeccable flavor. With more than twenty-six hundred miles of coastline it is not surprising that Chile is one of the world's largest fish exporters. I've noticed that exquisite Chilean sea bass and salmon have become popular in restaurants across the United States.

Over the centuries, Chilean cuisine has integrated ideas from a variety of settlers who followed the Spanish to Chile: the Yugoslavs, the Germans, the Swiss, the Arabs, the French, the English, and the Italians. Recently, Chinese and

Japanese restaurants and food stores are starting to pop up in the large cities. The intriguing medley continues to evolve. On trips to the spectacular southern Vulcan and Lake districts, I was surprised to discover *beerstubbes,* German-style beer houses boasting of their sauerkraut, sausages, and kuchen (rich cream-and-fruit-filled pastries). Chileans do have an incurable sweet tooth! Their traditional sweet repertoire, the dulces Chilenos (Spain's wicked legacy), amazes me by the sheer respect it shows to tradition and to the desire to keep century-old recipes alive and thriving.

And last, but not least, in this land of wine and honey, an exciting evolution is going on in Chile's vineyards and *bodegas.* In the late twentieth century, Chile's growing and ambitious viticulture is causing serious waves on the international fine-wine scene, offering not only low-priced and high-quality variety wines but also some outstanding and noble nectars. Chile, blessed with unique natural conditions and a sound experience based on some of the oldest wine-making traditions of the Americas, is forging itself a sound reputation. And I can't be thankful enough to be a firsthand observer (and taster) of this movement!

Maybe the biggest gift Chile, which to some may seem primitive and poor, has given me is a renewed appreciation of the richness hidden in the *simple* pleasures of life. Rustic country foods evoke the warmth and gaiety with which these dishes are shared in Chile, as well as the harshness and the bare existence of those making a living on the land.

Don't worry if all ingredients are not at hand or if the bread is a touch drier than usual; it truly doesn't matter. The dishes in this book will nevertheless taste good, especially when you share them in the Chilean style, celebrating their simplicity and serving them with a big heart.

To me, the Chilean table brings back images of a sea of sunlight bathing my kitchen, while I shell peas on the porch (a chilled glass of wine within reach), listen to the *flip-flop* of linen drying in the evening breeze, and caress my dog's nose resting in my lap. These simple pleasures in life are so often overlooked in our competitive, stressful, and wanna-be-sophisticated world.

Appetizers, Small Meals, and Drinks

Bocadillos y Aperitivos

We will never know with certainty if we should credit the Spanish conquistadores for introducing tapas to the Americas or attribute them to an innate predisposition of its inhabitants. I am talking about the delightful habit of lingering in good company; indulging in small, tasty bites, a few drinks, and good conversation; and watching the world go by. I quickly found, to my great delight, that the similarities between Chile and the Mediterranean countries don't start or end with their fondness for tapas, which are called *bocadillos* or *picadillos* in these parts of South America.

In the Chilean countryside, we gather under a shady *parrón*—a veranda covered with vines that is found in even the most humble houses—sip refreshing drinks, feast on wonderful little snacks, and enjoy the good company of family and friends. These are simple, earthy, basic pleasures. In more urban settings, Chileans love to meet in one of the many little bars and restaurants concentrated around the main square. They like to relax after a stressful day at work or simply share a drink before lunch or dinner. Any excuse is used to have a good time.

The higher you climb up the social ladder, the less spontaneous the outing. Eventually, complicated details have to be taken into consideration, such as being seen in the right place, in the right company, and wearing the right outfit!

Bocadillos can be as simple as a bowl of pungent Chilean salsa scooped up with homemade bread, as rustic and robust as La Pichanga (a medley of cured meats, cheeses, and pickles, p. 24), or as lavish as delicately fried seafood turnovers and elegant canapés topped with smoked salmon or sea urchin mousse. Seafood appetizers are in. And no wonder, with thousands of miles of coastline, Chileans have an enormous variety of outstanding seafood to choose from.

The ideal showcase for a cook's culinary creativity is the cocktail party. To say that Chileans have a soft spot for these social events would be an understatement. From the lavish parties given by the socialites (duly reported in local magazines and newspapers) to casual family gatherings to celebrate birthdays, anniversaries, christenings, and victories of the local soccer team, all evolve around the cocktail party. It's serious business. Not only are a wide variety of aperitivos served but also an endless number of beautifully decorated platters of exquisite hors d'oeuvres, hot and cold, savory and sweet, are offered to guests. Even the most inexperienced cook will make an extra effort to decorate a platter of canapés with style or will look for Grandma's recipe for empanaditas fritas or salmon mousse. A reputation is at stake!

In Chile, food is abundant and portions are generous. Very often, an evening out enjoying drinks and bocadillos turns into a whole meal. There's a fine line between hors d'oeuvres and appetizers, so I discuss them in the same chapter. As you will notice, many hors d'oeuvres can easily be served as an appetizer or even as a light meal, accompanied by some interesting salads.

Fresh Clams in Pungent Green Sauce

Almejas a la Ostra

Makes 2 servings

*T*he consumption of seafood reaches an all-time high during *la semana santa*, the week preceding Easter. A true penitence for the avid meat lovers, but a blessing for people like me who really prefer the fruits of the ocean.

Marinated clams, prepared in the Peruvian seviche style, act like pure medicine; you will feel revitalized enough to confront the toughest oceans! Delicate stomachs may want to abstain.

> **2 dozen littleneck clams, well scrubbed**
> **1 cup finely chopped onion**
> **2 cloves garlic, finely minced**
> **Salt and freshly ground black pepper, to taste**
> **Juice of 2 lemons**
> **1 tablespoon finely minced fresh parsley**
> **1 tablespoon finely minced fresh cilantro**

Shuck the clams and place the meat in a bowl with the juices. Add the onion, garlic, salt, pepper, and lemon juice. Toss to combine, and let marinate at room temperature no more than 30 minutes.

Add the herbs, and mix well. Divide the clams with the juices into 2 deep earthenware bowls and serve at once.

Tiny Fried Cheese or Seafood Pastries

Empanaditas Fritas de Queso o de Mariscos

Makes about sixteen 4-inch rounds or ten 6-inch rounds

Empanaditas fritas, the unmistakable favorite of every Chilean cocktail party, come in many versions: simply cheesy, succulent with an oniony meat filling, or stuffed with delicious mixed seafood. In the more sophisticated restaurants, the empanaditas may be wrapped with puff pastry; but the authentic ones are made with an ever so flaky pastry based on flour and good-quality lard. They are quickly fried until crunchy (the puff pastry version can also be baked). Empanaditas fritas taste great with a Pisco Sour (p. 50), the national cocktail. *Salud!*

> 2½ cups all-purpose flour
> 1 teaspoon baking powder
> 1 teaspoon salt
> 1 teaspoon sugar
> 4 tablespoons good-quality lard or solid vegetable shortening,
>   at room temperature
> 2 tablespoons butter, at room temperature
> About 1 cup warm water
> Easygoing Cheese Filling (below), Delicate Seafood Filling (below),
>   or 1½ cups Meat and Onion Filling (p. 17)
> About 3 cups vegetable oil, for frying

To make the dough by hand: In a large mixing bowl or on a clean work surface, sift the flour with the baking powder. Make a well in the center; add the salt, sugar, lard, butter, and water. Using your fingertips, work the ingredients quickly into the flour, adding as much flour as needed to obtain a soft, pliable dough. Knead the dough on a lightly floured surface 3 minutes.

To make the dough in a food processor: Place the flour, baking powder, salt, sugar, lard, and butter into the bowl of a food processor fitted with a steel blade. Pulse a few times, until the mixture has a coarse texture. Add the water, and pulse just until the dough comes together into a ball. Knead the dough on a lightly floured surface 1 minute.

On a lightly floured surface, roll out the dough to a ⅛-inch thickness. Using a round cutter, cut out either 4-inch circles for cheese or meat empanaditas or 6-inch circles for the seafood ones. Gather up all the scraps of the dough into a ball, roll out, and cut into circles until all of the dough is used.

Place 1 or 2 tablespoons of the filling in the center of each circle, leaving a ½-inch margin. Brush the edges lightly with water, and fold the circles in half to enclose the filling. Seal each empanadita securely by pressing the edges with your fingertips or pinching with a fork. With a toothpick, prick 3 to 4 holes in each empanadita, to prevent it from opening while frying. If making ahead, cover the prepared empanaditas and refrigerate until ready to fry or up to 1 day. (The empanaditas can be frozen up to 1 month.)

Just before serving, heat the oil in a wok, heavy skillet, or electric frying pan over high heat to 350F (175C). Fry a few empanaditas at a time, turning them over with a slotted spoon, until golden brown on both sides, about 2 minutes total. Bring the oil back to temperature before frying the next batch. Drain the empanaditas on paper towels and serve at once, piping hot.

Easygoing Cheese Filling

Makes 1¼ cups

For an unusual but great flavor, try adding the Quince Paste.

> **5 ounces hard cheese, such as Gouda or Swiss**
> **1 thin slice Dulce de Membrillo (p. 292) (optional)**

Finely dice the cheese. If desired, mix in the Quince Paste.

Delicate Seafood Filling

Makes 2 cups

Outstanding seafood empanaditas can be found along Chile's coastline. They can be filled with razor clams, small mussels, scallops, shrimp, or loco (abalone). Whatever is freshest will do. I have obtained satisfying results with frozen seafood, properly defrosted and drained. A filling that is too moist results in soggy empanaditas. If you are still experimenting with hot chiles, add them to taste at the end.

> **2 dozen razor or littleneck clams**
> **1 cup dry white wine**
> **2 dozen mussels, debearded**
> **1 pound medium shrimp, peeled, or bay scallops**
> **3 tablespoons vegetable oil**
> **1½ cups finely chopped onions**
> **1 tablespoon all-purpose flour**
> **3 cloves garlic, finely minced**
> **½ serrano or jalapeño chile, finely minced, or to taste**
> **½ tablespoon sweet paprika**
> **1 teaspoon dried oregano**
> **1 tablespoon finely minced fresh parsley**
> **Salt and freshly ground black pepper, to taste**

Place the clams in a medium saucepan. Add ¾ cup of the wine, cover, and cook over high heat until the shells open, 4 to 6 minutes. Using a slotted spoon, remove the clams and reserve, discarding any that haven't opened.

In the same cooking liquid, steam the mussels over high heat until the shells open, 4 to 6 minutes. Remove the mussels and reserve, discarding any that haven't opened.

Remove the mussels and clams from their shells and chop coarsely. Keep small shellfish whole for texture.

Strain the cooking liquid through cheesecloth or a paper coffee filter to remove any sand and grit. Return the strained liquid to the saucepan and poach the shrimp until firm, about 3 minutes. Remove the shrimp from the broth, let cool, and chop coarsely. Reserve the cooking liquid.

In a heavy skillet, heat the oil over medium heat. Add the onions, sauté, stirring occasionally, until translucent but not browned, about 5 minutes. Sprinkle the flour evenly over the onions, and add the garlic, chile, paprika, oregano, ¾ cup of the reserved cooking liquid, and the remaining ¼ cup of wine. Cook, stirring occasionally, for 3 minutes. Add the seafood and cook over high heat until most of the liquid has evaporated, 1 to 2 minutes. The mixture should be moist but not runny. Don't overcook the seafood or it will have a chewy consistency.

Add the parsley and season with salt and pepper. Let the filling cool completely, over ice if possible, before filling the empanaditas.

Onion and Meat-Filled Baked Turnovers

Empanadas de Horno

Makes 16 empanadas

The popular empanada, a flaky and savory filled pastry, is mentioned in Spanish manuscripts as early as the fourteenth century. Like the conquistadores, the empanada conquered the Spanish Caribbean and Latin America, albeit in a much more efficient and charming way.

Indigenous populations favored a juicy, sweet, and salty combination of meat, onions, spices, eggs, raisins, and olives. The filling is called pino, a word derived from the native Araucana Indian word *pinu*.

Empanadas de Horno, traditionally baked in a mud oven, can be considered Chile's favorite national snack. No holiday or Sunday outing would be complete without enjoying a few empanadas! The empanada is to Chile what a hamburger is to the United States.

Making empanadas is rather time-consuming and requires some experience, which explains why it has become a popular take-out food. The cook must have an experienced hand, as they say in Chile. Here are some important rules:

- **The secret for a juicy filling that won't run while you're assembling the empanada is to prepare it a day ahead and keep it refrigerated. I've obtained good results by preparing the pino in the early morning and holding it over a bowl of ice until the juices congeal.**

- **The dough should be flaky and cooked all the way through. So don't overwork your dough, and be sure to bake the empanadas in a preheated, hot oven.**

The results are worth the effort!

Chileans will never agree on the best recipe; they all have their secret ingredient for the pastry, for example, egg yolks, margarine, vinegar, or wine. I've opted for the most basic recipe (and still the best to my taste): flour, water, and good-quality lard (or a mixture of vegetable shortening and butter).

MEAT AND ONION FILLING (PINO)

3 tablespoons vegetable oil

6 cups finely chopped onions (about 4 large)

2 cloves garlic, finely minced

1 tablespoon sweet paprika

2½ teaspoon ground cumin

2½ teaspoons dried oregano

½ teaspoon cayenne pepper, or to taste

¾ pound beef for stewing, cut into ¼-inch cubes, or ground beef,
      or mixed beef and pork

1 tablespoon all-purpose flour

¾ cup beef broth (preferably homemade, p. 93)

Salt and freshly ground black pepper, to taste

DOUGH

7 to 8 cups all-purpose flour

4 ounces (8 tablespoons) good-quality lard or 4 tablespoons solid
      vegetable shortening plus 4 tablespoons butter, at room
      temperature

1 tablespoon salt dissolved in 2 cups warm water

ASSEMBLY

3 hard-cooked eggs, shelled and quartered

36 raisins

24 ripe whole olives, pitted

1 egg yolk mixed with 1 tablespoon water, for glaze

To make the filling: Heat the oil in a large skillet over medium heat. Add the onions and cook, stirring occasionally, until softened but not browned, 5 minutes. Add the garlic, paprika, cumin, oregano, salt, and cayenne. Add the meat and cook, stirring occasionally, 5 minutes. Sprinkle 1 tablespoon flour over the meat mixture, and mix well.

Stir in the broth. Cook uncovered over medium heat, stirring occasionally, until most of the juices have evaporated, 10 to 15 minutes. The mixture should be moist but not runny. Season with salt and black pepper to taste.

To make the dough: On a clean work surface, sift the flour. Make a well in the center, add the lard and some of the salted water; add more water as needed. Using a wooden spoon, combine all the ingredients as quickly as possible, adding water as necessary; knead very well about 5 minutes, until a soft dough is formed. Overworking the dough will result in a tough pastry. Wrap the dough in a clean kitchen towel to keep it warm and workable; let it rest 15 minutes.

Cooking with Lard: So What?

Like Spanish and most Latin American cooks, Chileans rely heavily on lard for baking and cooking. For many centuries, the annual slaughter of the family pig provided the pantry with a stock of durable food and lard, a precious source of calories and flavor.

In the late twentieth century, lard has received bad press in the United States. This is somewhat undeserved. According to the U.S. Department of Agriculture, pure pork fat contains less than half the amount of cholesterol found in butter; and if it has not been hydrogenated, lard is also low in saturated fat. My Chilean friends have taught me that the quality of the lard (pure unhydrogenated pork fat) is of the utmost importance as much for its unique flavor as for its nutritional value. But, like all sources of fat, it should be used with common sense.

Meanwhile, set up a station for filling the empanadas. Have all the ingredients ready: the cold meat mixture, eggs, raisins, olives, and glaze.

Preheat the oven to 400F(205C).

Shape the dough into a large sausage, and slice into 12 equal pieces. Work with one piece at a time, keeping the remaining dough covered. Roll out each piece of dough into an 8-inch round about ¼-inch thick. Spoon about ¼ cup of the filling onto each circle, leaving a ¾-inch margin. Top each with 1 egg quarter, 3 raisins, and 2 olives. Brush the margins all around with water, and fold the circles in half. To enclose the filling securely, fold each half-circle into a square: Place the straight edge of the half-circle toward you; then fold in left edge, the right edge, and the top to make the square. Seal the corners with your thumb by making a deep imprint in each one.

Brush each empanada with the egg yolk mixture. With a toothpick, prick 3 to 4 holes in each one to prevent it from opening up while baking. Bake 15 to 20 minutes, until the pastry is nicely browned and the filling is piping hot. Serve at once. Baked empanadas can easily be reheated.

Por una empanada y un cacho de vino . . .

No Chilean, no matter how urban or sophisticated he or she may appear, stays insensitive to the countryside's charming appeal or to the temptation of savoring *una rica empanada con un cacho de vino* ("a tasty empanada and a cow's horn filled with wine").

During the weekends, the highways are crowded with stressed-out Santiaguinos and their jittery offspring, seeking clean air and peace. El Cajón del Maipo is the ideal destination for a day's outing, with its winding roads to the mountain's heart, its picturesque villages, and its wide riverbed spreading out over the rich agricultural plains of Chile's Central Valley.

When driving through the country, you'll see many small stands along the road, often marked by a white flag. The white flag indicates that someone is selling genuine homemade food, such as pan amasado, dense, round, little breads baked in traditional cone-shaped mud ovens; the curious tortilla de rescoldo, an even denser bread that's baked in ashes; jams made from the many regional fruits; walnuts and local honey; and the ubiquitous empanadas de horno. Traditionally, empanadas are baked in mud ovens, which almost guarantees success, similar to the superior flavor brick oven–baked pizzas have over those baked at home.

Tasting my way through the country (my kind of traveling), I've come across many variations of empanadas. An interesting one is based on a pino made with cochayuyo (dried seaweed) that has been soaked, finely chopped, and used instead of the meat. In the south, when times were difficult and cooks may have had only a few onions, an ají verde (green chile), and a piece of lard, Pequenes were created. They are poor in ingredients but rich in flavor. Empanadas can also be filled with cheese or seafood; and of course, they become a dessert when filled with pear, apple, quince, or walnut mixtures.

The empanada celebration day, however, coincides with the national holiday on September 18. Patriotic feelings are reinforced during the morning military parades, serious displays of discipline and rigor that are easily forgotten during the afternoon's chaotic, exuberant Latin festivities. The evening is crowned by the traditional fireworks. Needless to say, it's a day of serious eating and drinking. Time for celebrating spring, and time for the Chilean kids to launch their colorful kites into the blue sky.

Seafood in a Hot, Garlicky Sauce

Mariscos al Pil-Pil

Makes 6 to 8 hors d'oeuvres or 4 appetizer servings

Hot red chiles, garlic, and olive oil: three simple ingredients that can make magic! In Chile, this winning combination is called *al pil-pil*, and it enhances just about everything, including camarones (shrimp), langostinos (crawfish), ostiones (scallops), angulas (tiny fresh eels), and even ranas (frog legs, a regional delicacy). There is definitely a strong Spanish influence in this dish, but the shared passion with which this bocadillo is devoured is truly Chilean. Be careful with the chiles though; you're looking for flavor not just blazing heat! If you'd like the garlic to be more discreet, add crushed cloves to the hot oil and discard them before serving. Serve with a crunchy loaf of bread.

> **1 cup extra-virgin olive oil**
> **2 to 3 large cloves garlic, finely minced, or to taste**
> **1 to 2 hot red or serrano chile peppers (preferably dried), seeded**
> **and finely chopped, or to taste**
> **1½ pounds medium shrimp, peeled**
> **Salt, to taste**

Warm individual earthenware dishes in a 300F(150C) oven.

In a small skillet, heat the oil over medium heat. When warm, but not smoking, add the garlic and chiles; cook 30 seconds. Increase the heat to high, and add the shrimp. Bring to a quick boil, stirring occasionally, and cook 1 minute. (Do not burn the garlic or chiles, which would give a very unpleasant bitter taste to the dish.)

Divide the seafood and its divine juices onto the warm dishes, and serve at once.

Broiled Razor Clams with Parmesan Cheese

Machas a la Parmesana

Makes 8 hors d'oeuvres, or 6 appetizer servings

This is a popular appetizer savored with a crisp Chilean sauvignon blanc. In Chile, machas, or razor clams, are a much-prized seafood, usually served raw, as in a Mariscal (p. 170), or simply broiled on the half-shell and dusted with a crusty layer of buttery cheese. If razor clams are not available, use cherrystone clams, oysters, scallops, or even mussels for an equally delicious and elegant dish.

> **3 dozen razor clams**
> **Coarse salt**
> **Freshly ground black pepper, to taste**
> **6 tablespoons butter**
> **1 cup grated Gouda or Swiss cheese or queso Mantecoso**
> **½ cup dry white wine or sherry**
> **¼ cup freshly grated Parmesan cheese**

Preheat the broiler.

Shuck the clams, reserving the bottom shell. Discard the dark stomach. Pound the clams with a wooden spoon for about 1 minute; according to Chilean chefs, this step tenderizes the meat.

Arrange the shellfish in the bottom shells, and place them on a baking sheet filled with a fine layer of coarse salt, just enough to hold the shells straight up. Grind some black pepper over the clams. Dab ½ teaspoon butter and 1 teaspoon Gouda cheese on each clam; sprinkle with the wine. Sprinkle the Parmesan cheese evenly over the clams. Broil, about 4 inches from the element, 2 minutes, until the cheese has melted and is lightly browned. Serve at once, piping hot.

One Holy Friday, my Parisian girlfriend and I were roaming the country market in Curicó, shopping for the holidays, when we noticed that our friendly fruit vendor was having a little feast all by himself. On the back of his truck, we spotted a plate of freshly shucked clams that he happily gulped down with a splash of freshly squeezed lemon juice. My friend, an adventurous and fine gourmet, was immediately interested to try this out in the little restaurant the man recommended to us.

Through a shabby opaque glass door we caught a glimpse of a dark, little bar. A few stern faces stared at us with surprise. It was the kind of place one would never enter alone; but we did. Passing through the backyard crowded with big bags of fresh clams and a few cats, we headed toward a small dining room, colorfully decorated with paintings of fishing and oceanside scenes.

The waiter, who sensed that he had some serious amateurs in front of him, offered us the almejas a la ostra; a plate of fried congrio; and of course, a nice bottle of a local white wine. We were in heaven.

Chilean-Style One-Bite Snacks

La Pichanga

Makes 4 to 6 servings

*T*he pichanga can be served in two ways: mix all the ingredients with the pungent sauce or ask for a *tabula,* which means that the neatly cubed meats, cheeses, and pickles will be served on a small wooden board (the *tabula*) without the dressing. A Chilean salsa is a great side dish. This is a wonderful accompaniment for a Pisco Sour (p. 50) or a glass of Chilean merlot or cabernet sauvignon.

> ½ **pound ripe olives**
>
> ½ **pound hard cheese such as Gouda or Swiss, cut into ½-inch**
> **cubes**
>
> ½ **pound quesillo fresco or fresh mozzarella cheese, cut into ½-inch**
> **cubes, optional**
>
> ½ **pound Arrollado de Malaya (p. 28), ham, or mortadella, cut into**
> **½-inch cubes**
>
> ¼ **pound headcheese, cut into ½-inch cubes, optional**
>
> ½ **pound pickled onions or mixed pickles, diced**
>
> 2 **hard-cooked eggs, peeled and cut into 8 slices**
>
> ½ **cup vegetable or olive oil**
>
> 1 **clove garlic, finely minced**
>
> 1 **tablespoon finely minced fresh parsley**
>
> 1 **tablespoon Salsa de Ají Colorado a la Chilena (p. 66), ground chili**
> **paste, sambal oelek, or harissa sauce, or 1 to 2 serrano or**
> **jalapeño chile peppers, seeds removed**

Combine the olives, cheeses, meats, pickled onions, and eggs in a decorative earthenware dish.

Mix the oil with the garlic, parsley, and Salsa de Ají in a small bowl. Pour over the cheese mixture, and toss gently to combine. If using, place the chili peppers in a separate small serving dish. Serve with toothpicks so guests can *pinchar* ("prick") the little cubes of their choice.

If you ask the young Santiaguinos if they like La Pichanga, they'll answer you, "Who's that?" The old guard will shake their heads in disbelief, agreeing on at least one point: that the youngsters no longer understand what life is all about. How can they forget about La Pichanga, one of the tastiest snacks Chile has to offer? Ah, this new generation, they seem to be on the run all the time—I am told—wasting their appetites on such strange things as pizzas, potato chips, and peanuts.

The old men are right; even in Chile the traditional dishes prepared with so much love and care are in a decline, as everywhere else in the world. I was lucky enough to find some more than decent versions of this reputed dish all over the country! You just ask the old guys where to go for La Pichanga.

Spicy Shrimp in Fresh Tomato Sauce

Camarones en Salsa Chilena

Makes 6 hors d'oeuvres or 4 appetizer servings

Shrimp are always everyone's favorite, but served with this pungent, Chilean-style tomato sauce, they'll steal your heart and stomach! This wonderful *bocadillo* is easily turned into a light, delicious lunch, accompanied by a bowl of fresh greens and a crisp white wine.

> 3 tablespoons butter
> 1 cup finely chopped onion
> 2 cloves garlic, finely minced
> 3 large ripe tomatoes, peeled, seeded, and chopped
> ½ teaspoon dried oregano
> 1 tablespoon Salsa de Ají Colorado a la Chilena (p. 66), ground fresh
>   chili paste, sambal oelek, or harissa sauce, to taste
> Salt and freshly ground black pepper, to taste
> 2 pounds large shrimp, peeled and deveined
> 1 tablespoon finely minced fresh parsley

Preheat the oven to 375F (190C).

Melt the butter in a medium saucepan over medium heat. Add the onion and cook, covered, until softened but not browned, 7 minutes. Add the garlic, tomatoes, oregano and salsa de ají. Simmer, stirring occasionally, 10 minutes more. Taste for seasoning and add salt and black pepper. Pour the mixture into an earthenware baking dish.

Toss the shrimp with salt and black pepper, and push them slightly into the tomato mixture sauce. Bake 10 minutes, until the shrimp are cooked. Garnish with parsley. Serve immediately.

Sautéed Scallops with Garlic, Scallions, and Parsley

Ostiones con Ajo, Cebollines, y Peregil

Makes 6 bocadillos or 4 appetizer servings

Sweet scallops make the most delicious bocadillos. In Chile, they're sold on the shell with the crescent-shaped orange coral still attached to the white flesh. Chileans like scallops quickly sautéed in a buttery sauce flavored with garlic, scallions, and parsley. The addition of cream makes it sinfully good. It's great served over pasta or Arroz Graneado (p. 214), but I leave this entirely up to you.

6 tablespoons butter
6 tablespoons finely minced scallions
2 tablespoons finely minced garlic
60 bay or 32 sea scallops, sliced in half on the diagonal
Salt and freshly ground black pepper, to taste
½ cup dry white wine
¾ cup heavy cream, optional
2 tablespoons finely minced fresh parsley

Melt the butter in a large skillet over medium heat. Add the scallions, and sauté 1 minute; add the garlic and scallops and sauté, stirring occasionally, 2 minutes more. Increase the heat to high. Pour in the wine and cream, if using, season with salt and pepper, and bring to a boil.

Arrange the scallops on a warm earthenware platter; sprinkle the parsley on top. Serve at once.

Spicy Rolled Flank Steak Stuffed with Eggs, Carrots, and Peppers

Arrollado de Malaya

Makes 6 to 8 servings

My mother-in-law, la Tia Julita, is without a doubt the champion of the malaya, a well-flavored beef roulade, colorfully stuffed with eggs and vegetables. Although la Tia is well into her sixties, she still often entertains her family of seven children and nineteen grandchildren. Arrollado de Malaya is her favorite party dish. She conveniently prepares the beef roulade the day before and lets it cool overnight in the rich broth. The next day, the malaya is sliced and served as an appetizer with a variety of salads and a pungent pebre or Chilean salsa on the side. It's her way of pleasing her sons, as she well knows that the younger generations are losing touch with the family's culinary traditions.

In Chile, this dish is sometimes prepared with a less expensive, less meaty, and tougher cut of meat that I find hard to locate in the United States. This particular cut of meat, also called malaya, is usually soaked for a few hours in vinegary water to soften the connective tissues. This step is not necessary when flank steak is used.

2 carrots, peeled and halved lengthwise
5 cloves garlic, peeled
1 teaspoon salt
1½ teaspoons ground cumin
¾ teaspoon freshly ground black pepper
2 teaspoons dried oregano
1½ pounds beef flank steak, butterflied
3 hard-cooked eggs, shelled
½ large green bell pepper, sliced in 1-inch strips

½ large red bell pepper, sliced in 1-inch strips
1 celery rib, 3 parsley sprigs, and 3 fresh oregano sprigs tied
    together

Place the carrots in a small saucepan and cover with cold, salted water. Cook over medium heat until tender, 25 to 30 minutes. Drain.

Using a mortar and pestle or a small spice grinder, crush the garlic with the salt. Add the cumin, black pepper, and oregano; mix well.

Place the steak on a work surface. Rub the spice mixture into the meat. Arrange the whole eggs lengthwise over the meat, flanked on both sides by the carrots. Top with the bell pepper strips, alternating between green and red.

Starting with one long side, roll the steak up, jelly-roll style, as tightly as possible. Tie it with kitchen string at 1-inch intervals. To secure the ends, I usually close them with a needle and thread (or unwaxed dental floss).

Place the rolled steak in a deep skillet just big enough to hold it snugly; cover with salted, cold water. Bring to a boil, reduce the heat to a simmer, and add the celery and herb bundle. Cook, covered, until tender when pierced with a sharp knife, 2 to 2½ hours. Leave the meat in the broth, and cool in the refrigerator, overnight if possible. Before serving, lift the rolled steak out of the broth, and slice it into ½-inch-thick pieces. Save the flavorful broth for soups and sauces.

Romaine Omelet Flavored with Bell Pepper and Caramelized Onion

Tortilla de Lechuga y Pimentón

Makes 2 servings

*C*hileans are fond of their tortillas, and I have tasted many original and delicious combinations. Prepare this tortilla with Romaine lettuce in the summer months and with Swiss chard or spinach in the winter.

> **3 cups finely shredded Romaine lettuce**
> **4 large eggs, separated**
> **Salt and freshly ground black pepper, to taste**
> **2 tablespoons all-purpose flour**
> **2½ tablespoons vegetable oil**
> **3 tablespoons finely chopped onion**
> **3 tablespoons finely diced red bell pepper**

Rinse the shredded greens thoroughly under cold running water and drain.

In a large bowl, beat the egg whites with a pinch of salt until soft peaks form. Carefully fold the yolks into the whites, one by one, alternating with the flour. Season with salt and black pepper. Squeeze the greens dry with your hands, and add them to the egg mixture.

Heat 1½ tablespoons of the oil in an 8-inch nonstick skillet over medium heat. Add the onion and bell pepper, and cook until soft and lightly browned, 3 to 4 minutes.

Pour the egg mixture into the skillet and cook over medium heat until the eggs are set, 3 to 4 minutes. Shake the skillet occasionally to make sure the omelet isn't sticking. Invert the omelet onto a plate.

Add the remaining 1 tablespoon oil to the pan, and slide the omelet, uncooked side down, back into the skillet. Cook until set and lightly browned, 2 to 3 minutes. Serve warm or at room temperature.

Tortillas de Verduras

The Tortilla de Verdura represents the Chilean version of the thick Spanish omelet or the Italian frittata.

The creative variations I've included here are all based on savory vegetables bound together with an egg mixture. In fact, a tortilla is a nutritious, inexpensive, and simply delicious dish that can be whipped together in no time, which explains its success all over the world.

Sliced into thin wedges, the tortilla elegantly accompanies an aperitif, makes a quick appetizer, or serves as a satisfying light meal when served with a salad and a pungent salsa on the side.

Chilean Carrot Omelet

Tortilla de Zanahorias

Makes 2 servings

This subtle, sweet carrot omelet was served to me one day by my mother-in-law, la Tia Julita. The dish was accompanied by Julita's Fresh Tomato Salsa (p. 59), boldly flavored with fresh garlic and cilantro.

> 3 large eggs, separated
> 2 tablespoons all-purpose flour
> Salt and freshly ground black pepper, to taste
> 1 clove garlic, finely minced
> 2½ cups peeled and grated carrots (2 to 3)
> 2 tablespoons vegetable oil

In a large bowl, beat the egg whites with a pinch of salt until soft peaks form. Carefully fold the yolks into the whites, one by one, alternating with the flour. Season with salt and black pepper. Add the garlic and carrots, and combine with a fork.

Heat 1 tablespoon of the oil in an 8-inch nonstick skillet over medium heat. Add the egg mixture, and cook until the omelet is set, 3 to 4 minutes. Shake the pan occasionally to make sure that the omelet isn't sticking. Invert the omelet onto a plate.

Add the remaining 1 tablespoon oil to the pan, and slide the omelet, uncooked side down, back into the skillet. Cook until set and lightly browned, for 2 to 3 minutes more. Serve warm or at room temperature.

Cheesy Cauliflower Omelet

Tortilla de Coliflor y Mantecoso Queso

Makes 2 servings

Leftover cooked cauliflower or green beans, some grated Swiss cheese, a few eggs: You're all set for this delicious snack that's prepared in no time.

> 3 large eggs, separated
> 2 tablespoons all-purpose flour
> 1 clove garlic, finely minced
> 1 tablespoon finely minced fresh parsley or cilantro
> ½ cup grated Swiss or Gouda cheese
> Salt and freshly ground black pepper, to taste
> 2½ tablespoons vegetable oil
> 2 cups cooked cauliflower, cut into small florets, or green beans

In a large bowl, beat the egg whites with a pinch of salt until soft peaks form. Carefully fold the yolks into the whites, one by one, alternating with the flour. Add the garlic, parsley, and Swiss cheese. Season with salt and black pepper.

Heat 1½ tablespoons of the oil in an 8-inch nonstick skillet over medium heat. Add the cauliflower, and cook, stirring occasionally, 3 minutes. Pour the egg mixture evenly over the cauliflower, and cook until the omelet is set, 3 to 4 minutes. Shake the skillet occasionally to make sure omelet isn't sticking. Invert the omelet onto a plate.

Add the remaining 1 tablespoon oil to the pan, and slide the omelet, uncooked side down, back into the skillet. Cook until set and lightly browned, 2 to 3 minutes more. Serve warm or at room temperature.

Baked Eggs with Chunky Tomato Sauce and Spicy Sausage

Paila de Huevos del Huaso

Makes 4 servings

When you spend your life outdoors, like the Chilean cowboy, or *huaso*, on horseback or laboring in the fields, you need a breakfast that sticks to the ribs. This egg dish is just the right thing, served in a shallow earthenware dish filled with a chunky tomato and pepper sauce, spicy chorizo sausages, and *unos ricos huevos de campo*, wonderful country eggs with fat yolks the color of gold. My own chickens devastate my garden but pay me back with golden eggs. Now I know what I missed all those years.

When I lead a more urban existence, I serve this dish for winter Sunday brunch, accompanied by a big bowl of tossed greens.

> **3 tablespoons vegetable or olive oil**
> **1 onion, halved lengthwise and thinly sliced**
> **1 red or green bell pepper, diced**
> **2 cloves garlic, finely minced**
> **4 large ripe tomatoes, peeled, seeded, and coarsely chopped**
> **$\frac{1}{2}$ serrano or jalapeño chile pepper, seeded and finely chopped, or**
>   **to taste**
> **Salt and freshly ground black pepper, to taste**
> **12 $\frac{1}{2}$-inch-thick slices chorizo or other spicy sausage**
> **8 large eggs**
> **$\frac{1}{4}$ cup grated Gouda or Swiss cheese**

Preheat the oven to 400F(205C).

Heat the oil in a large skillet. Add the onion and bell pepper, and cook over low heat stirring frequently, until softened but not browned, 7 to 10 minutes. Add the garlic, tomatoes, and chile peppers, and sauté over medium heat, stirring, until most of the liquid has evaporated, 7 to 10 minutes. Season generously with salt and black pepper.

In the meantime, sauté the sausage in a nonstick skillet until lightly browned on both sides, 2 to 3 minutes.

Divide the tomato sauce evenly among 4 individual flameproof gratin dishes or one large one. Make an indentation in the tomato sauce in the center of each for the eggs. Carefully break 2 eggs at a time into a bowl; slide them into the indentation. Season with salt and black pepper. Dot each with 1 tablespoon of cheese. Arrange 3 slices of sausage around the eggs.

Bake 7 to 10 minutes, until the egg whites are milky and the yolks are set but still soft. Serve immediately.

Avocados

The avocado, or palta as it is referred to in Chile, is a highly regarded fruit. The wide range of climates in Chile allows a year-round supply of this staple in our markets. Avocados are big business here and most are destined for exportation. The Californian-style Haas avocado, with its wrinkled dark green skin and excellent taste and texture, is the leading variety. It is great for stuffing. Huge, majestic-looking avocado trees often grace the parks and gardens of the colonial-style mansions and haciendas. The trees bear small, dark fruit that are somewhat stringy but have an outstanding, rich flavor. These are the avocados Chilean connoisseurs prefer.

Another common Chilean avocado is the Fuerte or Florida-style variety. This one is larger, sweeter, and moister than the Haas avocado. With its smooth, bright green skin and nutty flavor, the Fuerte avocado is the favorite for preparing spreads and velvety soups. A great plus of this variety is that it contains far less fat and calories than the Haas.

Baked Eggs in Creamy Corn Sauce with Basil

Huevos con Pilco de Choclo

Makes 4 servings

El pilco, a native corn dish, has a name that sounds like a song. This thick, creamy corn sauce, somehow always flavored with basil, turns up in many local dishes. Sometimes meat is cooked in the sauce, sometimes it is paired with other vegetables such as green beans, potatoes, or white beans for a purely vegetarian meal; and sometimes it is simply served as a side dish with roasted meats or poultry.

The following recipe has become my favorite brunch dish. The chunky, tasty corn mixture makes a wonderful accompaniment to baked eggs. It's easy, healthy, and surprisingly good. Just don't forget to serve a pungent fresh tomato salsa, for example, Chancho en Piedra (p. 60), alongside in the pure Chilean tradition.

> 1 tablespoon butter
> 3 tablespoons finely chopped onion
> 4 cups fresh or frozen corn kernels
> 1½ cups whole milk or half-and-half
> Salt and freshly ground black pepper, to taste
> 1 tablespoon finely minced fresh basil
> 4 or 8 eggs (1 or 2 per person)
> 2 tablespoons butter

Preheat the oven to 400F (205C). Butter 4 individual earthenware dishes or 1 large one.

Melt the butter in a medium saucepan over low heat. Add the onion and sauté until softened but not browned, 4 minutes. Add the corn and milk. Bring to a boil, reduce the heat, and simmer, uncovered, stirring occasionally, until the corn is tender and most of the liquid is absorbed, 10 to 15 minutes. (Frozen corn will take a little longer than fresh because it releases more water.) Season generously with salt, black pepper, and basil. (The dish can be prepared in advance up to this point. Reheat the corn mixture, adding a little milk if necessary, before continuing.)

Spoon the corn mixture evenly into the prepared dishes. Make an indentation in the corn mixture in the center of each dish for the eggs. Carefully break 1 or 2 eggs at a time into a bowl, and let them slide into each indentation. Season with salt and black pepper, and dot with the butter. Bake 7 to 10 minutes, until the egg white is milky and the yolk is set but still soft. Serve immediately.

Avocado-Butter Spread

A spread of mashed ripe avocados—generously seasoned with salt, freshly ground black pepper, and a little oil—is as common on Chilean tables as the jar of peanut butter in the United States. The spread is simply smeared on lightly toasted bread, much like butter. It's also an indispensable spread for most Chilean sandwiches, from the *completo* (hot dog served with avocado, tomatoes or sauerkraut, and mayonnaise) to the *chacarero* (a combination of roast beef, green beans, tomatoes, avocado, and hot chiles) and the many Chilean churrasco (roast beef) sandwiches.

Avocados with Chicken and Red Pepper Filling, Chilean Style

Palta Reina

Makes 4 servings

Palta Reina, a richly stuffed avocado "fit for a queen," is considered a real delicacy and presides on the menu of every respectable restaurant featuring Chilean cooking. Diced cooked chicken, red bell pepper, and mayonnaise is certainly the most common filling; but the buttery avocado is, to my taste, the perfect match for the delicate and refined flavor of seafood. You don't have to be a kitchen wizard or spend hours shopping for exotic ingredients to prepare this tasty appetizer. The most important thing is to serve *ripe* avocados, so it's wise to buy them a few days in advance and let them ripen wrapped in a brown paper bag.

> 2 ripe but firm avocados, preferably Haas
> Juice of ½ lemon
> Salt and freshly ground black pepper, to taste
> 1 whole chicken breast, cooked and cooled
> 1 cup mayonnaise
> ¼ red bell pepper, roasted, skinned, and finely chopped, or canned
>   pimientos
> 1 tablespoon minced fresh chives
> 1 head Boston lettuce, rinsed and finely shredded
> 1 tablespoon finely minced fresh parsley
> 8 ripe olives, garnish

Peel the avocados, cut into halves lengthwise, and remove the pits. Sprinkle each half with a little lemon juice and salt.

Discard the skin and the bones of the chicken and chop the meat finely. In a bowl, combine the chicken with about half of the mayonnaise, the bell pepper, chives, salt, and black pepper.

Fill the avocado halves with the chicken mixture. Arrange the lettuce on 4 small plates. Top with the filled avocado, and garnish with the parsley and olives. Serve the remaining mayonnaise on the side.

Variations

Avocados Stuffed with Shrimp or Crabmeat
Paltas Rellenas con Camarones

Arrange the peeled and halved avocados on a bed of shredded lettuce. Pour 1 tablespoon cocktail sauce in each half, and fill with 1¼ cups cooked shrimp or 1¼ cups lump crabmeat, picked over. Garnish with finely chopped hard-cooked egg and minced parsley. Serve some extra cocktail sauce on the side.

Avocados Stuffed with Russian Salad
Paltas Rellenas con Rusa

Arrange the peeled and halved avocados on a bed of shredded lettuce. Fill with Ensalada Rusa (p. 80), and garnish with a handful of ripe olives.

Avocados Stuffed with Rice and Ham
Paltas Rellenas con Arroz y Jamon

Arrange the peeled and halved avocados on a bed of shredded lettuce. Mix together 1 cup cooked rice, 1 mashed avocado, ½ cup diced cooked ham, ¼ cup extra-virgin olive oil, 2 tablespoons freshly squeezed lemon juice, and salt and freshly ground black pepper to taste. Fill the avocados with the rice mixture, garnish with minced parsley or cilantro.

Baby Artichokes Marinated in Green Herb Vinaigrette

Alcachofas Rellenas con Salsa Verde

Makes 4 servings

In Chile, artichokes grow profusely. This somewhat bizarre-looking vegetable with its well-hidden heart is just as popular here as it is in the Mediterranean area. Out in the country, artichokes are picked at an early stage and are available for the local aficionados, like me, when they are still firm with tender tightly closed leaves. In the city markets, the larger ones, ideal for stuffing, are sold. Both are delicious as long as they are picked and eaten on the same day, or not much longer.

Most Chileans prefer their artichokes pure and simply prepared. Blanched to tenderness, the vegetable is patiently dismantled at the table, each leaf dipped in a refreshing vinaigrette. In Chile, cooks add a tablespoon each of vinegar and flour to the cooking water to keep the artichokes green.

For this recipe, use the smallest artichokes available. At this early stage, the choke hasn't formed yet; and the yellowish central cones, attached to the bottom part, are still tender and edible. Served with a salsa verde, a pungent vinaigrette chock-full of fresh herbs, they are a real delicacy. This vinaigrette is often paired with young asparagus.

> **16 tender, baby artichokes, left whole, part of the stem still attached**
> **Salt and freshly ground black pepper, to taste**
> **½ cup vegetable oil**
> **¼ cup freshly squeezed lemon juice**
> **2 tablespoons finely minced fresh parsley**
> **2 tablespoons finely minced fresh cilantro**
> **1 hard-cooked egg, white and yolk chopped separately**

Bring 5 quarts of salted water to a boil in a large, nonreactive pot over medium heat. Add the artichokes, stem side down. Boil uncovered until a leaf can be pulled out easily, 20 to 25 minutes. Drain the artichokes upside down in a colander.

Meanwhile, whisk the oil with the lemon juice in a small bowl. Add the salt, pepper, 1 tablespoon of the parsley, and 1 tablespoon of the cilantro.

When the artichokes are cool enough to handle, carefully discard the tough green leaves, leaving the central yellow cone still attached to the bottom. Cut off the stem, and trim the base. Make sure to reserve all the edible parts from the leaves and stem. Chop these bits and pieces finely and add to the vinaigrette.

Arrange the artichoke cones on a colorful platter, and drizzle the vinaigrette evenly over the top.

Before serving, garnish the platter with the remaining 1 tablespoon of parsley and 1 tablespoon cilantro and chopped egg yolk and white.

Variation

If baby artichokes are not available, substitute artichoke bottoms for the preparing as directed on page 42.

Artichokes Stuffed with Tuna Fish and Celery Salad

Alcachofas Rellenas con Atún

Makes 4 servings

A nicely turned artichoke bottom is the ideal vessel for any kind of filling. This recipe is made with readily available ingredients: canned tuna, celery, onion, and mayonnaise. You can easily upgrade this appetizer by replacing the tuna with cooked diced shrimp, crabmeat, chicken, or ham or by filling with a vegetable salad or even caviar. I don't recommend using canned artichoke bottoms; they are overly acidic and high in sodium.

> 8 large artichokes
> 1 lemon, halved, and one-half cut into slices
> 2 tablespoons salt
> 6½ ounces water-packed tuna, well drained
> 1 hard-cooked egg, coarsely chopped
> 2 tablespoons finely chopped onion
> 3 tablespoons finely diced celery
> ½ cup mayonnaise, preferably homemade
> Freshly ground black pepper, to taste
> 8 lettuce leaves, patted dry
> 1 ripe tomato, cut into 8 wedges
> 2 tablespoons finely minced fresh parsley

Using a sharp stainless-steel knife, trim off the artichoke stems and slice 1 inch off the top. Rub the cuts with the lemon half.

Place the artichokes, stem side down, in a large nonreactive pot and cover with water. Add the salt and 4 lemon slices. Bring to a boil, reduce the heat, and boil gently uncovered until tender, 35 to 45 minutes. To test for doneness, pull a leaf out; if it comes out easily without resistance, the artichoke is done. Drain the artichokes upside down in a colander or on a rack.

When cool enough to handle, discard all the green leaves, scraping off and saving all the edible parts in a small bowl. Scoop out the fuzzy choke with a small spoon. Trim the bottom to a nice round shape.

Combine the tuna, egg, onion, celery, and the reserved artichoke pieces in a medium bowl. Add the mayonnaise and black pepper; toss gently with a fork. Adjust the seasoning.

Stuff the artichoke bottoms with the tuna and celery salad. Arrange the lettuce on a serving platter. Place the stuffed artichokes on top of the lettuce, and garnish with the tomato wedges and parsley.

Composed Salad, Chilean Style

Salpicón

Makes 4 to 6 servings

*S*alpicón is an ingenious way for the creative cook to use leftover roast meat, poultry, or cooked vegetables and turn it into an interesting salad. Along the Chilean coast, I've tasted my favorite versions, which are made with mussels, clams, or crabmeat. Anything goes; as long as you use good-quality and flavorful ingredients, the result will be wonderful and satisfying. Use this recipe as a guideline; the only limit is your imagination.

> 2 medium potatoes, unpeeled
> 1 large carrot, unpeeled
> Salt, to taste
> 1/2 cup fresh or frozen green peas
> 1/2 cup fresh or frozen corn kernels
> 1/2 cup fresh or frozen green beans, cut into 1/4-inch pieces, optional
> 2 hard-cooked eggs, cubed
> 2 cups cooked poultry, beef, pork or lamb or cooked shellfish, cut
>   into 1/4-inch cubes
> 1/4 cup whole ripe olives
> 1 scallion, chopped
> 1 head Boston lettuce, finely shredded
> 1 ripe avocado, cut into 1/4-inch cubes, optional
> 1 ripe tomato, peeled, seeded, and diced, optional
> 1/2 cup vegetable or extra-virgin olive oil
> 3 tablespoons freshly squeezed lemon juice or white wine vinegar
> Freshly ground black pepper, to taste
> 2 tablespoons finely minced fresh parsley or cilantro

Place the potatoes and carrot in a medium saucepan; cover with cold water, and add salt. Bring to a boil, reduce the heat, and simmer partly covered until tender, 20 to 25 minutes Drain, and let cool. Peel the vegetables, and cut into a ¼-inch dice.

Bring a pot of salted water to a boil. Add the peas, corn, and green beans, and cook uncovered until crisp-tender, 10 minutes. Drain and refresh under cold running water.

In a large bowl, combine the cooked vegetables with the eggs, meat, olives, scallion, lettuce, avocado, and tomato. Add the oil, lemon juice, salt, and black pepper. Toss to combine. Sprinkle with the fresh parsley, and serve at once.

Potatoes Stuffed with Watercress, Orange, and Cheese

Entrada de Berros con Papas y Queso

Makes 6 servings

In this tasty and refreshing appetizer, the peppery bite of the watercress is paired with creamy potatoes and tangy oranges. In Chile, watercress is mostly served as a salad, dressed with a splash of fresh lemon and olive oil, or as an uneaten garnish for the serving platter. Truly a shame considering the interesting, bold flavor of these decorative leaves.

Where I live, at the foot of the Andean Mountains, watercress grows freely in the many brooks that are fed by melting snow. But, according to my old kitchen manual, watercress can harbor harmful parasites so one must be sure that the water isn't polluted, and always rinse the watercress thoroughly under cold running water before serving.

> 6 large baking potatoes, unpeeled
> 1 tablespoon salt
> 1 bay leaf
> 1 bunch watercress (about 4 ounces) or 3 cups leaves, packed
> 2 hard-cooked eggs, peeled
> 2 teaspoons Dijon mustard
> ½ cup plus 3 tablespoons vegetables oil
> 2 tablespoons finely minced fresh chives or scallions
> 1 orange, peeled, sliced, and cut into ¼-inch cubes
> 5 ounces Gouda, Swiss, or other hard cheese, cut into
>   ¼-inch cubes
> Freshly ground black pepper, to taste

Place the potatoes in a large saucepan, cover with cold water, and add the salt and bay leaf. Bring to a boil, reduce the heat, and simmer partially covered until fork-tender, 40 to 50 minutes. Drain, and let cool.

In the meantime, discard the tough stems of the watercress. Rinse the leaves thoroughly under cold running water, and drain.

Peel the cooled potatoes, and slice off about ½ inch of the top of each potato. Using a small spoon, carefully scoop out the potato meat, leaving a ½-inch shell all around. Cut the scooped-out potato into ¼-inch cubes and reserve.

In a medium bowl, mash 1 of the eggs with a fork. Add the mustard, oil, and chives. Mix well. Add the watercress leaves, reserving some for garnish, orange, cheese, and about 1½ cups of the potato cubes; toss to combine. Adjust the seasonings with salt and black pepper, and fill the potato shells.

Arrange the reserved watercress leaves in a decorative pattern on individual plates; place 1 filled potato in the center of each. Finely chop the remaining 1 egg, and sprinkle evenly over the potatoes. Serve at once.

A Taste of Chilean Aperitivos

The inspired combination of tart lime or lemon juice, sugar, and a heady aguardiente gave birth to some of the most famous aperitivos of South and Central America: the Mexican margarita, the Peruvian sour, the Brazilian caipirinha, and the Chilean pisco sour.

La Serena and Coquimbo, two charming coastal towns north of Santiago, and the dry and sun-washed nearby Elquí Valley present just the right microclimate for the production of pink Moscatel grapes, the base of the national brandy-like liquor named *pisco*. Another area appreciated for its pisco is the Limari Valley.

Stored in wooden casks for two to twelve months pisco develops its distinctive, mellow grape flavor. The oldest brandy, called *gran pisco*, is the most sought after.

The younger and fruitier pisco (with also less alcohol) is an excellent base for the national Pisco Sour (p. 50) or other fruit-based cocktail. The farther north you go, the hotter the climate, the more arid the scenery, and the more exotic the drinks. Everything from papaya, passion fruit, mango, pineapple, and guava to the exquisite cherimoya (custard apple) is blended and shaken into refreshing cocktails.

Aguardiente de uva, a distillation of grapes grown south of Santiago, is an important ingredient in the second most popular aperitivo: Vaina (p. 51), a sweet blend of vino añejo, a portlike wine, aguardiente, cocoa, and egg yolks. It is very pleasant and most appreciated by the ladies.

The abundance of fruity young wines, red and white, and the cornucopia of seasonal fruits inspired many chefs to concoct light and easy-drinking cocktails, such as the Bourgogna (p. 55), ripe strawberries steeped in wine, and Ponche de Duraznos (p. 53), sweet peaches and sparkling wine.

The farther south you travel from Santiago, the lusher and greener the scenery, right into the spectacular Lake District—a region admired for its rivers, volcanoes, forests, and natural lakes and feared for its treacherous climate! Even in the middle of summer, we sometimes stay indoors around a gentle fireplace, hiding from the chilly showers. It's a reminder of my childhood in Belgium. And when we're visiting friends and our host produces a number of interesting-looking bottles that contain a selection of locally made liqueurs, I feel completely at home. It seems to me that *guindado*, an intensely flavored sour-cherry liqueur, comes straight out of my grandmother's cellar. It isn't really surprising, because many descendants of German settlers still make their home in the south of Chile.

I've tasted *manzanilla* (chamomile liqueur), *apiado* (celery liqueur), and *liquor de oro*, a syrupy, dense, herbed liquid with the color of gold; liqueurs with honey, blackberries, and raspberries; and liqueurs from a variety of wild herbs. I suspect Chileans have distilled about everything imaginable!

Whenever you're invited to someone's home, you wouldn't think of leaving the table after the meal without tasting and discussing the merits of the host's *bajativos*, or after-dinner drinks. I must admit, I find myself quite fascinated by the mystery of this timeless occupation; and I have a few concoctions in my own cellar, waiting to be degusted, and "passionately" discussed.

Pisco Sour

Makes 1 cocktail

Pisco (Chilean brandy) is mostly produced with the aromatic grapes that grow in the mysterious Elquí Valley, north of Santiago. Over the years the outlying hills of the same valley have attracted a host of esoteric movements and guru-led communities, in part, no doubt, owing to the great clarity of the night skies and the sensation that heaven is close. The valley, also known for its thermal springs and observatories, was made famous by the writings of Gabriela Mistral, the first Nobel Prize laureate for literature in the Americas.

> 1½ ounces (3 tablespoons) freshly squeezed lemon juice
> 4½ ounces (½ cup plus 1 tablespoon) pisco
> 2 teaspoons powdered sugar, or to taste
> ½ teaspoon egg white
> Cracked ice

Place lemon juice, pisco, sugar, and egg white into a cocktail shaker over cracked ice. Shake well until foamy. Strain into a small glass. No garnish is needed.

Note

Raw eggs may contain salmonella and should never be served to anyone who is ill or has a compromised immune system.

Sweet Port and Egg Cocktail

Vaina

Makes 4 cocktails

This smooth, sweet cocktail is a much-praised *aperitivo* in Chile, especially by the ladies. I like to serve it as an after-dinner drink, to be slowly sipped and enjoyed while sitting next to a fireplace on a cold and endless winter night.

> **1 cup port wine or sweet sherry**
> **½ cup crème de cacao liqueur**
> **⅓ cup cognac**
> **4 egg yolks**
> **Cracked ice**
> **Cinnamon for sprinkling**

Place all the ingredients, except the cinnamon, in a blender or cocktail shaker, and mix. Pour into sherry glasses or champagne flutes. Sprinkle cinnamon on top.

N o t e
Raw eggs may contain salmonella and should never be served to anyone who is ill or has a compromised immune system.

Monkey's Tale

Cola de Mono

Makes 5 cups, about 7 servings

Cola de Mono is much like a cooled and spiced version of café con latte with a generous shot of aguardiente to give it a kick. It's indeed a very pleasant drink, bearing the strange name of Monkey's Tale. I never found out why. What I did find out is that around the Christmas holidays, it's wise to have a serious reserve of Cola de Mono in the house along with sweet Pan de Pascua de la Mami Clara (p. 262) a dense bread studded with nuts and candied fruits. It's the busiest "family visits" period of the year, and traditionally the hungry travelers are welcomed with a glass of Cola de Mono and a slice of the sweet bread.

> **1 quart whole milk**
> **½ cup sugar**
> **1 cinnamon stick**
> **2 whole cloves**
> **1 tablespoon pure vanilla extract**
> **3 tablespoons powdered coffee**
> **1 cup 100-proof aguardiente de uva, brandy, or rum**

Combine the milk, sugar, cinnamon stick, cloves, and vanilla in a heavy saucepan. Simmer over low heat or until the spices infuse the milk with their flavors, about 15 minutes. Bring the milk just to a boil and remove the pan from the heat.

Add the coffee and liquor. Strain the mixture into clean bottle(s). Cover and refrigerate until ready to serve, up to 3 days.

Peach Punch

Ponche de Duraznos

Makes 4 servings

In Chile, punches are traditionally served in an earthenware bowl from Quin-chamali, a small community known for its pottery. There is nothing like a tree-ripened white peach eaten in the summer sun—a luxury I rediscovered in Chile. Their exquisite fragrance turns this popular refreshing aperitif into divine nectar.

> **6 ripe white or yellow peaches or nectarines, peeled, pitted, and diced**
> **Sugar to taste**
> **1 (750-milliliter) bottle fruity white wine or sparkling wine**
> **Ice cubes for serving**

Place the diced peaches and sugar in a large glass jar. Pour all the white wine or half the sparkling wine over the fruit, and let steep in the refrigerator 2 to 6 hours.

Serve in tall glasses filled with ice cubes. If using sparkling wine, pour the remaining wine into the glasses just before serving.

Variation

Slice off the top of a ripe honeydew or cantaloupe melon. Scoop out the seeds and use a melon baller to take out the fruit. Fill the melon shell with melon balls, fruity white wine, and 2 tablespoons sugar. Cover with plastic wrap, and refrigerate until chilled. Use a small ladle to pour the aromatic wine and fruit into wide glasses; garnish each with a sprig of fresh mint.

Strawberries, a Fragrant Chilean Gift to the World

Between the years 1714 and 1716, an adventuresome French lad named Amédée Francois Frézier traveled extensively in the narrow country called Chile. In his travel journal, he described a delicious, unique fruit he had found in the woods. A few plants of the juicy, big strawberries were shipped to France and handed to Monsieur Jussieu, the head gardener of the imperial gardens of Versailles. This fragrant New World fruit adapted well to its new environment and delighted the French court. Before this the tiny wild strawberries were the only ones known in the Old World.

Almost a century later, Charles Darwin found more strawberries in the southern Chilean islands of Chiloé. The rest is history.

The Chilean strawberry, *Fragaria chilensis*, is indeed one of the mother plants of the plump, sweet fruits we find in our markets. A fact all my Chilean friends are extremely proud of . . . and for good reason!

Strawberry Wine

Bourgogna

Makes 4 servings

This is a beautifully, refreshing drink, ideal for outdoor events, barbecues, or garden parties. Strain any leftover wine and serve the next day with a whole, frozen strawberry in the glass.

> 1½ cups ripe strawberries, hulled and sliced into small cubes (¾
>   pound) or raspberries, slightly crushed
> About 5 tablespoons sugar, depending on sweetness of fruit
> 2-inch piece orange zest
> 3 cups young Chilean red wine
> 2 tablespoons orange liqueur (optional)
> 4 orange slices or mint sprigs, garnish

Combine all the ingredients, except the orange slices, in a glass jar, and steep in the refrigerator 2 to 6 hours. Serve chilled. Decorate the glasses with a slice of orange.

Almond-Flavored Wine

Vino de Durazno

Makes about 2 cups, 2 or 3 servings

In the Chilean countryside, I've tasted the wildest combinations of liqueurs made with all sorts of leaves, berries, roots, and . . . well, you name it. But this refreshing wine with a distinctive and pleasant almond flavor caught my attention. If you happen to have a peach tree in your garden, surprise your friends with this wonderful aperitif wine.

> **20 peach leaves, washed and dried**
> **3 tablespoons sugar**
> **2 cups rosé wine**
> **3 tablespoons aguardiente**

Arrange the peach leaves in a glass jar. Add the sugar, and pour the wine and aguardiente on top; the leaves should be completely immersed. Cover, and let macerate in a cool place for 45 days.

Strain the wine, and refrigerate until ready to serve.

Chilean Salsas

Fiery, sizzling salsas or vibrant, refreshing, and chunky sauces seem to be the hot item on every menu in the United States. Many recipes have included exotic fruits, rare herbs, and vegetables but the one thing they all have in common is the chile.

In Chile, this popular ingredient is called ají. Chile is a Mexican word adopted in the United States for both mild and hot chiles.

Chiles are members of the Solanaceae, or nightshade family, as are tomatoes and potatoes. Chiles may have originated in South America, where they were prized by the pre-Colombian Incas and Mayas and later by other indigenous populations for their vibrant flavor and curative powers.

But, contrary to what the country's name may suggest, Chile isn't really the hot pepper's paradise or the secret birthplace of the popular chili stew. The name *Chile* is believed to have come from an Indian word for "snow," referring to the eternally snow-capped Andes Mountains.

In fact, the cuisine of Chile can hardly be considered a spicy cuisine. Its hearty dishes, deeply rooted in rural traditions, are rich in texture, nutritious, and satisfying but are rather discreetly flavored with sweet paprika, ground cumin, and dried oregano. The heat is served as side dishes, in pungent salsas or sizzling pevres.

Since pre-Colombian times, indigenous cooks understood the power of the chile as a wonderful flavor enhancer. In the seventeenth century, Spanish chronicler Gómez de Vidaurre warned his fellow countrymen of the fiery condiment but noted that once one's used to the heat, it's easy to become addicted to the ají for its many benefits. But never in Chile was the ají to become the torturous ingredient it has turned into in the United States, where too many times the blazing heat of a dish sets your mouth on fire and toasts your taste buds to ashes.

The most widely used chile is the lime green ají verde, a plump, thick-fleshed, medium-hot chile. It resembles the yellow wax chile, which is also called the Hungarian wax chile. Its fruity, vivid flavor enlivens salsas, pevres, and tomato salads. Halved and the seeds removed, the ají verde is often dipped in salt and eaten with a bowl of beans or a hearty meat and vegetable stew. A good substitute for the ají verde is the fresh green serrano or jalapeño chile pepper.

The hotter ají cacho de cabra—a thin, reddish, and fiery chile—is commonly used in dried and powder forms, and is known as ají picante. Substitute with cayenne pepper.

The mild-mannered pimentón, the crunchy, sweet bell pepper, is enjoyed raw in salads and omelets or cooked, adding a vibrant note to popular stews and casseroles. Roasted red sweet peppers, packed in jars or cans, are referred to as *pimentones morrones* and seem to be the most popular garnish for cocktail fare and appetizers.

Dried and powdered sweet pepper is the base of *ají de color*, or paprika, a staple spice in the Chilean cuisine.

And to make matters a bit confusing, *pimiento*, the Spanish word for "pepper," refers to peppercorns (whether black or white), which are not even part of the abundant *Capsicum* genus but are *Piper nigrum*.

Julita's Fresh Tomato Salsa

Salsa de Tomate de la Tia Julita

Makes 2 servings

My mother-in-law, Tia Julita, likes bold flavors; and fresh salsa is her way to add zest to a subtle carrot omelet, an ordinary hot dog, or about anything in life that needs some spice!

> 1 large, ripe tomato, peeled and coarsely chopped
> 1 large clove garlic, finely minced
> ½ serrano or jalapeño chile, seeded and finely minced, or to taste
> 1 tablespoon vegetable oil
> Salt and freshly ground black pepper, to taste

Combine all the ingredients in a small bowl. Let the salsa stand for about 30 minutes, so the tomato can release its precious juices.

Know Your Chiles and Be Cautious!

Chiles have the reputation of being unpredictable. Two chile peppers, even grown on the same plant, can differ greatly in level of heat. My advice: Always taste them and the dish you're preparing.

I usually recommend removing the ribs and all the seeds of the little devils. Most of the flavor is concentrated in the fleshy parts, whereas the heat is in the seeds and ribs. I especially like my toothed grapefruit spoon for removing the seeds.

It's a good idea to wear rubber gloves when mincing chiles. And don't forget: *Never touch your eyes or face when handling chile peppers.* It's risky business.

Chilean Salsa

Chancho en Piedra

Makes about 2 cups

Select juicy red tomatoes, pungent green chiles, sweet onions, and young garlic to capture the Chilean summer on your table. This is the national salsa. It's an exhilarating complement to the grilled meats and roasted chicken or fish and a zesty companion to Chilean specialties, such as empanadas (p. 16), humitas (p. 206), and Pastel de Choclo (p. 130). Indeed, this delicious salsa combines with nearly everything, and it easily becomes a hot addiction!

> **6 cloves garlic, peeled**
> **2 green serrano or jalapeño chiles, seeded and chopped**
> **1½ teaspoons coarse sea salt or kosher salt**
> **6 ripe tomatoes, peeled, seeded, and chopped**
> **1 cup finely chopped sweet Spanish or Vidalia onion**
> **1 tablespoon finely minced fresh cilantro**
> **½ teaspoon dried oregano**
> **½ cup vegetable oil**
> **2 tablespoons red wine vinegar**

In a large mortar, crush the garlic, chile peppers, and salt to a paste, using a circular motion with your pestle. If you don't have a mortar, use a knife to chop the garlic and chiles with the salt as fine as possible; then use the broad side of the knife against the chopping board to purée the mixture.

In the same mortar or in a serving bowl, add all the other ingredients, and combine well. To control the heat, set some of the puréed chile mixture aside and add at the end to taste. This salsa is best when freshly prepared, but leftovers will keep well 2 to 3 days in the refrigerator.

What's in a Name?

In Chile, the heavy mortar, commonly called *la piedra*, is still a much-used kitchen utensil. Carved out of grayish lava stone, the mortar is a beautiful object, and I like to bring salsa to the table right in the mortar. My Chilean friends, however, serve salsa in common earthenware bowls, which are often shaped in the form of a pig.

No modern kitchen gadget crushes garlic, chiles, and other ingredients to a fragrant paste as effectively as does the mortar and pestle. This motion of *chancar en piedra*, (crushing or grinding in the stone) is said to be the origin of Chilean salsa's name chancho en piedra, which literally means "little pig in stone."

In the south of the country, this popular salsa is affectionately referred to as pebre cuchareado. It's the local cowboys' favorite salsa to have with tapas. I've seen them spoon the addictive salsa on pieces of pan amasado, dense homemade breads, and on sopaipillas, flat and tasty pumpkin fritters. Either way, there's never enough of it!

Southern Hot Green Sauce

Pebre Verde del Sur de Chile

Makes about 1½ cups

This is a hot variation of Salsa Verde (p. 64) with, of course, plenty of hot chiles. What's the secret ingredient? Merquén, a pungent dried spice mixture. It is made up of oregano, coriander, salt, and the hotter than hot ají cacho de cabra. Merquén is popular in southern Chile and is widely used to enliven stews, salsas, and sausages. I think it's the perfect dry spice rub for grilled meats and poultry. In this recipe, I've listed the ingredients so you can make your own merquén.

> 1 cup finely chopped Spanish or Vidalia onion
> 1½ teaspoons coarse sea salt or kosher salt
> 1 large clove garlic, peeled
> 1½ serrano or jalapeño chiles, seeded and finely chopped, or to taste
> 1½ cups packed finely minced fresh cilantro leaves
> 1 teaspoon merquén or ½ teaspoon dried oregano, ¼ teaspoon
>   ground coriander, and ⅛ teaspoon cayenne pepper
> 2 tablespoons vegetable oil
> 2 tablespoons red wine vinegar
> ¼ cup lukewarm water

Place the onion and ½ teaspoon of the salt in a small bowl. Cover with cold water, and soak 15 minutes. Drain in a colander, and rinse briefly under cold running water. Shake well.

In a large mortar, crush the garlic, chiles, and the remaining 1 teaspoon of salt to a paste, using a circular motion with your pestle. If you don't have a mortar, use a knife to chop the garlic, chiles, and salt as fine as possible. Then use the broad side of the knife against the chopping board to purée the mixture. Transfer the paste to a serving bowl.

Add the onion to the chile paste along with all the remaining ingredients. Mix well and taste for seasoning. This salsa keeps for 3 to 4 days in the refrigerator.

Green Herb Sauce

Salsa Verde

Makes about 1½ cups

With its overtones of fresh green herbs, this mild, green salsa is actually a vinaigrette. It tastes great with grilled meats and vegetables. In Chile, it traditionally accompanies poached tongue, trout, and shellfish. The secret is to use a mild vegetable oil, fresh herbs bursting with flavor, and enough salt to bring it all together.

½ cup finely chopped Spanish or Vidalia onion
1 teaspoon sugar
½ cup finely minced fresh cilantro leaves
¼ cup finely minced fresh parsley leaves
4 fresh celery leaves, finely minced
1 clove garlic, finely minced
½ serrano or jalapeño chile, seeded and chopped, or 1 tablespoon ground fresh chile paste, such as the sambal oelek or Moroccan harissa sauce, or to taste
6 tablespoons mild vegetable oil, such as safflower or corn
2 tablespoons white wine vinegar or freshly squeezed lemon juice
1 tablespoon coarse sea salt
¼ cup warm water

Place the onion and sugar in a bowl and cover with cold water; soak 15 minutes. Drain in a colander and rinse briefly under cold running water. Shake well.

Combine the onion with all the remaining ingredients in a serving bowl. Taste for seasonings, and adjust as needed; this vinaigrette should be brimming with flavor. Refrigerate until ready to serve or up to 1 week.

Chunky Red Chile Salsa

Pebre Chileno

Makes about 1½ cups

This enticing salsa is based on the ubiquitous salsa de ají (red chile sauce). In the *picadas,* popular food joints, there's always a plastic jar of salsa de ají sitting on the table, next to the ketchup and mustard.

In every store, you'll find several brands of red sauce, some are smoothly puréed, others are chunky with fiery seeds. You can make it from scratch or substitute a commercial Caribbean hot sauce, Indonesian sambal oelek, or Moroccan harissa sauce. Experiment with the heat!

In Chile, pebre is often served in the ubiquitous earthenware dish shaped in the form of a little pig. Transfer any leftovers to a glass or plastic jar; this salsa is so explosive and acidic that it corrodes pottery!

> 1 cup Salsa de Ají Colorado a la Chilena (p. 66) or ground fresh
>   chile paste, such as Caribbean hot sauce, Indonesian sambal
>   oelek, or Moroccan harissa sauce
> 2 tablespoons finely minced fresh cilantro leaves
> 1 clove garlic, finely minced
> 2 tablespoons finely chopped onion
> 1 tablespoon vegetable oil

Combine all the ingredients in a glass or plastic jar. Cover and refrigerate up to 1 week.

Red Chile Sauce

Salsa de Ají Colorado a la Chilena

Makes about 1 cup

On as hot a subject as this one, no one will ever agree! There just isn't only one recipe. This concoction is basically liquefied, ripe chiles with a little seasoning to underscore their flavor. Some recipes use vinegar, others oil, to preserve the chiles.

This recipe was given to me by my dear friend Angelica when I was trying to find a way to use up all the chiles from my prolific garden. If you like fiery hot stuff, leave the seeds in the chiles; if you like to play it cooler, take them out. Remember to wear rubber gloves when handling the chiles.

> **15 ripe red serrano or jalapeño chiles**
> **1 cup red wine vinegar**
> **1 clove garlic, crushed**
> **1 tablespoon salt**

Cut off the little stems from the chiles and discard the seeds, for a milder salsa. Place the chiles in a glass bowl, and add the vinegar, garlic, and salt. Cover and let marinate overnight. This step will slightly soften the skin of the chiles.

Transfer the chiles and ½ cup of the vinegar mixture to a blender. Purée until the mixture has the consistency of a barbecue sauce (seeds still intact) or, if you discarded the seeds, purée to absolute smoothness. Store this salsa in tightly sealed jars. It will keep in the refrigerator for several months, and it just gets better with age.

Creole Salsa

Salsa Criolla

Makes 2¹/₂ cups

*T*his mild, chunky, and delicious salsa—made with juicy tomatoes, avocado, and sweet corn—is guaranteed to be a star at your next barbecue or summer picnic.

> 2 large, ripe tomatoes, peeled, seeded, and diced
> 1 ripe avocado, diced
> 1 cup fresh or frozen corn kernels, cooked and cooled
> ¹/₄ cup finely chopped onion
> 1 clove garlic, finely chopped
> 1 serrano or jalapeño chile, seeded and minced, or to taste
> 2 tablespoons chopped fresh cilantro
> ¹/₄ cup vegetable oil
> 1 tablespoon freshly squeezed lemon juice
> Salt, to taste

Combine all the ingredients in a serving bowl. Taste for seasoning. Serve at once.

A Taste of Chilean Salads and Soups

Ensaladas, Sopas, y Caldos

Who wants to spend hours cooking in the kitchen when the sun is out? Nobody. That's exactly how Chilean cooks look at it. And when you live in a country with farmers markets overflowing with beautiful produce on every street corner, the solution is obvious. Make salads. Apart from hardy vegetables, such as celery, carrots, beets, and cabbages, the subtropical northern regions provide the rest of the country with the usual summer specials.

Chileans love salads, and the selection goes further than a bowl of lettuce with a few sliced tomatoes. Actually, the accompaniment of choice to grilled or roasted meats or fish is an appetizing plate of mixed salads. This can include a selection of corn, green beans, cooked beets, a bean and spring onion salad, avocados, broccoli, peas, carrots, tomato and onion rings, crisp celery sticks—every imaginable vegetable is shredded, sliced, cooked, and diced and served in a colorful display. Dressings are minimal: freshly squeezed lemon juice, a drizzle of oil, and enough salt to bring out the natural flavor of each vegetable.

With produce that slowly ripened on the plant and is picked the same morning you bring it to the table, that's all you need! This doesn't mean that you won't find plastic-wrapped, picture-perfect carrots, tomatoes, and lettuces in the supermarkets that taste like . . . nothing! The price we pay for progress. Fortunately, farmers markets that offer locally grown produce are sprouting up all over the United States with increasing success. Do support them!

If you believe the Chileans, salads can be served with about everything: the Sunday barbecue, a summer buffet, pasta and pizza, a bowl of Porotos Granados (p. 208; fresh bean and corn casserole), or Humitas (p. 206; seasoned corn steamed in the husks).

Trying to summarize all the different Chilean salads is an impossible task. As abundant and varied are the offerings of fresh vegetables in the market, so also are the salad combinations numerous and creative. The more elaborate salads, often paired with seafood or cold cuts, are usually served as appetizers and are found in that chapter.

If you look through the recipes in this chapter, you will notice that many vegetables are cooked first and are always peeled. This was once (and sometimes still is) a necessary precaution against cholera when the safety of the produce was in doubt.

Hearty, nourishing, soulful soups are the backbone of the peasant's diet when the fields lay still and dormant. Nevertheless, these slow-simmered concoctions with an overtone of vegetables and a little meat for flavor and consistency have proven to be the perfect antidote for a stressful day, an upset stomach, or those lingering winter blues.

Chile's *cocina criolla* offers an interesting repertoire of original and great soups. Some are satisfying enough to be served as a whole meal and can be found in the "Poultry and Meats" chapter. This chapter also includes a famous fish soup, summer favorites made with fresh corn and tomatoes, a silky cold avocado soup, and many more to choose from.

The Chagual and the Penca

Always on the lookout for new things to taste, I noticed two strange-looking vegetables on a visit to the markets in the Central Valley. One is a whitish, cone-shaped root vegetable, known as *chagual*, that reminds me of the artichoke. It consists of a series of tough leaves tightly held together. These are shredded in the finest julienne and simply dressed with lemon juice, oil, and salt. Another unusual vegetable is *penca*, a member of the thistle family. It takes an experienced hand to peel the long stalks, which are studded with sharp thorns. What's left is a juicy stem, very much resembling a celery stalk in texture and taste. Both vegetables grow wild in the Cerros, the arid rolling hills stretching out between the coastal line and the valley. They are unique in taste and texture and solely found in Chile.

Chilean Tomato and Sweet Onion Salad

Ensalada a la Chilena

Makes 6 servings

This salad is without a doubt the queen of the Chilean salads. Juicy red tomatoes are paired with lots of paper-thin onion fans, and the flavors are heightened with a sprinkle of hot chiles and cilantro. In the Central Valley we are blessed with a warm and endless summer and sun-ripened, sweet tomatoes are abundant in our country markets for several months a year.

The sweet tomato offers us *el regalo de su color fogoso y la totalidad de su frescura,* "the gift of its fiery color and its total fresh coolness," as Pablo Neruda sings in his "Ode to the Tomato."

> 1 large Spanish or Vidalia onion, halved lengthwise and very thinly sliced
> 1 tablespoon salt
> 5 large ripe tomatoes, peeled and sliced
> 1 serrano or jalapeño chile, seeded and finely minced
> 1 tablespoon minced fresh cilantro or parsley
> 3 tablespoons vegetable or extra-virgin olive oil

Place the onion slices and salt in a bowl; cover with cold water, and soak for about 10 minutes. Drain in a colander and rinse briefly under cold running water. Shake well. This step will eliminate most of the sharpness of the onion.

Arrange the tomatoes on a platter. Salt generously. Top with the onion, chile, and cilantro. Sprinkle the oil evenly over the salad, toss to combine, and serve at once.

Sweet Onion Salad with Lemon and Parsley

Ensalada de Cebolla y Perejil

Makes 4 servings

At first, I was somewhat suspicious about this most unusual yet delicious combination. We all love onions but we do know that, when eaten raw, they tend to stick with you. To my surprise the onions in this salad tasted sweet and mild. The secret? Chilean cooks soak the sliced onions in salted or sugared water, which eliminates their unpleasant sharpness. Dressed with plenty of freshly squeezed lemon juice and flavored with fresh parsley or cilantro, you have a pure delight at hand. This salad is the perfect companion for summer barbecues.

> 1 large Spanish or Vidalia onion
> 1 tablespoon sugar
> ¾ cup freshly squeezed lemon juice
> 2 tablespoons vegetable oil
> 2 tablespoons coarsely chopped fresh parsley or cilantro
> 2 teaspoons salt, or to taste

Cut the onion in half lengthwise and slice as thinly as possible using a sharp knife or a mandoline.

Place the onion slices and the sugar in a bowl; cover with cold water, and soak for about 10 minutes. Drain in a colander and rinse briefly under cold running water. Shake well.

Before serving, arrange the sliced onion in a serving bowl. Dress with the lemon juice, oil, and parsley. Salt generously to bring out the intensity of all the flavors.

Chilean housewives have a peculiar way of slicing their favorite but treacherous bulb. Most recipes in local cookbooks call for *cebolla en pluma*, paper-thin slices, resembling feathers. The onion is cut in half horizontally through the root. Holding the rounded side in the palm of the hand, slice the onion from the stem toward the root, making long, very thin fans. When I asked Chilean cooks how they avoided suffering from irritated eyes, they answered me: "Slice very fast, so the onion doesn't even get a chance to torture you!" This is obviously a technique that calls for many years of practice.

An Ode to the Onion

I never came across a nation so devoted, so captivated by the humble onion as Chile is. Its abundance or scarcity, its price, its size, and its hidden juiciness seem to be the main preoccupations, animating the conversations around the marketplace. True, the onion is an indispensable ingredient; and more so, it is the backbone of most national specialties. What would the ubiquitous empanada, the beloved pastel de choclo, the famous tomato salad—affectionately named *la Chilena*—be without onions?

Even the celebrated poet Pablo Neruda felt inspired and praised the onion as a "fairy godmother in delicate paper, whose skin is peeled away, one layer after another to reveal a new and perfectly shaped entity . . . "

In Chile, the entire onion family is present in the country's markets, from the sweet yellow, red, and precious pearl onions to the mild scallions, intense shallots, sweet leeks, and pungent garlic. The large yellow onion, sweet and mild owing to local growing conditions and a sunny climate, is the most widely used in Chilean cooking. In the United States, look for the sweet Spanish or Vidalia onion for the best results.

Crispy Celery Sticks

Ensalada de Apio

Makes 4 to 6 servings

These crispy celery sticks are a popular winter salad in Chile and one to remember. It's simplicity itself: fresh, crunchy celery sticks, a generous squeeze of lemon juice, and enough salt to bring out these refreshing flavors. What's the trick? Choose young celery stalks that snap under your fingers when bent. Give the sticks an ice bath, which will keep them crunchy and make them curl attractively. Dress only as much celery as needed; the lemon juice "cooks" the celery and will leave it limp. Any leftover celery sticks keep perfectly fine in cold water until the next day, when you're ready to prepare another salad.

> **6 to 8 young celery ribs, leaves removed**
> **$\frac{1}{2}$ cup freshly squeezed lemon juice**
> **$\frac{1}{3}$ cup vegetable oil**
> **1 tablespoon salt, or to taste**
> **1 tablespoon finely minced fresh cilantro (optional)**

If the celery is stringy, peel off the long strings with a sharp knife. Cut the stalks into 2 × $\frac{1}{2}$-inch pieces. Make 3 to 4 lengthwise slits on one side to fan them out.

Place the celery sticks in a bowl filled with ice water; let sit at least 1 hour, or refrigerate overnight.

Before serving, drain the celery, and place in a bowl. Add the lemon juice, oil, and salt and toss to combine. If desired, sprinkle with cilantro.

Tricolored Festive Rice Salad

Ensalada de Arroz Tricolor

Makes 4 servings

Yellow corn, avocado, green rice, and deep ruby red beets—my mother-in-law is truly a wizard when creating beauty with vegetables. For this festive recipe, she layers the corn and the rice salad in a bowl, then unmolds it right before serving. If you use covered plastic bowls, you've found the ideal picnic salad! I like to serve it with a grilled chicken breast, hard-cooked eggs, shrimp, or a good-quality ham for a satisfying light meal.

> 3 cups fresh or frozen corn kernels, cooked and cooled
> 6 tablespoons mayonnaise
> 1 ripe Haas avocado
> 1 tablespoon freshly squeezed lemon juice
> 4 tablespoons vegetable oil
> Salt and freshly ground black pepper, to taste
> 2 cups cooked rice, cooled
> 1½ cups fresh or frozen green beans, cooked and cooled
> 1 tablespoon finely minced chives or scallions
> 2 large red beets, cooked and cooled
> 3 tablespoons red wine vinegar
> Lettuce leaves
> Freshly minced parsley or chives, whole ripe olives, or roasted red
>   pepper strips for garnish

In a small bowl, combine the corn with the mayonnaise.

Peel the avocado, halve, and remove the pit. In a large bowl, mash the avocado with a fork. Add the lemon juice, 1 tablespoon of the vegetable oil, the salt, and black pepper. Add the rice, green beans, and chives; stir to combine.

Press the corn mixture firmly into a round bowl just large enough to hold the corn and rice mixtures. Top with rice mixture, pressing firmly again. Cover the bowl with plastic wrap and refrigerate until ready to serve, or overnight.

Meanwhile, peel the beets, and cut into julienne. Place in a small bowl, and toss with the vinegar, remaining 3 tablespoons of oil, the salt, and black pepper. Cover the bowl with plastic wrap and refrigerate until ready to serve, or overnight.

To serve, arrange a few lettuce leaves on a large round platter. Unmold the corn and rice salad in the center, and arrange the beets around it. Sprinkle the top with freshly minced parsley, and garnish with a few olives or pepper strips.

Hearty Bean Salad with Scallions and Olives

Ensalada de Porotos, Cebollin y Aceitunas

Makes 4 to 6 servings

Leftover cooked beans are ideal for creating interesting salads. Dress them with a flavorful vinaigrette, fresh herbs, and a handful of olives and you have a quick, satisfying light meal. Or turn the bean salad into a trendy appetizer by adding cooked shrimp, a grilled chicken breast, quickly seared tuna steak, or whatever you fancy.

> **2 cups cooked or canned dried beans of any type or color, drained**
> **½ cup finely chopped onion**
> **1 teaspoon salt**
> **¼ cup diced red or green bell pepper**
> **3 tablespoons minced fresh parsley or cilantro**
> **1 serrano or jalapeño chile, seeded and finely minced, or to taste**
> **3 tablespoons vegetable or extra-virgin olive oil**
> **2 tablespoons red wine vinegar**
> **Salt and freshly ground black pepper, to taste**
> **½ cup ripe olives**

If using canned beans, rinse them in a colander under cold running water. Drain well.

Place the onion and 1 teaspoon salt in a small bowl. Cover with cold water, and soak for 10 minutes. Drain and rinse under cold running water. This step eliminates most of the sharpness of the onion and makes the salad more digestible.

In a serving bowl, combine the beans, onion, bell pepper, parsley, and chile.

In a small bowl, whisk together the oil, vinegar, salt, and black pepper. Pour the vinaigrette over the salad, and toss well. Taste for seasonings, and adjust as necessary. Place the salad on a serving platter, and garnish with the olives.

Russian Salad

Ensalada Rusa

Makes 6 servings

This colorful medley of vegetables is definitely an old-timer that some-what disappeared off our tables. In Chile, where traditions seem to survive longer than in trendier societies, la Rusa is still firmly leading the salad parade. I have to admit, when made from scratch with only fresh ingredients, it is better than any potato salad I have ever tasted and is certainly a far cry from the insipid version we have grown accustomed to that uses canned vegetables. The salad is open for interpretation, but the first five ingredients (not including salt) are considered staples. Aside from these, you can add as many of the suggested vegetables—or others—as you fancy, following the season's offerings.

> 2 medium potatoes, unpeeled
> 1 large carrot, unpeeled
> Salt to taste
> 1 cup fresh or frozen green peas
> 1 cup ¼-inch pieces fresh or frozen green beans
> ½ cup cooked fresh or frozen corn kernels, optional
> 1 celery rib (optional), diced
> 1 red beet (optional), cooked and diced
> ½ cup ¼-inch pieces cooked asparagus (optional)
> ½ green apple, peeled and diced
> ¼ cup pickled cucumbers or pearl onions (optional), diced
> ¼ cup coarsely chopped walnuts (optional)
> ¼ cup mayonnaise for every 1 cup vegetables
> Finely minced fresh parsley, cilantro, or chives, garnish

Place the potatoes, carrot, and salt in a medium saucepan, and cover with cold water. Bring to a boil over medium heat, reduce the heat to a simmer, and cook partially covered until tender, 20 to 25 minutes. Drain and let the vegetables cool. Peel and cut into a ¼-inch dice.

Bring a large pot of salted water to a boil. Add the peas and green beans, and cook uncovered until tender, 10 minutes. Drain, and refresh under cold running water.

Combine all the vegetables in a large serving bowl. Before serving, add the walnuts and mayonnaise; toss gently to combine. Garnish with parsley.

Variation

Substitute 2 cups cooked rice for the potatoes. Chilean cooks like to serve this Russian rice salad in a ring mold: Press the salad firmly into the mold using a spoon. Unmold on a serving platter and decorate with shredded lettuce, and a few wedges of hard-cooked egg and sliced tomatoes.

Swiss Chard, Egg, and Olive Salad

Ensalada de Acelga con Aceitunas

Makes 4 servings

Touring the Chilean country markets, I am often reminded of the French Provence region and the Italian Riviera, not only for the abundance and the quality of the offered produce but also for the shared respect and passion reserved for the dishes prepared with the same beautiful vegetables. One of these vegetables is the earthy tasting, leafy Swiss chard. In Chile, it is available almost year-round and is widely used in tortillas, soups, stews, and even in this unusual but tasty salad.

> **1 bunch Swiss chard, leaves and ribs separated, trimmed, and**
> **coarsely chopped**
> **¼ cup freshly squeezed lemon juice**
> **3 tablespoons extra-virgin olive or vegetable oil**
> **Salt and freshly ground black pepper, to taste**
> **2 hard-cooked eggs, sliced**
> **½ cup whole ripe olives**

Bring a large pot of salted water to a boil. Add the chard ribs, and boil about 5 minutes. Add the chard leaves, and boil 3 minutes more. Drain and refresh under cold running water. Gently squeeze the chard dry. If the pieces are still too big, chop them into bite-sized pieces.

In a medium bowl, combine the lemon juice, oil, salt, and black pepper. Add the chard and mix to combine.

Using a slotted spoon, transfer the chard to a colorful platter. Garnish with the egg slices and olives. Serve at once.

Avocado, Celery, and Pomegranate Salad

Ensalada de Paltas, Apio, y Granada

Makes 4 servings

The red pomegranate is mostly appreciated in Chile as a garden ornament and is rarely eaten. The juicy red kernels, however, are edible and lend a crunchy, tart bite to both savory and sweet salads. This recipe makes an elegant accompaniment to fish or poultry dishes.

> **2 ripe avocados, preferably Haas**
> **1 teaspoon Dijon mustard**
> **3 tablespoons freshly squeezed lemon juice**
> **6 tablespoons vegetable or extra-virgin olive oil**
> **Salt and freshly ground black pepper, to taste**
> **1 cup thinly sliced celery**
> **½ pomegranate, seeds removed**

Halve the avocados, pit, and scoop out the flesh using a melon baller.

Whisk the mustard, lemon juice, and oil in a medium bowl until well combined. Season with the salt and black pepper. Add the avocado balls and celery, and mix carefully. Garnish with the pomegranate seeds. Serve at once.

Maria-Theresa's Lentil Salad

Ensalada de Lentejas

Makes 4 servings

A hearty lentil salad is the ideal starter for your winter menu. This satisfying and delicious recipe comes from my friend, and excellent cook, Maria-Theresa. What's her trick? She infuses the lentils while they are still warm with a pungent vinaigrette that's flavored with a hint of cumin and plenty of fresh herbs. This salad will keep well for 2 or 3 days in the refrigerator.

> $1\frac{1}{2}$ **cups brown lentils, picked over and soaked in cold water for 4 hours**
> **1 large carrot, peeled and diced**
> **Salt and freshly ground black pepper, to taste**
> **1 bay leaf**
> **5 tablespoons vegetable or extra-virgin olive oil**
> **2 to 3 tablespoons red wine vinegar**
> $\frac{1}{2}$ **teaspoon ground cumin**
> **1 scallion, finely chopped, or $\frac{1}{4}$ cup finely chopped onion**
> **2 tablespoons minced fresh cilantro**
> **2 tablespoons minced fresh parsley**
> **1 hard-cooked egg (optional), chopped**

Drain the lentils, and place them in a large saucepan with 4 cups of cold water. Add the carrot, salt and pepper, and bay leaf. Bring to a boil, reduce the heat, and simmer covered until tender but not mushy, 25 to 40 minutes, depending on their size and age. Drain.

Meanwhile, in a small bowl, whisk the oil with the vinegar, cumin, salt, and black pepper.

Place the warm lentils and carrot in a serving bowl, and add two-thirds of the vinaigrette and the scallion. Toss well. (The recipe can be made to this step several hours before serving.)

Before serving, pour the rest of the vinaigrette over the lentils, add the herbs, and toss to combine. Taste for seasoning, adjusting as necessary; this salad should be well seasoned. Sprinkle with the chopped egg to serve the salad the Chilean way.

Early Pea and Spring Onion Salad

Ensalada Primavera

Makes 4 servings

*I*n Chile, the country markets clearly reflect the seasonal changes. One of the best parts of living in the fertile Central Valley with its mild winters is the availability of a wide variety of wonderful produce all year round. Yet no season equals the magic of spring, when the first sweet peas, fava beans, artichokes, tender asparagus, new onions, and tiny carrots come to market. Along with nature, the country folks seem to awaken. You can actually feel the difference; there's that touch of *alegría* that floats in the air . . . or is it a sigh of relief that winter is finally over?

Celebrate spring, and prepare this wonderful salad with all the best things the earth has to offer.

> **2 pounds fresh green peas, shelled and rinsed, or about 2¼ cups tiny frozen peas**
> **½ cup finely chopped spring onions or scallions**
> **1 teaspoon salt**
> **3 tablespoons vegetable oil**
> **1 tablespoon freshly squeezed lemon juice**
> **2 tablespoons finely minced fresh parsley or chives**

Bring 3 cups of salted water to a boil in a medium saucepan. Add the peas, and simmer uncovered until tender, 10 to 20 minutes. (Frozen peas need less time.) Drain, and refresh the peas under cold running water. Drain.

Meanwhile, place the onions and salt in a small bowl filled with cold water; let stand 10 minutes. Drain the onions, and rinse under cold running water. This step will eliminate most of the sharpness of the onion and make the salad more digestible.

In a serving bowl, whisk the oil and lemon juice. Add the peas, onions, and parsley, and toss to combine. Taste for seasonings, adjusting as necessary. Serve at once.

Variation

Substitute fresh fava beans for the peas. In Chile, fava beans come to market when they are still young and tender. It is not necessary to remove the light green skin. The more mature the bean, the harder the skin becomes, and the more starchy the bean. The skin can be easily slipped off after cooking.

Sweet Corn and Green Bean Salad

Ensalada de Choclo y Porotos Verdes

Makes 6 servings

This colorful salad is simplicity itself, but it never fails to delight. I must admit, I perked it up by adding a handful of zesty scallions, fresh basil, and a hot chile. In most Chilean restaurants, cooks seem shy to use the wonderful fresh herbs and chiles that grow so profusely in local gardens. The salads are too often plain and boring—a shame indeed.

> ¾ cup mayonnaise
> 1 tablespoon Dijon mustard
> 1½ tablespoon freshly squeezed lemon juice, or to taste
> ½ red bell pepper, diced
> 2 scallions, minced (⅓ cup)
> 1½ cups cooked fresh or frozen corn kernels, cooled
> 3 cups 1-inch pieces cooked fresh or frozen green beans, cooled
> 4 tablespoons finely minced fresh basil or cilantro
> Salt and freshly ground black pepper, to taste
> ½ serrano or jalapeño chile, seeded and finely minced, or to taste

In a large serving bowl, mix together the mayonnaise, mustard, and lemon juice. Add the vegetables and basil; toss gently to combine. Season with salt and black pepper. Sprinkle with the chile and serve at once.

Chilean Quinoa Salad

Ensalada de Quinoa

Makes 4 servings

From time immemorial, the diet of the Aymara Indians in the Andean altiplano has been based on corn, potatoes, meat, milk from the goats and llamas, and the tiny pearl-like grains of quinoa. The Incas called this nutritious grain, which is high in protein, calcium, and iron, "the mother grain." Until recently, it was hardly known outside its native Andes, where it still plays a vital role in completing vegetable stews and side dishes.

This recipe is an updated version of a traditional dish. The grassy, springy grains are flavored with a fresh Chilean salsa.

> 1½ cups quinoa, rinsed until water runs clear
> Salt, to taste
> 2 tomatoes, peeled, seeded, and diced
> 1 red bell pepper, diced
> 1 cup finely chopped sweet onion, rinsed under cold water
> 2 jalapeño or serrano chiles, seeded and finely minced, or to taste
> ½ cup finely minced fresh cilantro or parsley
> ¼ cup freshly squeezed lemon juice
> ½ cup olive oil

Place the quinoa in a medium saucepan and cover with 3 cups water. Bring to a boil, reduce the heat, and simmer covered until translucent, 12 to 15 minutes. Drain, and let cool. Place the quinoa in a large bowl, and fluff with a fork.

Add the vegetables, cilantro, lemon juice, and oil, and mix well. Taste for seasonings, and adjust as necessary. Cover and refrigerate for 30 minutes before serving.

It's best to rinse quinoa thoroughly to remove any residue of saponin, a soapy, bitter substance that naturally coats the grains. Quinoa is cooked much like rice, in salted water or a light broth; the ratio is 2 cups of liquid for every 1 cup of quinoa. Cook covered until the grains are translucent, 12 to 15 minutes. Let the quinoa rest briefly; then fluff with a fork. Lightly toasting the quinoa in a hot skillet for a few minutes before cooking adds a nice flavor.

The Andean altiplano is a place of austere but great beauty. It's the home of the stoic and proud Aymara people, who live in adobe cottages in much the same way as their ancestors did during the reign of the Incas.

The sleepy mountain villages come to life once a year, drawing large crowds, during the colorful fiestas that celebrate their patron saints in a strange mixture of Catholic and ancestral traditions. The most famous one is *La Fiesta de la Virgen de la Tirana*. Every July 16, more than sixty thousand people are drawn to a tiny village in the middle of the high desert to pass a magical night dancing, celebrating, praying, and asking favors of the Virgin of La Tirana.

The celebrations are the ideal times to visit these unique places and to sample some of the typical dishes, which are strongly influenced by the culinary traditions of the neighboring countries of Peru and Bolivia. Remember, no alcohol is served during the festivities.

Beet and Carrot Salad

Ensalada de Betarragas

Makes 4 to 6 servings

For some reason, earthy red beets and sweet carrots are often overlooked in the vegetable department. Yet they make a colorful, fresh winter salad that presents a welcome alternative to the eternal mixed greens. In most Chilean restaurants, salads and cooked vegetables are served plain. I substituted a simple vinaigrette for the usual oil and vinegar served on the side, to bring all the subtle flavors together.

5 small beets, unpeeled, with a little of the green tops left on
Salt and freshly ground black pepper, to taste
3 young carrots, unpeeled
2 teaspoons Dijon mustard
2 tablespoons red wine vinegar
6 tablespoons vegetable or extra-virgin olive oil
2 tablespoons finely minced fresh parsley

Place the beets in a medium saucepan, cover with cold water, add salt, and bring to a boil. Reduce the heat to a simmer, and cook until tender, 25 to 40 minutes, depending on their size. Drain, and let cool a little.

In a separate small saucepan, cover the carrots with cold water, add salt, and bring to a boil. Reduce the heat to a simmer, and cook until tender, about 20 minutes, depending on their size. Drain, and let cool a little.

In a small bowl, whisk together the mustard, vinegar, salt, and black pepper. Whisk in the oil in a thin stream. Adjust the seasonings to taste.

When the beets and carrots are cool enough to handle, peel them and cut into thin slices. Arrange the slices on a round platter or big plate, alternating colors and overlapping the slices, working from the outside of the platter to the inside. Spoon the vinaigrette over all, and garnish with parsley. Serve at once.

Zesty Carrot Salad with Garlic and Cilantro

Ensalada de Zanahorias con Cilantro

Makes 4 servings

One of the best things about living in Chile is the availability of wonderful fresh produce all year round. Even a simple carrot is brimming with flavor: intense, sweet, and juicy. Look for young carrots when they are in season to prepare this salad, rich in vitamins and simply delicious.

> **5 young carrots, peeled and coarsely grated**
> **1 clove garlic, finely minced**
> **1 tablespoon finely minced fresh cilantro**
> **¼ cup freshly squeezed lemon juice**
> **Salt and freshly ground black pepper, to taste**
> **1 tablespoon vegetable oil (optional)**

Combine all the ingredients in a serving bowl. Serve at once.

Rich Beef Broth

Caldo de Huesos

Makes about 6 cups

The secret to a flavorful soup lies, of course, in the quality of the broth, or as my Chilean kitchen assistant and mentor, Angelica, puts it, *"Se prepare un caldo bien sabroso, de esos que son capaces de hacer andar a los muertos."* ("Prepare one of those rich broths that will keep even the dead going.")

> **2 pounds beef and/or veal bones, with some meat attached**
> **2 quarts cold water**
> **1 carrot, peeled and quartered**
> **1 onion studded with 2 cloves**
> **2 small celery ribs with leaves, 3 sprigs parsley, and 3 sprigs**
> **oregano, tied together with kitchen string**

Place the bones in a large stockpot, add the cold water, and bring to a boil over high heat. Let boil 5 minutes, and skim off as much of the foam and fat that has risen to the surface as possible.

Reduce the heat and add the carrot, onion, and herb bundle. Simmer partly covered over low heat, skimming occasionally, 2 to 2½ hours.

Strain the broth, and let cool, if possible, over a bowl of ice. Refrigerate overnight, and remove the fat that has congealed on the surface. This broth will keep 3 to 4 days refrigerated or up to 6 months in the freezer. Remember that this broth is unsalted.

Cream of Corn Soup with Basil and Tomatoes

Crema de Choclo y Tomate

Makes 4 servings

A wonderful, creamy soup made with the best the summer garden has to offer: golden, sweet corn, spring onions, juicy tomatoes, and fresh basil. Unfortunately, many Chilean cooks, even professional ones, are following modern trends and rely on the dehydrated soups. I have been disappointed more than once, even in the better restaurants. Needless to say, there isn't the slightest comparison between a bowl of freshly made soup and the artificial, starchy make-believe imitations!

> 2 tablespoons butter
> 1 medium onion, chopped
> 4 cups fresh or frozen corn kernels
> 3 cups chicken broth
> 2 cups milk
> 5 fresh basil leaves
> 1 tablespoon sugar
> Salt and freshly ground black pepper, to taste
> 1 tomato, peeled, seeded, and diced
> 2 tablespoons finely minced fresh basil or cilantro

Melt the butter in a heavy soup pot over medium heat. Add the onion, and cook, stirring, until softened but not browned, 3 minutes.

Add the corn, broth, milk, basil leaves, and sugar to the onion, and season with salt and black pepper. Bring to a boil, reduce the heat, and simmer covered for 25 minutes. Taste for seasoning.

Remove the soup from the heat, and let cool a little. Press the soup through a fine-meshed food mill or purée in batches in a blender or food processor. For a smooth texture, pass the soup through a sieve to remove the skins. Return the puréed soup to the pot, and reheat before serving. If the soup is too thick, add a little more milk. Garnish each soup plate with tomato and basil.

White Bean Soup with Croutons

Sopa de Porotos con Pancitos Fritos

Makes 4 to 6 servings

An elegant, smooth and delicious winter soup, it contains white beans, pumpkin, sweet onions, and lots of garlic.

SOUP

1½ cups dried white beans, picked over and soaked overnight in
       cold water to cover
1 bay leaf
1 chicken bouillon cube, crumbled
7 cups water
3 tablespoons butter or vegetable oil
1 cup chopped onion
1 cup ½-inch cubes pumpkin
1 carrot, peeled and grated
8 cloves garlic, peeled
1 teaspoon sweet paprika
½ teaspoon ground cumin
1 cup milk (optional)
Salt and freshly ground black pepper, to taste
2 tablespoons finely minced fresh parsley

CROUTONS

3 tablespoons butter or olive oil
4 to 6 slices firm white bread, crusts removed and cut into ¼-inch
       cubes

Drain the beans, and place in a heavy soup pot with the bay leaf, crumbled bouillon cube, and the water. Bring to a boil. Reduce the heat, and simmer covered until soft, 1½ hours.

Heat the butter or oil in a heavy pot. Add the onion, pumpkin, carrot, garlic, paprika, and cumin. Cook, stirring frequently, until softened but not browned, about 6 minutes.

Add the vegetables to the beans, and simmer until the beans are very soft, 30 to 45 minutes. Discard the bay leaf. Remove the soup from the heat, and let cool slightly. Press the soup through a food mill or purée, in batches, in a blender or food processor. Return soup to the pot and add the milk or more water if the soup is too thick, and season with salt and black pepper to bring out all the flavors. Reheat the soup and make the croutons.

To make the croutons, heat the butter in a small skillet over medium heat; add the bread cubes. Sauté the cubes, turning them over frequently, until nicely browned on all sides. Serve the soup piping hot garnished with parsley and the bread croutons.

Hearty Beef and Potato Soup

Ajiaco

Makes 4 or 5 servings

On Mondays, this satisfying beef and potato soup is often on the menu for the *huasos,* the local cowboys. It is said to be the perfect cure for chasing away the Sunday blues or a lingering hangover. It's certainly a clever way to use leftover meats from Sunday's grill or roast. This recipe is filling enough to be served as a meal, especially if you add a poached egg to each plate. Serve a variety of Chilean salads on the side.

> 3 tablespoons vegetable oil
> 1 medium onion, halved and thinly sliced
> 1 teaspoon sweet paprika
> 1 teaspoon dried oregano
> 2 cloves garlic, finely minced
> ¾ to 1 pound cooked roast or grilled beef, cut into 1 × ¼-inch strips
> Salt and freshly ground black pepper, to taste
> 6 cups water
> ½ carrot, peeled and cut into 1 × ¼-inch strips
> ½ carrot, peeled and grated
> 3 parsley sprigs
> 3 medium potatoes, peeled, cut into 1 × ¼-inch strips
> 4 or 5 eggs (optional)
> 1½ tablespoons finely minced fresh parsley
> 1½ tablespoons finely minced fresh cilantro

Heat the oil in a Dutch oven over medium heat. Add the onion and sauté until softened but not browned, 3 minutes. Add the paprika, oregano, garlic, and beef; cook, stirring occasionally, about 4 minutes. Season with salt and black pepper.

Add the water, both types of carrot, and parsley. Simmer covered over medium heat, 20 minutes. Add the potatoes, and simmer until soft, 15 to 20 minutes more.

In a shallow sauté pan with a lid, bring 2½ inches of lightly salted water to a boil. Turn off the heat and carefully break the eggs directly into the water. Cover the pan, and allow the eggs to cook until the whites are set and the yolks still soft, 4 to 5 minutes, or use a commercial egg poacher.

To serve, ladle the hot soup into individual soup plates. If desired, use a slotted spoon to place 1 poached egg in each plate. Sprinkle the soup generously with parsley and cilantro. Serve at once.

Variation

If you don't have any cooked beef on hand, sauté 1 pound flank steak, cut into 1 × ¼-inch strips, in the vegetable oil. When the beef is brown all over, add the onion, and continue with the recipe.

Some older Chileans who are connoisseurs of good cooking like to add the aromatic juice of a bitter orange (Seville orange) to this soup to give it a special touch. This is possibly a Cuban influence. There, traditional island cooks once used tangy orange juice to replace scarce vinegars. However, the Cuban version of this soup is a hearty root vegetable stew.

Living Like a Lord in
La Hacienda los Lingues

Traveling through the Chilean countryside, tourists may observe huge Spanish-style mansions, hidden away in stately parks of native palm trees and centenary trees. These vestiges of the colonial past often remain clouded in mystery, as one rarely passes through the closed, forged-iron gates.

Many haciendas, and the smaller *fundos*, will surprise you by their disheveled, abandoned look. The frequent earthquakes, revolutions, and impoverished owners have taken their toll on these estates. Other properties have evolved into thriving working farms; the glorious estates of successful wine-producing families are the best example.

A remarkable example is *La Hacienda los Lingues*, which opened its doors to the public and has turned itself into a distinguished member of the international hotel chain Relais & Chateaux.

A visit to the hacienda, only a mere seventy-five miles from the bustling capital, is like stepping into the life of an aristocratic Chilean landowner of one hundred years ago.

This vast property of a thousand acres of farmland and another eight thousand acres of Andean foothills has gained international recognition as a breeding farm for the Aculeo horses, the descendants of the Berber horses brought to the Americas by the Spaniards. The land and the colonial-style buildings, some dating as far back as the late seventeenth and early eighteenth centuries, are still intact and have remained in the hands of the family of the current owner, Don Germán Claro Lira, for more than four centuries.

With the same tenacious conviction they used to hold on to their land, the family became passionate defenders of *La cocina criolla*, Chile's rich culinary heritage. And as with everything else, they do it with style.

Guests enjoy traditional Chilean dishes from centuries-old recipes, handed down over generations. The food is served on one of the many interior patios or in the stylish dining room. To my knowledge, this opportunity to sample traditional dishes is quite unique. All too often, the cuisine in some of the top-class Chilean restaurants imitate the big trendsetters; Europe and the United States, denying and bastardizing their own, rich culinary background.

However, I honestly cannot think of a better place to begin your Chilean culinary education or of being introduced to better hosts than at the *Hacienda*. Every guest is welcomed with such a warm and generous simplicity by the family you instantly feel at home.

The thick-walled adobe buildings are tucked away against the backdrop of the imposing Andean Mountains. The picturesque, sun-faded clay tiles are enlivened by the lush surroundings of dense vegetation and radiant flowers.

The houses are encircled by the shady corridors and vine-covered paths where an almost sacred silence seems to reign, inducing one to immediately lower one's voice in order to continue the conversation in a respectful whisper. Wherever you look, you are constantly reminded of the still lifes by Velásquez or the serenity in a Vermeer painting.

Even inside the house, one feels somewhat overwhelmed by the vast decor of the colonial furniture, the Epoque paintings, native Mapuche or Diaguita Indian artifacts, and an incredible collection of silver objects. They seem to have more artifacts than a museum.

Over the centuries the family has filled the house with their memories. It leaves one with a very strange feeling, when wandering around, of not quite being alone, a deep sensation of being accompanied.

Hearty Lentil Chowder with Chorizo

Sopa de Lentejas de la Tía Julita

Makes 6 to 8 servings

I seem to have a lot in common with la Tía Julita, my mother-in-law; but above all we share a profound attraction and love for the bounty of Mother Earth. We're constantly exchanging little secrets, plant clippings, flower seeds, and recipes! More precisely, la Tía is digging, explaining, and cooking; and I am mostly listening and watching. As always, our days wind up in the kitchen, where she treats me to one of her heartwarming preparations, like this delicious lentil soup, chock-full of the vegetables we gather in her garden and spiced with a link of chorizo.

> 2 tablespoons vegetable oil
> 5 ounces chorizo sausage, peeled and sliced into 8 parts
> 1 cup coarsely chopped onion
> 1 cup ¼-inch pieces pumpkin
> 2 leeks, white and light green parts only, sliced into 1-inch rings
> 5 cloves garlic, coarsely chopped
> 1 large tomato, peeled, seeded, and coarsely chopped
> 1½ cups lentils, picked over and rinsed
> 1 small celery rib with leaves, 3 sprigs parsley, and 2 bay leaves, tied
>   together with kitchen string
> 2½ to 3 quarts water
> Salt and freshly ground black pepper, to taste
> 4 small potatoes, peeled and cut into ¼-inch dice
> 2 tablespoons finely minced fresh parsley

Heat the oil in a heavy soup pot. Add the chorizo, onion, and pumpkin; cook over high heat, stirring, for a few minutes. Add the leeks, garlic, and tomato, and cook for 3 minutes more. Add the lentils and the herb bundle.

Add enough water to cover the lentils by 2 inches, and bring to a boil. Reduce the heat, and simmer covered for about 30 minutes. Season with salt and black pepper, add the potato cubes, and simmer until the vegetables are soft, 20 minutes. If necessary, add more water.

Before serving, discard the herb bundle, and taste for seasonings. Serve the soup piping hot, garnished with the parsley.

Rich Chicken Broth with Polenta Dumplings

Caldo de Gallina con Sopones de Polenta

Makes 4 servings

These airy polenta dumplings, delicately flavored with fresh herbs and a touch of nutmeg, turn any broth into an elegant and satisfying first course. In Chile, most cooks prefer the typically cooked, dried and ground cornmeal, called chuchoca (p. 123), but polenta works just as well. It is interesting to notice that similar dishes were created in both the New and the Old Worlds.

SOUP

2 tablespoons butter

¼ teaspoon sweet paprika

1 cup finely chopped onion

1 carrot, peeled and grated

1 celery rib, finely diced

½ red bell pepper, finely diced

6 cups good-quality chicken broth

Salt and freshly ground black pepper, to taste

2 tablespoons finely minced fresh parsley or cilantro

DUMPLINGS

1 cup water

⅓ cup finely ground cornmeal

½ teaspoon salt

1 large egg

1 tablespoon finely minced fresh cilantro or parsley

Pinch of freshly grated nutmeg

½ tablespoon finely minced seeded serrano or jalapeño chile, or to taste (optional)

2 tablespoons all-purpose flour

To prepare the soup: Melt the butter in a large saucepan over low heat, and add the paprika. Cook, stirring, 30 seconds. Add the onion, carrot, celery, and bell pepper; sauté, stirring occasionally, 5 minutes. Add the broth, and season with salt, black pepper, and 1 tablespoon of the parsley. Bring the broth to a boil, reduce the heat, and simmer covered, 25 minutes.

To prepare the dumplings: Bring the water to a boil in a small saucepan, and reduce the heat to low. Using a wooden spoon to stir constantly, pour the cornmeal in a thin stream into the water; add the salt. Cook the polenta, stirring frequently, 15 to 20 minutes. In a bowl, whisk the egg until frothy, and add the cilantro, nutmeg, and chile. Stir the egg mixture into the polenta to combine. Sift enough flour into the mixture to make a soft but thick paste. Cover and keep warm until ready to use.

To finish: Drop spoonfuls of the polenta into the simmering soup. Simmer until the dumplings are cooked and rise to the surface, 7 to 10 minutes. Ladle at once into deep soup plates, and sprinkle with the remaining parsley.

Rich Broth with Fresh Pasta, Chilean Style

Pancutras

Makes 4 servings

It's unlikely you'll find this hearty, robust peasant fare on a restaurant menu, not even in the tiniest hole-in-the-wall eatery. A shame indeed, as these are precisely the nutritious, comforting dishes we all crave in our fast-moving modern society. In the midst of the Chilean winter, when a chilly dampness settles into the poorly insulated houses, there's not a better remedy than a steaming bowl of this soup to warm body and soul. It consists mainly of a rich, gelatinous beef broth flavored with onion, carrot, and bell pepper, in which wide strips of fresh pasta—resembling the Italian *pappardelle*—are cooked until they soak up most of the richness of the broth. Is this the influence of a distant Italian past or is it pure coincidence? I haven't found the answer yet.

SOUP
2 tablespoons vegetable oil
½ cup finely chopped onion
1 clove garlic, finely minced
½ red bell pepper, finely diced
1 small carrot, peeled and grated
6 cups Caldo de Huesos (p. 93) or canned beef broth
Salt and freshly ground black pepper, to taste
3 tablespoons finely minced fresh cilantro or parsley

PASTA
1½ teaspoons salt
¾ cup warm beef broth or warm water
2 cups all-purpose flour

To prepare the soup: Heat the oil in a large saucepan over medium heat. Add the onion, garlic, bell pepper, and carrot; cook, stirring occasionally, 3 minutes. Add the Caldo de Huesos, and season with salt and black pepper. Bring to a boil, reduce the heat, and simmer 10 minutes.

To prepare the pasta: Dissolve the salt in the broth. Sift the flour onto a clean work surface. Make a well in the center and add the broth. Using a fork, work the liquid gradually into the flour, adding as much flour as needed to obtain a soft, nonsticky dough. Knead the dough with the palms of your hands on a lightly floured surface until smooth and pliable, about 3 minutes. Flour your work surface again and roll the dough out into a large circle that's as thin as possible. Using a sharp knife, cut the pasta into ½-inch-wide strips to resemble Italian *pappardelle*. Arrange the strips on a clean kitchen towel until ready to finish the soup.

To finish: Before serving, bring the broth to a boil. Add the pasta strips, one at the time. Reduce the heat and simmer, stirring carefully, until the pasta is tender yet firm to the bite, 2 to 3 minutes. Serve the soup at once in deep soup plates, generously sprinkled with fresh cilantro.

If the soup stands, the pasta will absorb most of the broth and get soggy—some Chileans prefer this "dry" version.

Hearty Beef Jerky and Onion Soup

Valdiviano

Makes 8 servings

This is an original dish based on the common onion, lots of sweet paprika (which gives the soup a deep reddish-brown color), and sun-dried strips of beef, known as *sharqui*, or jerky.

The story goes that many centuries ago, this hearty soup fed the humble and the peasant. Over the years, valdiviano has been adapted to more demanding palates, enriched with a poached egg for consistency and flavored with the intriguing bitter-sweet juice of Seville oranges. This is a wonderful soup you'll rarely find on a restaurant menu and one that may soon appear on the list of endangered dishes.

If you have trouble finding good-quality dried meat or jerky, substitute finely shredded cooked roast beef.

3 tablespoons vegetable oil
4 large onions, halved lengthwise and thinly sliced
2½ tablespoons sweet paprika
1 cup ½-inch cubes pumpkin
½ pound beef jerky, sliced or finely shredded
1 teaspoon ground cumin
1 teaspoon dried oregano
6 cups Caldo de Huesos (p. 93) or canned beef broth
1 cup crumbled white bread without crusts soaked in 1 cup milk
Salt and freshly ground black pepper, to taste
8 eggs
2 tablespoons finely minced fresh parsley
Juice of 2 bitter (Seville) oranges or juice of 1 lemon and 1 sweet
    orange

Heat the oil in a large soup pot over low heat. Add the onions and paprika; cover, and cook, stirring occasionally, until softened but not browned, 10 to 15 minutes.

Meanwhile, cook the pumpkin in salted water until soft, 15 to 20 minutes. Drain, and set aside.

If you have a stovetop grill, toast the jerky for a few minutes on each side. If not, toast under the broiler until somewhat dried out and hardened. Slice into small strips, and add the onions along with the cumin, oregano, and Caldo de Huesos. Simmer covered over low heat, 25 minutes.

Purée the bread and cooked pumpkin to a smooth paste in a blender. Add to the soup, and cook, stirring constantly, over low heat until the soup has thickened slightly, 5 minutes. Season generously with salt and black pepper.

In a shallow sauté pan with a lid, bring 2½ inches of lightly salted water to a boil. Turn off the heat and carefully break the eggs directly into the water. Cover the pan, and allow the eggs to cook until the whites are set and the yolks still soft, 4 to 5 minutes, or use a commercial egg poacher.

Serve the hot soup in individual earthenware soup bowls. Use a slotted spoon to place 1 poached egg in each bowl. Sprinkle with parsley and the orange juice to taste. Serve at once.

Fisherman's Soup with Fresh Tomatoes and White Wine

Caldillo de Congrio con Vino Blanco

Makes 4 to 6 servings

El congrio dorado (p. 188) is considered the king of fish in Chile. Its firm, sweet, and delicate white flesh makes it a perfect choice for this popular fisherman's soup.

Caldillo starts with a flavorful broth, made with the head and bones of the fish. The addition of other ingredients, such as potatoes, milk, cream, or other shellfish, is passionately disputed. Everyone seems to have his own strong opinion. The most famous opinion is expressed by none other than the celebrated poet Pablo Neruda, a devoted gourmet, who dedicated an entire ode to this humble soup.

Congrio isn't available in the United States; but for an equally delicious version use Chilean sea bass, monkfish, red snapper, halibut, John Dory, grouper, tilefish, or a mixture.

> 3 tablespoons vegetable oil
> 1 large onion, cut in half and thinly sliced
> 1 clove garlic, finely minced
> ½ tablespoon sweet paprika
> ¼ red bell pepper, thinly sliced
> ½ carrot, peeled and grated
> 3 ripe tomatoes, peeled, seeded, and coarsely chopped
> 4 cups fish broth (preferably homemade)
> ¾ cup dry white wine
> 1 bay leaf
> 4 parsley sprigs

Salt and freshly ground black pepper, to taste

4 (2-inch-thick) pieces of firm, white-fleshed fish

1 pound small mussels, clams, scallops, or shrimp (optional)

6 small potatoes (optional), peeled and cooked

1 cup heavy cream

1 egg yolk

½ cup finely minced fresh parsley

Heat the oil in a large saucepan over medium heat. Add the onion, and sauté until softened but not browned, 4 minutes. Add the garlic, paprika, bell pepper, and carrot; cook, stirring occasionally, 2 minutes more. Add the tomatoes, broth, wine, bay leaf, and parsley sprigs. Season with salt and black pepper. Bring to a boil, reduce the heat, and simmer 20 minutes. (The soup can be prepared in advance up to this point.)

Add the fish, shellfish, and potatoes. Simmer over low heat until the fish has changed from translucent to opaque and the shellfish has opened, 10 to 15 minutes. In a small bowl, whisk the cream with the egg yolk, and gradually ladle some of the hot soup into the egg mixture before adding the egg mixture to the soup. This step prevents the egg and cream from curdling. For the same reason, don't let the soup boil. Serve the soup at once sprinkled with parsley.

Cold Avocado Soup

Crema Fria de Palta

Makes 4 servings

This is a beautiful, soft green soup with a rich velvety smoothness. No wonder that the guests of *La Hacienda los Lingues* (p. 100) are intrigued and often ask for the recipe. La Señora María Elena prefers the smooth-skinned, bright green avocados (the Florida type) for this recipe. They are moister and seemingly lower in fat than the Haas variety.

> 2 large or 4 small ripe avocados, diced (about 2 cups)
> 2 cups good-quality cold chicken broth
> About 2 cups cold milk
> 1½ tablespoons freshly squeezed lemon juice
> Salt and freshly ground black pepper, to taste
> Pinch of cayenne pepper
> 2 tablespoons finely minced fresh cilantro or chives
> 1 tomato, peeled, seeded, and finely diced

Purée the avocados with the chicken broth in a blender until smooth. Pour in enough milk to make a thick but pourable soup. Add the lemon juice and season with salt, black pepper, and cayenne to bring out the delicate flavors.

Garnish with the cilantro and tomato. Serve at once, because the soup tends to discolor rapidly.

The Poet's Recipe . . .

One of the most important and beloved poets in the Spanish language and a 1971 Nobel Prize winner, Pablo Neruda (1904–1973) served both poetry and politics with his pen during his full, adventurous existence. Yet *el poeta* lives in the memory of his compatriots not only for his social consciousness but mostly as a famous bon vivant and a great romantic who knew how to embrace life to the fullest—characteristics many Chileans like to identify with. In many regards, Neruda left more than his writings to the world.

His three homes, left intact, reveal even more of the playful, generous host; the eccentric collector, and his strong artistic sensibility. No wonder that after his death, the houses turned into true pilgrimage destinations; *La Isla Negra*, his favorite haunt by the ocean and his burial place, is the most visited.

Through his words one gains an invaluable insight into the people, places, plants, and animals of his beloved country. He took Chile to heart and sang its everyday reality. He wrote numerous poems celebrating the ocean, his loved ones, friendship, and good eats and drinks.

Neruda was known as a devoted gourmand; and the story goes that even at the very end of his life, his biggest preoccupation was the late delivery of some empanadas he had ordered to share with friends over a bottle of *un buen tinto*.

In his *Odas Elementales,* he glorifies the simple, essential things in life; he sings of the artichoke, the large tuna in the market, the onion, and the tomato. . . . One feels his deep love for his generous country in every word. Verses such as*: "un sol fresco, / profundo, / inagotable, / llena las ensaladas / de Chile"* ("A cool sun, / profound, / inexhaustible, / populates the salads / of Chile.") And listen to this sublime recipe for el caldillo de congrio:

Ode to Conger Chowder

In the storm-tossed
Chilean
sea
lives the rosy conger,
giant eel
of snowy flesh.
And in Chilean
stewpots,
along the coast,
was born the chowder,
thick and succulent,
a boon to man
You bring the conger, skinned,
to the kitchen
(its mottled skin slips off
like a glove,
leaving the
grape of the sea
exposed to the world),
naked,
the tender eel
glistens,
prepared
to serve our appetites.

Now
you take
garlic,
first, caress

that precious
ivory,
smell
its innate fragrance,
then
blend the minced garlic
with onion
and tomato
until the onion
is the color of gold.
Meanwhile
steam
our regal
ocean prawns,
and when
they are
tender,
when the savor is
set in a sauce
combining the liquors
of the ocean
and the clear water
released from the light of the onion,
then
you add the eel
that it may be immersed in glory,
that it may steep in the oils
of the pot,
shrink and be saturated.

Now all that remains is to
drop a dollop of cream
into the concoction,
a heavy rose,
then slowly
deliver
the treasure to the flame,
until in the chowder

are warmed
the essences of Chile,
and to the table
come, newlywed,
the savors
of land and sea
that in this dish
you may know heaven.

Poultry and Meats

Pollo y Carne

Ever since the Spanish conquistadores introduced European livestock—cattle, sheep, and horses—to the Americas, the eating habits in our vast continents underwent a drastic and long-lasting change. In the United States, up to this very day, steakhouses are still some of the most popular restaurants, despite the recent health craze; and barbecues are lit all over the nation with an intense passion! Let's admit it, is there anything more satisfying in the world than a juicy piece of meat grilled over a smoldering fire?

In Chile, the concern over fat and cholesterol blew over without much of an impact, except perhaps for the capital, where they mostly just talk about it a lot. In Chile, the preferred macho traditional restaurant was and remains the rustic Argentine-style steakhouses, where skillfully grilled beef or a mixture of meats is brought to the table on a small brazier. This is a clever way to finish the cooking to the customer's personal preference and to keep the meat hot. Chileans openly *love* meat, and they can devour huge quantities of it!

When Chileans invite friends or family for a meal, nine times out of ten they'll gather around an outdoor grill under a shady, vine-covered terrace. These cherished social events take up most of the afternoon, during which impressive amounts of meat are grilled and eaten with gusto, accompanied by a wide selection of Chilean salads, and washed down with a few bottles of the excellent local cabernet sauvignon.

Cattle is mostly grass fed in Chile; and because the animals often have to travel long distances to reach fresh pastures, the meat is leaner and tougher than the tender, marbled beef of the United States or the famous Argentinean beef raised in the Pampas. Yet, for the same reason, Chilean beef gains in flavor what it loses in tenderness. Actually, most connoisseurs prefer the chewier, richer cuts for grilling over the hot coals, such as skirt steak, London broil, and even a whole rib roast.

The meat of choice for the *parilla* is beef, but Chileans just as frequently eat chicken and pork. Another misconception would be to think that all meat finishes on the grill!

Chilean cooks are very inventive with cuts that are really too chewy and tough to be grilled. They have a whole repertoire of hearty stews and soups to choose from, including *arrollados*, rolled and stuffed pieces of beef or pork slowly simmered to tenderness in a flavorful broth.

Some local rustic restaurants specialize in *chancho* (pork) and serve every single piece of the animal: from ribs, to spicy strips of meat cooked to tenderness in pork skin, the much-prized blood sausages, and tripe. Eating pork products is still mostly reserved to the winter months. In the colder southern parts of the country, a strong German influence is responsible for a wide variety of good-quality charcuterie, such as hams, sausages, pâtés, and the popular *chucrut con pernil*, pickled cabbage with cooked ham. Surprising in this remote part of South America!

Lamb and young goat are not as widely available in the urban centers. But if you live out in the country, it is easy to find, especially in spring. In the wind swept inhospitable southern tip, in Patagonia and Tierra del Fuego, guanacos (llamas) and sheep are the main sources of meat. In the arid areas of the north, goats, alpaca, and llamas seem to be the only animals willing to put up with the severe and extreme living conditions of the desert and Altiplano.

As everywhere else in the world, chickens and turkeys are raised on an industrial scale. They are inexpensive, plentiful, and uninteresting. But out in the country, people still keep poultry that scratches for its own food and clucks away to its hearts' content. If you ever have the chance to taste *una cazuela con gallina de campo*, a wonderful stew made with a real country bird, you'll know what I'm talking about!

In Chile, the broth is often served first as a consommé enriched with a whole egg. For each person, whisk an egg in a small bowl and add 2 to 3 ladles of the boiling broth in a thin stream. Serve at once sprinkled with some of the parsley. The chicken and vegetable medley is served as a second course with salads. If you prepare the stew ahead of time or if you plan to make a big pot of it, cook the potatoes separately and add just before serving for a fresher flavor.

Eating Eggs

Paging through these recipes, you may well be surprised by the considerable amount of eggs consumed by Chileans. Indeed, many salads, soups, and stews are fortified by the addition of an egg.

Don't forget that these recipes come from a country in which most of the people still lead a physically intense existence and can afford to eat a steady supply of fresh farm eggs. As in most rural areas around the world, meat is not on the menu on a daily basis, and legumes and eggs often provide the necessary protein.

Poultry and Vegetable Stew

Cazuela de Ave con Chuchoca

Makes 6 servings

An Old World classic, named after the earthenware pot the dish was originally prepared in, cazuela gets a New World twist in this rendition of Creole cuisine. It is an all-time favorite in the Chilean countryside and has everything to seduce us. It is rather easy to prepare, and it looks appealing with its yellow corn, orange pumpkin, green beans, and red pepper swimming in a rich broth. It's hearty, satisfying, and soulful.

A tender chicken is the meat of choice, but in the region of Curicó, a tasty variation is prepared with turkey, cazuela de pava con chuchoca. (see "Chuchoca or Polenta?" p. 123). In fact, any tasty, less-tender cut of meat lends itself to this type of long, slow cooking; try pork, beef, lamb, or even young goat. To my taste, the best cazuelas are the ones made with lots of vegetables and thickened with chuchoca (cooked, dried, and ground corn) or polenta.

A salad of fresh greens makes the perfect accompaniment.

1 (3- to 4-lb.) chicken, rinsed, patted dry, and cut into 8 pieces, or 3 pounds turkey breast and/or dark meat, cut into 1-inch-thick pieces

2½ quarts cold water

1 tablespoon salt, or to taste

2 tablespoons vegetable oil

Freshly ground black pepper, to taste

1 large onion, cut into 8 pieces

2 cloves garlic, minced

¾ teaspoon ground cumin

1½ teaspoons dried oregano

1 pound pumpkin, cut into 1-inch cubes

1 cup fresh or frozen green beans
1 cup fresh or frozen green peas
6 medium potatoes, peeled
$\frac{1}{2}$ red bell pepper, cut into 1-inch strips
2 ears fresh or frozen corn, each ear cut into 3 pieces
$\frac{3}{4}$ cup fresh or frozen fava beans, optional
$\frac{3}{4}$ cup instant polenta or chuchoca (see p. 123)
$\frac{1}{2}$ cup finely minced fresh parsley, fresh cilantro, and/or scallions
2 serrano or jalapeño chiles

Place the chicken in a large soup pot. Add the water and salt, and bring to a boil over high heat. Reduce the heat to a simmer, and cook 15 minutes. Skim the surface of the broth to remove any foam and fat. Using a slotted spoon, take out the chicken; pat the pieces dry with a paper towel. Reserve the broth.

Heat the oil in a large skillet over medium heat. Add the chicken and cook until browned, 3 to 4 minutes per side. Season with salt and black pepper. Add the onion, garlic, cumin, and oregano; cook, stirring, 3 minutes more. Transfer the chicken mixture to the reserved broth. Add the pumpkin and simmer covered over low heat, 15 minutes.

Add all the remaining vegetables, and simmer covered until all the vegetables are soft but still holding their shape, 20 minutes more. Season with salt and black pepper.

Skim off any fat that has risen to the surface. Stir in the polenta and half of the parsley. Simmer, stirring occasionally, until the broth thickens slightly, 5 to 7 minutes.

Split the chiles open, remove the seeds, and cut into strips. Divide the chicken and vegetables evenly into deep soup plates, and cover with the flavorful broth. Serve at once. Pass the remaining parsley at the table. Serve the chile peppers on the side with some salt for dipping.

Young Chicken Stew with Peas and Tomatoes

Pollo Arvejado

Makes 4 to 6 servings

The country table is never richer than in early summer, and unpretentious one-dish meals, chock-full of fresh vegetables, definitely offer an inspiration for the modern cook. Serve this tasty stew with Arroz Graneado (p. 214) or, better yet, a huge stack of crunchy French fries.

> **2 tablespoons vegetable oil**
> **1 (3- to 4-lb.) chicken, rinsed, patted dry, and cut into 8 serving pieces with all visible fat removed**
> **Salt and freshly ground black pepper, to taste**
> **1 large onion, coarsely chopped**
> **4 cloves garlic, minced**
> **1 red bell pepper, cut into ½-inch strips**
> **1 carrot, peeled and cut into ½-inch pieces**
> **1 teaspoon sweet paprika**
> **1 teaspoon dried oregano**
> **1 cup water**
> **1 cup dry white wine or rich chicken broth**
> **2 tablespoons tomato paste**
> **1 pound fresh green peas, shelled, or 1 (10-oz.) package frozen peas, thawed**
> **2 tablespoons finely minced fresh parsley**

Heat the oil in a large Dutch oven over medium heat. Add the chicken, in batches, and cook until golden brown all over, about 7 minutes. Remove the chicken to a platter, and season with salt and black pepper.

Discard all but 2 tablespoons fat from the Dutch oven. Add the onion, garlic, bell pepper, carrot, and paprika; cook, stirring frequently, over medium heat until softened but not browned, 3 to 4 minutes. Season with oregano, salt, and black pepper. Add the water, wine, and tomato paste; bring to a boil, stirring and scraping all the brown bits from the bottom of the pan. Arrange the chicken over the vegetables, cover partially, and simmer 30 minutes.

Add the peas, and simmer uncovered until the chicken is very tender, 20 to 30 minutes more. Taste for seasoning. Sprinkle with fresh parsley just before serving.

Chuchoca or Polenta?

The day Angelica introduced me to the tasty yellow cornmeal named chuchoca, I was intrigued. At the end of summer, she selected the freshest, plump corn and cooked it until tender in salted water. With a swift hand she sliced off all the kernels, spread them out on clean towels, and put them out to dry in the hot sun. This drying process took two to three days. Chilean nights are cool and damp in the Central Valley so the corn is taken inside after dark. The dried kernels are stored in cotton bags for later use. Angelica grinds the corn in a special grinder (a Moulinex grain mill does the trick) and told me that in the old days the job had to be done in a heavy stone mortar and that took forever.

Chuchoca is mainly used as a binder; it lends a wonderful special touch to any cazuela. I really like it with potatoes, as in Papas con Chuchoca (p. 216).

In all recipes chuchoca can be replaced by polenta. Polenta is ground, uncooked corn kernels and has a less pronounced corn flavor than the Chilean equivalent. Instant polenta meal is very easy to use. If you use stone-ground yellow cornmeal, let it soak for at least 3 hours in cold water before you add it to the dish as directed. Chuchoca is available, already made, in all Chilean supermarkets. Though I didn't come across it in the United States, that doesn't mean it isn't out there somewhere!

Braised Chicken with Cilantro

Pollo con Cilantro

Makes 4 to 5 servings

This may not be a typical Chilean dish but it's one that was whipped together by my assistant when we had nothing left in the house but a few Chilean staples: a string of garlic, onions, some local wine, and plenty of fresh cilantro from the garden. I was immediately seduced by the simplicity of the dish and the pungent intense flavor the cilantro imparted to the chicken and sauce.

> 3 tablespoons vegetable oil
> 1 (3- to 4-lb.) chicken, rinsed, patted dry, and cut into 8 serving
>   pieces with all visible fat removed
> Salt and freshly ground black pepper, to taste
> 1 cup coarsely chopped onion
> 4 cloves garlic, minced
> ¾ teaspoon dried oregano
> 2 tablespoons all-purpose flour
> 1 cup chicken broth
> ½ cup dry white wine
> 1 cup packed finely minced cilantro leaves
> ½ tablespoon serrano or jalapeño chile, seeded and minced
>   (optional)

Heat the oil in a large casserole or Dutch oven over medium heat. Add the chicken and cook until browned all over, about 3 minutes a side. Season with salt and black pepper. Transfer the chicken to a platter.

Add the onion and garlic to the drippings and sauté over medium heat for 2 minutes. Return the chicken to the pan, along with the oregano and flour; stir to mix. Pour the broth and wine into the Dutch oven, cover, and simmer over low heat until the chicken is just done (and still juicy inside), 20 to 30 minutes. Just before serving, stir the cilantro and chile into the sauce.

Cilantro, also known as Chinese parsley or fresh coriander, is widely used in Creole cuisine. One either loves it or hates it! Cilantro does have a pronounced flavor; therefore, it's better to add it to a dish right before serving, as cooking alters the flavor and darkens the leaves. If you really don't like cilantro, try a mixture of parsley, mint, and/or basil.

Rice with Chicken

Arroz con Pollo

Makes 6 servings

The tradition of Spain is still tangibly present in Chile in the huge colonial estate houses with their curved verandas and stone arches, their artwork and antique silverware. But perhaps this enduring influence is most noticeable in the cuisine, especially in the glorious rice dishes.

Never was a dish as much copied, adapted, and wholeheartedly embraced in the Hispanic community as the famous paella Valenciana. This rustic, satisfying, and easy one-pan meal knows as many variations as there are cooks.

This Chilean version is made with long-grain rice and flavored with the popular seasoning trio: cumin, sweet paprika, and oregano. A generous grinding of black pepper and its rather soupy and creamy consistency (much like a risotto) gives this dish an original touch.

¼ cup olive oil
3 pounds skinless, boneless chicken breasts, cut into 1-inch pieces
Salt and freshly ground black pepper, to taste
½ cup coarsely chopped onion
½ red bell pepper, cut into strips
1 carrot, peeled and coarsely grated
3 cloves garlic, finely minced
2 teaspoons sweet paprika
½ teaspoon ground cumin
1 teaspoon dried oregano
1 large ripe tomato, coarsely chopped
1½ cups long-grain rice
4 to 5 cups chicken broth, warmed
½ cup fresh or frozen green peas

Heat the oil in a wide skillet or paella pan over medium heat. Add the chicken, and cook, stirring occasionally, until browned evenly, 6 to 8 minutes. Season with salt and black pepper, and remove the chicken with a slotted spoon.

Add the onion, bell pepper, carrot, and garlic to the pan drippings; cook, stirring occasionally, over medium heat, 3 minutes. Season with the paprika, cumin, and oregano, and cook, stirring, 1 minute more. Stir in the tomato, and simmer until it releases its juice, about 3 minutes.

Add the rice, and stir until it has absorbed most of the oil. Place the chicken and peas on top of the rice, and pour 3 cups of the chicken broth over the top. Reduce the heat to low, cover the pan, and simmer until the liquid has been absorbed. It's important not to stir the rice. If the mixture starts to dry out, add more broth, and cook until the rice is soft, 25 to 35 minutes. The rice should be moist and creamy. Serve at once.

Rodeos

The Panamerican Highway travels almost the full length of Chile; like a vital spine, it connects Arica on the Peruvian border to Quellón Isla Grande in Chiloé. Chilean businesses maintain their headquarters along this road. It's the necessary link to the modern world.

But once you venture off the highway into the plains or toward the imposing Andes Mountains, you'll hit the dirt roads and enter another world. It's like taking a step backward in time, to a simpler and slower pace and a more relaxing lifestyle. And that's precisely where I chose to live for a while.

From the fertile Central Valley, blessed with a Mediterranean climate, to the southern Lake District, you'll encounter some of the richest farmland in the country, vast grazing lands for cattle, and immense orchards and vineyards, bordered by weeping willows, fast-growing eucalyptus, and gracious mimosa trees.

This is the domain of the *huaso,* the local cowboy, riding his sturdy mount, his inseparable companion. It's not at all unusual to spot herds of stocky horses roaming the vast riverbeds, seemingly wild and alone. These animals are descendants of the Berber horses, introduced to Spain by the Moors and brought by the conquistadores to the Americas.

In my little street (a dirt road to be more correct), the sound of a car painstakingly making its way is so unusual that it still draws everyone outside. But the sight of the cowboy, with his broad-rimmed sombrero and his short jacket or the colorfully patterned poncho, is a daily routine.

The perfect way to catch a glimpse of the cowboys' horsemanship, elegant attire, food, and folklore is to watch a rodeo. People gather from miles around to watch the competition, which is one of Chile's national sports. Most rodeos are held between September and May, crowned by the Chilean Championship in Rancagua.

In a Chilean rodeo, it's all about horsemanship. There's neither roping nor riding of wild beasts. A pair of riders use their mounts to waltz the young steers around in *la media luna* ("half-moon-shaped ring") and maneuver the beast to a padded section of the wall. The biggest difficulty consists in galloping sideways along the curved shape of the corral; it demands a perfect symbiosis between man and horse. Participants are rated by the way they keep their composure in the saddle, the way they treat the animals (brutality results in bad ratings), and even by their appearance. The Chilean cowboys have the reputation of being proud and honest men of the country and excellent horsemen.

After the rodeo, there is a long night of feasting, drinking, and dancing. In the club beside the rodeo ring, the women cook up a storm, making Empanadas de Horno (p. 16), hearty fresh bean dishes, Pastel de Choclo (p. 130), and cazuela (see chapter 2), all typical dishes of *la cocina criolla*. These are washed down with a local red wine or some heady chicha (a fermented raw grape or apple juice).

Later in the night, the women take out their white handkerchiefs, and the men prepare to dance *la cueca*, Chile's national dance. In a shuffling, courting manner, the man makes his first advances to his partner. She, keeping her distance and flicking her handkerchief, sets up a pattern of the pursuer and the pursued. Folklore says a rooster stalking a hen inspired the dance.

Meat and Onion Pie with a Crisp Corn Topping

Pastel de Choclo

Makes 6 servings

This is Chile's national dish and one of the most popular ways to prepare corn. Pastel de Choclo is a perfect example of the interaction between the cuisines of the Spanish conquistadores and the indigenous Mapuche population. The pie is based on a rich beef and onion mixture called pino, and the filling is topped with a sweet, creamy corn or choclo ("corn") purée. This dish is traditionally baked and served in a clay dish from Pomaire, a tiny village of potters located about an hour east of Santiago. Connoisseurs pretend that the red clay infuses its own particular flavor to the dish. To me it mostly adds a touch of local color. Honoring the Chilean tradition, serve the Pastel de Choclo with a zesty Ensalada a la Chilena (p. 72)

Salty and Sweet

Chileans, like other Latino-Americans, seem to be fond of dishes that are both salty and sweet. Raisins are an essential ingredient in pino; fried savory turnovers are often dusted with powdered sugar; and above all, traditional corn preparations are lightly sweetened at the table. It's a bit of an acquired taste, easily traced to the Moorish influences, and is certainly worth checking out!

FILLING

1 (3-pound) chicken, rinsed, patted dry, and cut into 8 serving pieces

1 celery rib, 3 parsley sprigs, and 3 oregano sprigs tied together with
kitchen string

3 tablespoons vegetable oil

3 cups finely chopped onions (about 4 large onions)

1½ pounds ground beef

3 cloves garlic, finely minced

1½ teaspoons ground cumin

2 teaspoons salt, or to taste

½ teaspoon freshly ground black pepper

2 teaspoons sweet paprika

¼ cup raisins soaked in hot water 20 minutes and drained

12 green whole olives, pitted

2 hard-cooked eggs, quartered lengthwise

CORN TOPPING

11 cups fresh or frozen corn kernels (p. 132)

¾ cup milk

4 tablespoons butter

1 teaspoon salt, or to taste

½ teaspoon freshly ground black pepper

1 egg, lightly beaten

8 tablespoons powdered sugar, optional

To prepare the filling: Arrange the chicken pieces and the herb bundle in a large saucepan, and cover with cold salted water. Bring to a boil, reduce the heat, and simmer covered until the chicken is tender, 35 to 45 minutes. Let cool in the broth.

Meanwhile, heat the oil over medium heat in a large skillet. Add the onions, and sauté stirring, until tender, 7 minutes. Add the ground beef, garlic, cumin, salt, and black pepper. Sauté, stirring frequently, until the meat and onions release their juices, 7 to 10 minutes. Add the paprika; cook 1 minute, and turn off the heat. (Paprika turns bitter when heated too long.) If the mixture is too dry, moisten with some of the chicken broth.

To prepare the topping: Puree the corn kernels, in batches, with the milk in a blender or food processor. For a smooth, pastry-like texture press the mixture through a sieve, if you'd like. Melt the butter over medium heat in a large skillet. Add the corn purée, salt, and black pepper. While stirring constantly with a wooden spoon, add the egg. Cook, stirring constantly, over low heat until the mixture has slightly thickened, 3 to 4 minutes. Taste for seasonings, and adjust if necessary.

Take the chicken pieces out of the broth. Discard the skin and pull the meat off the bones in big chunks. Many Chilean cooks leave the meat on the bone but I find it easier to eat if the chicken is boneless.

Fresh vs. Frozen Corn

In the country, Pastel de Choclo is summer or early fall fare, prepared when the plump, sweet corn is at its best in the farmers markets. Native cooks do not fancy frozen or canned substitutes, because they faithfully follow each season's offerings. I have obtained successful results using a good-quality frozen corn (to the surprise of my Chilean friends). It is best to defrost the corn first in a colander so that it can drain. Often frozen corn is less sweet than fresh corn; if this is the case, add 1 tablespoon powdered sugar to the topping. One three-pound bag of frozen corn, defrosted and drained, yields about nine cups of kernels.

Use fresh corn whenever it is available. Calculate two plump fresh ears for each cup of kernels. Shave the kernels from the ears with a sharp knife. For Pastel de Choclo you will need twenty to twenty-two ears, depending on their size.

To assemble and bake: Preheat oven to 375F(190C). Butter a large gratin dish or six 2-cup earthenware dishes. Spoon the beef mixture into the dish; arrange the chicken, raisins, olives, and eggs on top. (If using individual dishes, divide the beef mixture and other ingredients evenly among them. Cover with the topping. For an authentic Chilean touch, sprinkle the sugar on top of the pie. (The dish can be prepared ahead up to this point. Refrigerate until ready to bake and serve.)

Bake the pie 35 minutes, or until the topping is lightly caramelized. Serve piping hot.

Variation

When corn isn't available, a well-seasoned mashed potato mixture is often used to prepare an equally delicious Pastel de Papas. Sprinkle the potato topping with grated Parmesan cheese instead of sugar.

Rib Roast Studded with Bell Pepper and Carrot Sticks

Carne Mechada

Makes 4 to 6 servings

This is a most elegant and easy way to prepare a roast for company. To protect the meat from drying out, it is usually larded with fine slivers of pork fat. In this recipe, the roast is studded with red bell pepper and carrot sticks and braised in onions and white wine. Frequent basting will guarantee a moist and succulent piece of meat.

Chileans tend to eat their beef well done (internal temperature 160-170F, 70-75C). I recommend taking the roast out of the oven when the internal temperature registers 150F(65C), or medium, for beef that is a lot juicier.

1 (3-pound) beef rib roast or boneless beef loin roast
12 carrot sticks, about 1 inch long and ¼ inch thick
12 red bell pepper sticks, about 1 inch long and ¼ inch thick
1 large clove garlic, halved
4 tablespoons lard, butter, or margarine
1 large onion, sliced into rings
Salt and freshly ground black pepper, to taste
1 cup white wine
¾ cup beef broth
1½ teaspoons dried oregano

Preheat the oven to 375F(190C).

With the point of a sharp paring knife, make small slits into the meat about every 2 inches. Insert the carrot and bell pepper pieces, alternating them, into these pockets. Turn the roast over and repeat the procedure. Rub the garlic well over the entire roast.

Melt the lard in a roasting pan, large enough to hold the roast snugly, on the stovetop over high heat. Add the meat, and brown lightly on both sides. Reduce the heat to medium, add the onions, and sauté, stirring frequently, until softened but not browned, 5 to 7 minutes. Season the roast and onions with salt and black pepper. Pour wine and broth into the pan and sprinkle the oregano evenly over the meat.

Transfer the pan to the oven. Roast the meat 40 to 50 minutes for medium, or until a meat thermometer reads 150F (65C) or 50 to 60 minutes for well done, or until a meat thermometer reads 160–170F(70–75C). For juicy, tasty meat, it is very important to baste the roast every 15 minutes with the drippings.

Remove the pan from the oven, transfer the roast to a platter, and allow it to rest 10 minutes before carving. If the drippings are too thin for a sauce, place the pan over high heat, and reduce the drippings, stirring constantly, until the sauce has the consistency of heavy cream.

Slice the meat, and arrange it on top of the sauce on a warm serving platter.

Summer Pork Stew with Tomatoes and Sweet Corn

Tomaticán con Pulpa de Cerdo

Makes 4 to 5 servings

It's common knowledge in Chile that the country folk eat better and healthier than do their counterparts living in the big cities. Their diet is based on myriad vegetables, mostly grown in their own backyards; little meat; and hearty legume dishes in the damp winter months. This should be inspiring for the health conscious among us!

This summer stew is a perfect example: Little nuggets of pork are cooked until tender in juicy tomatoes, onions, and sweet corn. A handful of minced cilantro, parsley, and pungent chili peppers sprinkled over the stew before serving gives the dish an extra, welcome bite. Tomaticán is often prepared with chicken or beef for an equally tasty dish. Arroz Graneado (p. 214) makes a perfect accompaniment, or serve tomaticán with a variety of Chilean salads.

3 tablespoons lard or vegetable oil

1½ pounds pork stew meat, cut into ½-inch cubes

Salt and freshly ground black pepper, to taste

3 medium onions, halved and thinly sliced

1 large clove garlic, finely minced

1 teaspoon ground cumin

2 teaspoons dried oregano

2 pounds tomatoes, peeled and coarsely chopped

1½ cups fresh or frozen corn kernels

1 tablespoon finely minced fresh parsley

2 tablespoons finely minced fresh cilantro

1 serrano or jalapeño chile, seeded and finely chopped, or to taste

Heat the lard over high heat in a heavy saucepan or Dutch oven. Add the pork, and cook, stirring occasionally, until browned on all sides, about 10 minutes. Season with salt and black pepper.

Reduce the heat to low, add the onions, and cook, stirring occasionally, until softened but not browned, 8 minutes. Add the garlic, cumin, oregano, and tomatoes with their juices; simmer partly covered over low heat until the pork is tender, 45 minutes. Add the corn and simmer 15 minutes more. Taste for seasonings. Before serving, sprinkle with the cilantro, parsley, and chile.

Vegetable and Jerky Stew

Charquicán

Makes 6 servings

If we are to believe *Larousse Gastronomique,* there's only one authentic Chilean dish: charquicán and a close variation called valdiviano. This statement could easily be disputed . . . but, let's avoid an argument and take a closer look at this interesting dish. Its main ingredient is charqui, thin, long slivers of air-dried meat, which is combined with the native Indian staples of corn, pumpkin, and tomatoes.

> 1 pound pumpkin, cut into ¼-inch cubes
> 6 medium potatoes, peeled and cut into ¼-inch cubes
> 1 carrot, peeled and cut into ¼-inch cubes
> 1½ cups fresh or frozen green peas
> 1½ cups fresh or frozen corn kernels
> 2 cups beef or chicken broth
> Salt, to taste
> 3 tablespoons lard or vegetable oil
> ½ pound beef jerky or 1 pound cooked beef top round or rib-eye
>   steak, cut into ¼-inch cubes
> 1 medium onion, coarsely chopped
> 2 cloves garlic, finely minced
> 1 tablespoon sweet paprika
> 1 tablespoon dried oregano
> 1½ teaspoons ground cumin
> Freshly ground black pepper, to taste

In a large saucepan, bring the pumpkin, potatoes, carrot, peas, corn, and broth to a boil. Season with salt. Reduce the heat, and simmer partly covered for 15 minutes.

Meanwhile, heat the oil in a heavy skillet over medium heat. Add the beef and onion, and sauté until browned, 5 minutes. Add the garlic, paprika, oregano, cumin, salt, and black pepper. Cook, stirring, 3 minutes more. Add the beef mixture to the vegetables; simmer uncovered over low heat, stirring occasionally, until the liquid has evaporated, 15 to 20 minutes. Serve hot.

Adobo

Adobo, a popular spice rub, has for centuries been a valuable way to preserve meats in most Latin-American countries. Scientists have confirmed the intuitive folk wisdom, by discovering the antiseptic qualities of several popular flavoring agents. Garlic, onion, black pepper, and oregano seem to be the most effective agents in getting rid of many bacteria; thyme, tarragon, cumin, and chile peppers are also effective. Thus the seemingly direct link between hot climates and hot food is only natural.

In Chile, adobo is usually a mixture of cumin, garlic, sweet paprika, oregano, and (sometimes) hot chile peppers. The mix is a widely used flavoring agent. Variations of this seasoning mix are found in Cuba, Mexico, Peru, and other countries. In fact, the combination of chiles and oregano has been traced to the Aztecs. No wonder that chili powder, a Texan invention, has become a national best-seller in the United States! (This information on seasonings and bacteria is based on the findings of Jennifer Billing and Paul Sherman, who published their findings in the March 1998 issue of the *Quarterly Review of Biology*.)

It has become extremely difficult to purchase real charqui in Chile, unless you know an *arriero*, an altiplano herdsman. The superthin sheets that are for sale in the supermarkets and in the streets are dried in industrial ovens; they taste like salted cardboard and have nothing in common with the real thing. If you live in the southern part of the United States, you might be able to find a good-quality jerky, a staple of the North American cowboy's diet. If not, start with fresh meat and grill or roast it until it's completely dried out (and resembles jerky). This makes an acceptable substitute for the charqui.

This dish is traditionally served with a hot, pungent pevre, or chile sauce, and pickled pearl onions.

Life on the Altiplano

Drying meat in the high mountain wind is a way of preserving that goes back to pre-Colombian times. This method is still practiced by the *arrieros*, tough horsemen who take their herds of horses, sheep, and goats into the altiplano in search of greener pastures. These men often spend months away from home and family and survive on a strict minimum. Their existence is really less romantic than popular folk songs presume.

The diet of the *arrieros* consists of lots of charqui (jerky), which is easy to eat while traveling on horseback. At night, a few potatoes and onions are thrown into the ashes of a campfire or a tortilla de rescoldo—a dense bread (flour, liquid, and salt) that is assembled in a dried goatskin and baked in a dying fire covered by the ashes. All is washed down with sweetened maté, a popular herbal tea.

Callampas from the Cerro

Callampas forestas, Chilean wild mushrooms, are sold dried, seldom fresh. They have a deep earthy flavor, comparable to porcini mushrooms, and are ideal for perking up sauces, casseroles, and soups. A good part of the harvest is shipped to Spain; and in Chile, the imported and cultivated mushrooms (*champiñones*) are taking over the culinary scene, which I consider a real loss.

During the rainy winter months, Angelica, my initiator in the secrets of Chilean rural life, took me to the Cerros to search for the *callampas* and other wild mushrooms that grow between the rocks and under thorny bushes. The Cerros, a long chain of hills running from north to south between the Andes Mountains and Pacific Ocean, undergo the most wonderful metamorphosis as soon as the first raindrops hit the ground. Most of the year, the Cerros have an inhospitable look, an arid, dusty region where only the thorny hawthorn and cacti seem to thrive.

Angelica, like the people of the Cerros, knows where to gather medical herbs, roots, bark, and berries, remedies to cure about every imaginable illness, from sore muscles to the very frequent ailments caused by the evil eye (*el mal de ojo*) to a broken heart. Most of these herbal remedies are still commonly used and sold by vendors or *curanderos*, the healers, in every country or urban market.

The Cerros seem to exercise a strong attraction to the people living around them, whose universe is filled with legends and magic. The Cerro Dimanque rises immediately behind my house and in the late afternoon, when it hides the winter sun, its huge, chilly shadow covers the house and the garden like a somber blanket. It's the hour of *la cuca, la vieja lola* (the old, young one), the old woman with fingernails like claws who bewitches young men and lures them into the bushes where a cruel fate awaits them. Angelica couldn't be more specific because no one ever comes back. *"Palabra, palabra, es la pura verdad!"* (I give you my word, it's nothing but the truth.)

Braised Stuffed Scaloppine with Porcini Mushrooms

Niños Envueltos

Makes 6 servings

In spite of the country's geographic isolation, for centuries, Santiaguinos have looked to Europe for inspiration and guidelines. To this very day, the city's historic center reflects that certain Old World charm that seduces nostalgic visitors like me.

In the culinary world, the French left an undeniable imprint, affecting mostly the urban upper and middle classes. But many ladies of these classes seldom spend more time in the kitchen than it takes to give orders to the maid and cook. Fortunately, there have always been exceptions, and one can find some of the most refined cooks within their midst, such as Señora Chita Ponce. She rules her kitchen, putting a finishing touch on a sauce, completing a delicate crema de lucuma (p. 281), and arranging a bunch of roses for the table. Señora Chita graciously shared several recipes with me and, most important, her knowledge and deep love for the pleasures of the table!

In this recipe, tender scaloppine is stuffed with bacon, carrots, and egg for a colorful presentation. After stuffing, they are braised until tender in a flavorful red wine sauce infused with the woodsy aroma of *callampas*, Chilean dried mushrooms (p. 141). Serve with potato purée or a Chilean-style rice dish.

> 12 thin 2 × 3-inch slices veal or beef, pounded to ¼-inch thickness
> Salt and freshly ground black pepper, to taste
> 6 thin slices smoked bacon, halved
> 2 hard-cooked eggs, cut lengthwise into 6 pieces
> 2 carrots, cooked and cut into 1½ × ¼-inch strips
> 12 cilantro sprigs
> 2½ tablespoons all-purpose flour

¾ cup hot water

3 tablespoons butter or vegetable oil

½ cup dried porcini mushrooms

1 cup finely chopped onion

1 large clove garlic, finely minced

1 teaspoon dried oregano

½ cup red wine

½ cup beef broth

2 tablespoons minced fresh parsley

Place the veal flat on a work surface, season with salt and black pepper, and cover each piece with 1 piece of bacon. Place 1 piece of egg, 2 carrot strips, and 1 cilantro sprig in the center of each piece. Starting at a short side, roll the meat tightly around the filling twice, closing in the edges. Tie with kitchen string. Dust the meat bundles with the flour, shaking off any excess.

Soak the dried mushrooms in the water about 15 minutes. Drain the mushrooms and chop finely. Pass the soaking liquid through a coffee filter to remove any sand and reserve.

Heat the butter in a heavy Dutch oven over medium heat until it is hot but not smoking. Add the meat bundles, and sauté, turning, until browned on all sides, about 6 minutes. Be careful not to burn the drippings. Remove the meat bundles, and place on a platter.

Add the onion and garlic to the meat drippings, and sauté over medium heat about 3 minutes. Add the mushrooms, their soaking liquid, oregano, wine, and beef broth. Return the meat to the pan, cover, and simmer over low heat, 20 to 25 minutes. If the sauce is too thin, remove the meat from the pan, and reduce the juices over high heat, stirring, until the sauce has the desired consistency. Taste for seasonings.

For an elegant presentation, discard the kitchen string from the meat bundles and cut each one in half. Spoon the sauce into a warm serving platter, arrange the meat on top, cut side up to reveal the colorful spiral. Sprinkle with parsley and serve at once.

Oven-Roasted Leg of Lamb, Chilean Style

Pierna de Cordero Mechada

Makes 4 to 5 servings

Roasting a whole lamb over a pit of hot coals is a popular way of celebrating the New Year in the Chilean countryside. This recipe is a wonderful alternative, adapted for the home cook who may feel somewhat intimidated by such a huge production. A leg of lamb, infused with a pungent adobo or marinade is oven roasted and served simply, surrounded by golden brown potatoes. Definitely an easy, nourishing, and delicious way of presenting lamb in a one-dish meal!

> 1 tablespoon finely chopped onion
> 6 large cloves garlic, finely minced
> 2 tablespoons dried porcini mushrooms, soaked in hot water 20 minutes, drained and finely chopped
> 1 tablespoon finely minced fresh parsley
> 3 tablespoons red wine vinegar
> 1 teaspoon salt
> 1/2 teaspoon freshly ground black pepper
> 1 (about 4-pounds) rump part of leg of lamb with bone-in (for more flavor)
> 4 tablespoons lard or vegetable oil
> 1 teaspoon dried oregano
> 18 small potatoes, coated with 3 tablespoons olive oil and coarse salt
> 1/2 cup hot water
> 2 tablespoons chopped fresh parsley

In a small bowl, make adobo by mixing the onion, garlic, mushrooms, minced parsley, vinegar, salt, and black pepper. Place the lamb in a deep roasting pan.

Using a sharp paring knife, make little slits in the meat and push some of the adobo inside each one. Rub the rest of the adobo into the lamb, covering it all over. Cover the pan with plastic wrap and refrigerate for at least 1 hour or overnight.

Preheat the oven to 400F(205C). Sprinkle salt and pepper on each side of the meat, and cover with lard. Dust with the oregano. Roast 10 minutes on a side; reduce the heat to 375F(190C), and add the potatoes and water to the pan. Baste the meat with the drippings every 10 minutes, and turn the potatoes at least once during cooking. Roast 35 to 45 minutes, or until a meat thermometer reads 140F(60C) for medium-rare; roast 10 to 15 minutes more or until a thermometer reads 160–170F(70–75C) for well-done.

Remove the roasting pan from the oven, and wrap in foil to keep the lamb warm. Let rest 10 minutes before carving. Slice the lamb, and serve on a hot platter, surrounded by the golden brown potatoes and sprinkled with chopped parsley. Serve the drippings on the side in a sauceboat.

Rich Lamb Stew with Spring Vegetables

Estofado de Cordero Primavera

Makes 6 to 8 servings

After two years of small-town living, my family moved even farther away from civilization to a huge apple farm, or *fundo*, in the heart of the fertile Central Valley. The farm is a close, self-sufficient community. Our house, a rustic adobe construction surrounded by a large veranda overgrown with ivy and kiwifruit plants, seems lost in a sea of apple trees, pears, cherries, and grapevines.

The imposing, snow-topped Andes Mountains rise behind the house. We couldn't be in a more propitious spot to sample Chilean country life in all its glory and hardship. We had to serve a whole apprenticeship to fully appreciate the earthy pleasures of country life at a pace governed by seasons and not by days.

For one, we rediscovered the magic of spring with its bountiful revival that most clearly influenced our eating habits. A tasty stew of incredibly tender spring vegetables and young lamb, a cheerful table on a sun-drenched terrace— what more could one want from life?

Serve this estofado with plenty of crusty country bread to mop up all the wonderful flavors.

> **3 tablespoons lard or vegetable oil**
> **4 pounds boneless breast or shoulder of lamb, cut into 1-inch cubes, fat removed**
> **Salt and freshly ground black pepper, to taste**
> **1 large onion, halved lengthwise and thinly sliced**

½ **red bell pepper, cut into strips**

1 **carrot, peeled and coarsely grated**

3 **large cloves garlic, finely minced**

1½ **teaspoons dried oregano**

3 **cups beef broth**

12 **small or 8 medium artichoke bottoms (p. 43)**

3 **tomatoes, peeled and quartered**

1 **small bunch Swiss chard, rinsed and shredded**

1 **cup fresh or frozen fava beans**

1 **cup fresh or frozen green peas**

12 **small new potatoes, peeled**

2 **tablespoons finely chopped fresh parsley**

In a heavy casserole or Dutch oven, heat the oil over high heat. Add the lamb and sauté until brown on all sides. Season with salt and black pepper. Using a slotted spoon, remove the lamb from the pan, and set aside.

Add the onion to the drippings, and cook over low heat, stirring occasionally, until softened but not brown, about 8 minutes. Add the bell pepper, carrot, garlic, and oregano, and sauté 2 minutes more. Season with salt and black pepper. Return the lamb to the pan, add the broth, and simmer covered, 1 hour.

Meanwhile, blanch the artichoke bottoms in salted boiling water 5 minutes. Drain.

Preheat the oven to 375F (190C).

In the casserole, layer the artichokes, tomatoes, chard, fava beans, peas, and potatoes on top of the lamb. Season with salt and black pepper. Cover, and bake 40 to 50 minutes, until the potatoes are soft. Bring the casserole right to the table, and ladle the stew into deep soup plates. Sprinkle with the parsley.

Poor Man's Pork Chops

Chuletas a lo Pobre

Makes 4 servings

This dish might well be the best-deal meal in the country's local little restaurants. Two thin pork chops or slices of beef are covered with eggs, sunny side up, and flanked by sweet, caramelized onions, and a serious heap of French fries. This copious plate is curiously named Poor Man's Pork Chops. I strongly suspect this dish originated in the lush southern provinces of Chile, or even in the island of Chiloé where the inhabitants are known for their huge appetites.

I did make two small changes to the original recipe. First, I choose to serve one thick pork chop instead of two thin ones. Pork is remarkably leaner these days in the United States and thus can dry out quickly. Second, I fry the potatoes in the Belgian style, which means dipping them twice in the hot oil to get crispy outsides and soft insides.

> 6 tablespoons vegetable oil or butter
> 2 large onions, halved lengthwise and thinly sliced
> 1½ pounds baking potatoes
> Vegetable oil for frying
> 4 (1-inch-thick) center-cut pork chops
> 4 eggs

Heat 3 tablespoons of the oil in a large skillet over medium-low heat. Add the onions, and cook, stirring occasionally, until slightly caramelized, about 25 minutes. Season with salt and black pepper, and keep warm.

Bring the oil in a deep-fryer to 325F(165C). Peel the potatoes, cut into thin fries, and dry thoroughly in paper towels. Fry the potatoes, about 1 cup at a time, 3 to 4 minutes. They should not be brown at this point.

Heat the remaining 3 tablespoons of oil in a large skillet over medium heat. Season the pork chops with salt and black pepper. Add the pork to the skillet, and cook until brown on both sides, about 2 minutes per side. Reduce the heat, and cook, turning, until cooked through, 4 to 6 minutes more. Be careful not to overcook pork, as it will become dry and tough. Transfer the pork to a platter and keep warm.

Again, bring the oil in the deep-fryer to 375F (190C). Meanwhile, fry the eggs, sunny side up, in the meat drippings. While the eggs are cooking, add the potatoes to the oil in batches, and fry until golden brown, 1 to 3 minutes. Drain on paper towels, salt, and serve them at once.

Place a pork chop in the center of a dinner plate, and top with an egg. Place caramelized onions on one side and crusty fries on the other.

Pork Roast with Chilean Spice Rub

Lomo de Cerdo en Adobo

Makes 6 servings

Chilean regional cooking is an ever-evolving story of the home cook's artistry behind unpretentious dishes. This updated version of a hearty winter meal flavors a boneless pork loin with a garlicky adobo and roasts it with potatoes.

> **4 cloves garlic, peeled**
> **2 teaspoons salt**
> **1 tablespoon minced fresh oregano or 2 teaspoons dried**
> **3 tablespoons minced fresh parsley**
> **1 teaspoon freshly ground black pepper**
> **1 tablespoon sweet paprika**
> **¼ cup vegetable oil**
> **1 (3-pound) boneless pork loin roast, tied**
> **2 pounds small potatoes, peeled**

To prepare the adobo, pound the garlic with the salt in a mortar to a fine paste. Stir in the oregano and 1 tablespoon of the parsley; pound until incorporated. Add the black pepper and paprika, and slowly pour in the oil, stirring, until you have a thick, smooth mixture. Cover the pork loin evenly with the adobo, and refrigerate overnight, turning the pork occasionally. Bring to room temperature before roasting.

Preheat the oven to 400F(205C). Boil the potatoes in salted water for 10 minutes. Drain and reserve.

Place the pork loin in a roasting pan, and roast 20 minutes, turning once, until lightly brown on all sides. Reduce the oven temperature to 350F (175C). Add the potatoes, covering them evenly with the pan juices. Roast 45 minutes more, until the potatoes are brown and the juices run clear when the pork is pierced deeply.

Let the roast rest for 10 minutes before slicing. Serve on a warmed serving platter, surrounded by the potatoes. Garnish with the remaining parsley.

Grilling

In Chile, I've heard more than once that one is born *un verdadero maestro,* "a true master," in the primal art of cooking food directly over a smoldering fire. We're not talking here about grilling a few dainty lamb chops or the ubiquitous hamburgers and hot dogs we're used to in the United States but about impressive pieces of meat. It does take almost an instinct to know when a 5- to 10-pound slab of meat needs to be turned over, or when it needs a brush of marinade, more heat, or a sprinkle of salt and, more important, when exactly it is perfectly done: nicely brown and crispy on the outside and juicy tender on the inside. And this without any sophisticated piece of equipment!

Most *parrillas* ("grills") are quite rustic, a big oil drum sliced in half lengthwise and mounted on an iron framework. It is very important to have adjustable racks so the heat can be regulated. The fire is started from dried wood or hardwood charcoal; no chemicals are ever used.

Grilling is a matter of patience and full dedication to the task. Under *no* circumstances does the maestro ever leave the grill unattended, a condition Chileans seem to accept without a second thought. Automatically, all the men gather around the *parrilla,* passing around beers or Pisco Sours (p. 50), intently discussing the soccer games, the latest news in politics, and family affairs while impatiently eyeing the meat. A good maestro keeps his audience entertained, praising the benefits of his favorite cut of meat and offering his guests something to nibble on to soothe their by now ferocious appetites. Some spicy chorizo sausages wrapped in a crusty roll do the trick. While the meat is roasting, the host may slice small pieces off the end of the meat and pass them around.

I've seen some maestros moisten the roast in the most theatrical moves, for example, squirting a foaming beer bottle over the meat (beer does impart an interesting flavor). This is not the ideal way to avoid flare-ups!

Grilling is definitely a man's business in Chile, and no woman would dispute this macho prerogative. At least, it guarantees her a short moment of respite from the kitchen (although she is usually in charge of the salads, drinks, and general table management; of keeping kids and pets out of the men's way; and of the cleaning up).

Over the years, I've come to understand that there are at least two rules. First of all, if you don't want to miss out on the latest gossip and the juiciest pieces of beef, it's an absolute must to join the crowd around the grill. Second, if you're entertaining South American guests be aware that they can devour an astonishing amount of meat. This brings to mind an anecdote I would rather forget for the rest of my life. On the first occasion my husband invited his colleagues from the apple farm for a cookout at our home, I had the inspired idea to break with tradition and serve the meat threaded on skewers, intertwined with little vegetables and bacon. The huge stack of brochettes disappeared in no time. What surprised me was that no one had touched the bowls of salads. When I noticed the expectant and somewhat worried looks on my guests' faces, I understood that they were waiting for the *real* meat to come!

Strategies for Grilling

- In Chile I've learned that to a certain extent the fire is more important than the meat to be grilled. They use charcoal grills exclusively, as only charred wood imparts the unique and true grill flavor.

- Any type of charcoal grill will do, as long as it has an adjustable rack or another way to regulate the heat.

- I definitely recommend using only all-natural hardwood charcoal (or starting from scratch with chunks of hardwood, such as oak, cherry, apple, hickory, mesquite, and alder wood). Lump charcoal starts quicker and burns twice as hot as briquettes. Avoid any starters that contain chemicals; there are many alternative devices on the market.

- Expensive and exotic wood chips are, to me, a waste of money and energy. Don't forget we want to taste meat, not smoke.

- Grilling is all about timing. Start the fire early and allow the charcoal to burn for at least 25 minutes in a mound before you spread out the hot coals. The fire is ready when the coals are no longer flaming and are covered with a layer of white ash. In Chile, the fire is often started in a small brazier. When the coals are ready, they are placed in the grill. This is a clever way of working, especially if you are planning to grill large pieces of meat or if you plan to serve some grilled vegetables first, hamburgers next, and finally chicken legs. You can start the replacement coals in the brazier, so they don't get in the way of the grilling.

- Start the grilling only when the coals are ready, and your grill is clean.

- It's a good idea to sear the meat first over high heat; this will keep the juices in. Spread out the coals even more, salt the meat, and keep turning it, every 7 to 10 minutes for big pieces and every 2 to 3 minutes for small ones, over an *even* heat source. If the meat has a layer of fat on one side, score it; and place the fat side down on the grill.

- Avoid flare-ups, do not prick the meat with a fork (use tongs instead), and stoically resist every maneuver that may distract you from your noble task.

- For grilling, the meat should never be thicker than 1$\frac{1}{2}$ to 2 inches. One inch is ideal. Larger pieces such as leg of lamb should be butterflied to reduce the thickness before grilling.

- It's important to avoid letting the meat get dry and leathery. Cooking the meat until it is crusty outside and juicy-tender inside takes an experienced touch. It's perfectly acceptable, however, to make a small incision with a small sharp knife. When the meat is done, slice it and serve at once (bigger pieces and leftovers can rest for a while, covered with aluminum foil), and never return the meat to the flames.

- In Chile, experienced maestros will never agree on what type of marinade or adobo is best, and some swear that only sea salt will do, especially for beef. Pork, lamb, and chicken are traditionally marinated. None of the marinades I've tasted were overwhelmingly spicy or sweet. The point is to eat meat. The heat and spice is mostly served on the side as a salsa or pevre.

- As a general rule, marinate tougher and bigger cuts of meat with a mixture that contains some acid, such as wine, vinegar, or lemon juice, to tenderize the connective tissues and oil to protect it from drying out; herbs and spices add flavor. Marinades give a boost to lamb, cabrito (young goat), and pork ribs. Loin chops and nicely marbled steaks are best simply rubbed with olive oil and well seasoned with salt and black pepper, nothing else.

Mixed Grill, Chilean Style

Parrillada Mixta

Makes 8 servings

The pork chops and sirloin steaks are quickly seared and kept at the right distance from the hot coals so they cook to perfection. A pungent adobo made with Chilean wine is brushed on the meat to give it extra zest and keep it from drying out. Big bowls of Chilean salads and salsa bring everyone to the table where the grill master himself slices and distributes the pieces that are ready to be eaten. In the meantime, new charcoal revives the dying embers and is prepared for the last round: an extra steak for the diehards and the chicken thighs and drumsticks the kids have been waiting for the whole afternoon . . .

MARINADE
2 large cloves garlic, finely minced
¼ cup finely chopped onion
1 tablespoon dried oregano
1 tablespoon salt
1 teaspoon freshly ground black pepper
1 cup red wine
¼ cup red wine vinegar
½ cup vegetable oil

GRILL
8 (1-inch-thick) center-cut pork chops
8 chicken legs, separated into thighs and drumsticks
16 to 32 small spicy pork sausages
Buns for sausages
Salt, to taste
2 (2-inch-thick) beef sirloin, rib-eye, T-bone, or porterhouse steaks
        (about 2 pounds each)

Combine all the ingredients for the marinade in a small bowl. Place pork chops and chicken legs in separate nonreactive bowls. Pour half the marinade over the pork and the other half over the chicken, and refrigerate about 4 hours. Drain and reserve the marinades for basting.

Prepare the coals for grilling the sausages. When they're ready, start a new, bigger batch for the steaks and pork chops.

Grill the sausages over medium heat until cooked through and lightly charred, 5 to 7 minutes, depending on their size. Pass them around at once, each one pressed between a little bun.

To start the pork chops and beef, you'll need high heat to sear the meat quickly for about 1 minute on each side. Season the seared meat with salt. Scatter the charcoal evenly over the grill and cook the chops and steaks over moderate direct heat, turning and basting the meat every 3 to 4 minutes until it is done to your liking. The pork should take 12 to 15 minutes; the beef 10 to 15 minutes for medium-rare. Slice the pork and beef into 1-inch pieces and serve immediately.

Finally, grill the chicken over medium heat, turning and basting frequently, until lightly charred and cooked through, 20 to 30 minutes.

Organizing *un asado* ("a grill cookout") is serious business. First of all you give your butcher and family and friends a few days' notice; purchase a decent amount of charcoal, wine, beer, and other necessary thirst quenchers; and prepare to take a full day off. The secret for a successful cookout is to keep the fun going by offering guests at regular intervals an interesting variety of meats and giving everyone a chance to recuperate. It's always a good idea to have some juicy, spicy pork sausages ready for when your guests arrive. Chunky, hot Chancho en Piedra (p. 60) scooped up with pieces of crusty bread will keep everyone happy. When the last drop of Pisco Sour (p. 50) is served, it's time to do some serious grilling.

Grilled Lamb or Young Goat

Cordero o Cabrito a la Parrilla

Makes 6 servings

Whether you choose a rack or a whole leg, lamb or cabrito (young goat) grilled to tenderness, is simply marvelous! In the Chilean countryside, a simple seasoning of coarse salt is all that's used, but here I've used a pungent, garlicky adobo to give the meat an extra little bit of flavor and to mask the sometimes stronger taste of goat and older animals.

When you buy the roast, let the butcher butterfly it for you, so the meat will cook faster and more evenly. Most of the fat should be cut away; it imparts a strong flavor to the meat. An even, slow grilling is the secret; baste and turn the meat frequently. Watch out for flare-ups, which will result in charred meat and a bitter flavor.

> 1 red bell pepper, roasted, peeled and seeded (or 2 canned
>   pimientos)
> 6 large cloves garlic, peeled
> 2 teaspoons salt
> $\frac{1}{2}$ teaspoon freshly ground black pepper
> 2 tablespoons finely minced fresh parsley
> $\frac{1}{2}$ cup red wine vinegar
> $\frac{1}{3}$ cup vegetable oil
> 1 teaspoon dried oregano
> $\frac{1}{2}$ teaspoon dried or fresh rosemary
> 3 racks of lamb or cabrito ($4\frac{1}{2}$ to 5 pounds total weight) or
>   1 (4- to 5-pound), butterflied leg of lamb or cabrito

In a mortar or food processor make a paste with the bell pepper, garlic, salt, and black pepper. Add the remaining ingredients, except the lamb, and mix to combine.

Place the meat in a nonreactive deep dish or baking pan, and spread the marinade evenly over the meat. Cover, and marinate in the refrigerator 6 hours or overnight.

Prepare the coals for grilling. Remove the meat from the marinade, and reserve the marinade for basting. Grill the meat over moderate, direct heat, about 4 inches above the hot coals, basting with the marinade and turning frequently. The ribs will take 20 to 30 minutes; they should be fork-tender when pierced between the ribs. The leg will take 30 to 40 minutes, depending on the thickness of the meat and the temperature of the coals. Let the meat rest 10 minutes before carving; remember that it will continue to cook during this time.

Marinated and Grilled Steak

Plateada a la Parrilla

Makes 4 servings

Grilling a thick slab of red meat to juicy tenderness requires some skillful attention, but tasting it is a hard-to-beat experience. In Chile, meat lovers favor what we consider the less-tender cuts, such as top round and flank steak, because of their superior flavor. For Chileans, meat has to taste like meat, only a sprinkle of coarse salt is permitted. Interestingly enough, most of my Chilean friends like their beef well-done, and the chewiness doesn't seem to bother them one bit.

Keeping in mind the preference for tender, juicy meat of my North American friends, I marinate the steak in this recipe to tenderize it. For the same reason, the meat should be cooked to rare or medium-rare. If your prefer rare meat, it's a good idea to insist on it in most Chilean restaurants.

> 2 large cloves garlic, finely minced
> 3 tablespoons Salsa de Ají Colorado a la Chilena (p. 66)
>   or ground fresh chile paste, such as sambal oelek or harissa
>   sauce
> 1½ teaspoons dried oregano
> 1 teaspoon salt
> 1 tablespoon freshly squeezed lemon juice
> 2 tablespoons vegetable oil
> 1 (2-pound) top-round or flank steak, about 2 inches thick

Combine all the ingredients, except the beef, in a deep nonreactive dish. Add the beef, and coat thoroughly on both sides with the marinade. Cover, and let marinate at room temperature 1 to 3 hours in the refrigerator. Bring to room temperature before grilling.

Prepare the coals for grilling. Drain the beef, reserving the marinade. Sear the beef quickly over high heat on both sides. Scatter the coals evenly over the grill, and cook the beef over moderate, direct heat, basting with the remaining marinade and turning it every 4 to 5 minutes. Continue cooking 15 to 20 minutes for medium-rare. Check frequently for doneness, as it can quickly become too well done.

Spicy Pork Ribs, Chilean Style

Costillas de Chancho a la Parrilla

Makes 4 servings

In Chile, meaty pork ribs, generously dabbed with a pungent salsa de ají, are sold in most butcher shops. The hot salsa preserves (a necessary precaution in hot climates) and softens the meat while imparting it with a tantalizing bite. In Chile pork ribs are never precooked but are slowly and skillfully grilled over hot coals until the tender meat almost falls off the bone. Serve with a bowl of chunky Chancho en Piedra (p. 60), a delicious, fresh Chilean salsa.

If you feel intimidated by this time-consuming task, bake the ribs in a 300F(150C) oven for about 1 hour. Then finish the rack on the grill until the meat is nicely brown and very tender, about 1 hour more.

> **1 cup Salsa de Ají Colorado a la Chilena (p. 66) or ground fresh**
> **chile paste, sambal oelek, or harissa sauce**
> **2 large cloves garlic, finely minced**
> **1 tablespoon dried oregano**
> **4 pounds pork ribs**

Combine the salsa de ají, garlic, and oregano in a small bowl.

Place the ribs in a nonreactive dish; rub the chili mixture over all surfaces, cover the dish, and refrigerate for at least 12 hours or up to 2 days. Return to room temperature before cooking. Bake the ribs, if desired.

Prepare the coals for grilling; keep some new charcoal going to ensure a steady supply for 1 or 2 hours.

When the fire is ready, place the grill rack about 4 inches away from the hot coals. It's important that the ribs cook slowly and that the fat renders.

Avoid flare-ups, because the chile mixture will become bitter. Turn the ribs frequently, and grill for about 1 hour if they were prebaked or 2 hours if they were not, until the pork is cooked through and fork-tender when pierced between the ribs. It's important to keep the charcoal at an even, moderate heat the whole time.

When the ribs are done, transfer to a cutting board and slice into individual ribs. Serve hot.

All over Chile, small rustic eateries specialize in chancho (pork), often raised on the premises. During the winter months, these *picadas* are a sought-after Sunday-outing destination.

A mixed grill as served in the *picadas* consists of juicy pork chops; the *popular costillas* (ribs); and above all the very typical fresh and spicy sausages (*longanizas and chorizos*), tripe (*chunchules*), blood sausages (*prietas*), and other innards. You certainly have to acquire a taste for some of these exotic items, but they are worth it for any adventurous palate!

Just don't forget that these cuts get cold very fast and must be eaten piping hot. Chilean country folks believe that the drink of choice to accompany greasy foods, like sausages and the traditional empanadas is *un buen tinto*, a good red wine. They say that cold drinks, such as beer or soft drinks, make the grease congeal in your stomach, a sure source of trouble! An old wives' tale?

Grilled Chicken, Chilean Style

Pollo a la Parilla

Makes 4 servings

This is definitely a modern adaptation, a city grill party for an intimate group of four. Chileans are very social people, and most gatherings include extended family members. But times are changing. Accompany this grilled chicken with several Chilean salads.

Yet, big or small, the basic idea remains the same: Never forget to give your guests something to nibble on while they're waiting. For this recipe, start your guests with the tasty morsels of chicken livers, enrobed in thin bacon and grilled to juicy perfection. A bowl of pickled onions can be passed around. A great combination!

> 4 tablespoons softened butter
> 3 tablespoons freshly squeezed lemon juice
> 1 clove garlic, finely minced
> Salt and freshly ground black pepper, to taste
> 1 (3½- to 4-lb.) roasting chicken, cut into 6 serving pieces, rinsed
>   and patted dry
> ½ cup finely minced fresh parsley
> ⅓ cup vegetable or olive oil
> 2 tablespoons red wine vinegar
> 12 chicken livers, trimmed of fat and discolored spots, rinsed and
>   patted dry
> 12 thin slices of smoked bacon
> 3 scallions, each cut into 4 pieces, or pickled onions

In a small bowl, combine the softened butter with the lemon juice, garlic, salt and black pepper. Spread this mixture evenly over the chicken. Place the chicken in a deep plate, cover, and refrigerate for up to 4 hours.

In a small bowl, combine the parsley, oil, and vinegar.

Season the chicken livers with salt and black pepper. Wrap each liver tightly with a slice of bacon. Thread the wrapped livers, alternating with the scallions, on 3 or 4 skewers. (If you will be serving pickled onions on the side, omit the scallions.)

Prepare a charcoal grill (if possible, large enough to hold the chicken and the livers).

Place the chicken liver brochettes and the chicken pieces on the grill. Grill the livers, turning the skewers several times, until rosy inside, 8 to 10 minutes. Baste with the parsley mixture when they're done. Pass the livers around.

In the meantime, keep an eye on the chicken. Adjust the rack over the hot coals; do not let it burn. Remember that chicken takes a while to cook. Baste with the parsley mixture every now and then. When the chicken is cooked through and nicely colored, baste generously with the parsley mixture before serving.

A Fisherman's Paradise

In the narrow country of Chile, the ocean is never far off. From the northern city of Iquique, bordering Peru, along the fishing ports of the Central Valley and the Lake District, to the southern windswept island of Tierra del Fuego, Chile's coast provides an incredible wealth of fish and shellfish.

The famous Humboldt current, which carries the icy cold Antarctic waters up the Chilean coast, guarantees a wide variety of fish and seafood of impeccable flavor. Chile has a reputation of being one of the world's largest fish producers, and Japan and the United States are the main importers.

Unfortunately, this incredible natural resource will soon be exhausted unless more attention is paid to irresponsible and indiscriminate exploitation and overfishing.

Chile was always a real paradise for the adventurous seafood lover; and fortunately, it still is in many ways. When you are in the picturesque fishing villages, make your way to the beach where the brightly colored boats dock in the morning. It's not unusual to see a pair of sturdy oxen pulling the boats into the ocean. The fishermen will be more than pleased to help you choose from the refined lenguado y corvina (sole and sea bass), the meaty albacora y tollo (albacore tuna and shark), the exquisite congrio dorado o negro (a local fish), and the abundant sweet merluza (hake). And then, of course, there's a legion of local specimens, mostly known by their fisherman's names, la vieja (a white, mild-tasting fish), pichiguen y palometa (medium-size tuna), lisa y pejerreyes (small, silverish freshwater fish), and about a hundred more.

If you like fish, you'll adore the shellfish! There are only two conditions: It must be very fresh and must come from unpolluted waters. It's wise to check first! The most popular mariscos are the choritos (black-shelled small mussels), almejas (clams), machas (razor clams), ostras (oysters), ostiones (scallops), camarones (shrimp), langostinos (crawfish and/or prawns), calamares (squid), pulpo (octopus), centolla (red, spiny Patagonian king crab), and the large-bodied jaiva (common crab). For the real seafood lovers, there are the exotics; choros zapatos (mussels as big as a shoe) and erizo (the Chilean fat sea urchin). Within the spiny shell of the erizo lie five orange *lenguas,* or tongues (which are in fact the reproduction organs), also known as the much-prized *uni* in the Japanese sushi bars. The loco (Chilean abalone) is considered a rare and expensive delicacy. Because of their dwindling numbers, locos may only be harvested in certain seasons.

The potent piure, respectfully named *el ojo rojo* ("the red eye") by poet Pablo Nerudo, seems to have all the iodine of the ocean concentrated in its tiny body. My favorite seafood is the unusual picoroco, a large, rough-shelled barnacle that harbors sweet, somewhat stringy meat that resembles lobster meat.

Talking about lobsters is like talking about a mysterious place. The volcanic Archipelago de Juan Fernandez, 650 kilometers off the Chilean coast is a beautiful, forgotten group of islands known for its friendly inhabitants and the enormous langostas they catch. It's here that the real Robinson Crusoë (named Alexander Selkirk) lived the biggest adventure of his life and became a legend. His experience could still be repeated, because this remote place has hardly changed. Almost all of the archipelago's forty-five hundred inhabitants live in the lobster town of San Juan Bautista, and lobsters are the islanders' main source of income.

Where to Eat and What to Order

For obvious reasons, the closer to the water the better the seafood. The small, homey eateries overlooking the beached boats, the placid pelicans, and the fishermen repairing their nets are my favorites.

Actually, these places are often run by that same fisherman's wife or sister-in-law. Order the simpler dishes that the locals know best: paella marina, a concoction of fish, shellfish, broth, and vegetables; a plate of freshly shucked oysters or clams; sizzling hot scallops al pil-pil; moist pescado frito; or the ubiquitous fisherman's soup, caldillo, superb when prepared with the unusual congrio fish, potatoes, and onions. And my absolute favorite is chupe de jaiva o de locos, a rich, cheesy gratin made with lots of succulent crabmeat or, even better, Chilean abalone.

Interestingly enough, a great place to buy and to sample a wonderful variety of seafood is located in the heart of Santiago. *El Mercado Central,* a 120-year old monument of open-lace ironwork, and *La Feria,* a bustling, open market on the other side of the Mapocho River, are abundant with cheap eating places, especially the *marisquerías,* among rows of fish and vegetable stands.

Fish preparation is a delicate matter in Chile. To my biggest despair and disappointment, the fish is very often served hopelessly overcooked and devoid of all interest. In the better restaurants, cooks tend to hide their crime under a thick, starchy layer of something called salsa Margarita—a poor imitation of a French velouté sauce.

There seems to be no in between: It's either the humble fisherman's place or the trendy top restaurants situated in *El Barrio Alto,* Santiago's wealthy neighborhood. There, a new generation of Chilean chefs creates innovative dishes with a definite international influence but based on the wonderful produce the land and ocean have to offer.

An Ode to the Ocean

Mariscal

Makes 1 serving

Mariscal is a colorful plate filled to the rim with a wide assortment of mariscos (fruits of the sea), served over a pungent mixture of scallions, cilantro, and parsley; lots of lemon juice; ají verde, and ulte (cooked and finely chopped seaweed).

The best places to sample "the one and only" mariscal are the little, homey restaurants that lean against the fishing boat sheds or are found across from the fish market. From the *picadas* in Valparaiso to the market in Concepción or all the way south, pick places where the shellfish is opened in front of you, almost from the boat onto your plate.

You can be as adventurous as you like; a mariscal is open to variation. The clams, oysters, and mussels are often served raw on the half-shell or sometimes lightly cooked. A gourmet version includes delicate orange sea urchins, crab claws, and picorocos (huge barnacles). Some cooks like to serve the seafood whole, with the pungent green sauce on the side, others chop everything coarsely and marinate it in the flavorful juices, like a seviche. It's a matter of personal taste.

GREEN SAUCE, PER PERSON
1 tablespoon finely chopped onion
$\frac{1}{2}$ scallion, minced
$\frac{1}{2}$ tablespoon finely minced fresh cilantro
$\frac{1}{2}$ tablespoon finely minced fresh parsley
$\frac{1}{4}$ serrano or jalapeño chile, seeded and finely chopped, or to taste
2 tablespoons freshly squeezed lemon juice
1 tablespoon vegetable oil
Freshly ground pepper, to taste

SEAFOOD, PER PERSON; CHOOSE FROM THE
FOLLOWING:

**6 razor or cherrystone clams, shucked and served raw with juice or
   steamed**

6 mussels, shucked and served raw with juice or steamed

6 oysters, shucked and served raw with juice

6 scallops, cooked

6 large shrimp, cooked and peeled

In a small bowl, combine all the sauce ingredients.

Arrange your choice of seafood in an attractive pattern on a big platter. Serve the green sauce on the side.

Variation

Chop the seafood coarsely and combine with the sauce. Let the dish marinate 20 to 30 minutes before serving.

A Taste for Seaweed

Chileans and Japanese share a passion for the mysterious vegetables of the sea, so rich in minerals and vitamins A, B_{12}, and D. Since pre-Colombian times, the indigenous Indian tribes gathered the seaweed, which was a precious source of protein. The roots, called ulte, and the leafy parts, called luche, are still appreciated in traditional Chilean dishes. Fresh seaweed is steamed and seasoned with shallots and white wine. Dried, it is known as cochayuyo, and the neat bundles are widely available in the markets. The soaked and finely chopped cochayuyo often replaces the ground meat in many popular dishes. Unfortunately, it can be considered a cheap substitute for meat, which is a negative reputation hard to overcome!

Gratin of Chilean Crab

Chupe de Jaiva

Makes 8 servings

My favorite crab preparation in the Chilean repertoire is Chupe de Jaiva, a luxurious dish loaded with crabmeat and boldly flavored with spices, herbs, and Chilean hot sauce. It's baked to perfection in native clay dishes. Other seafood, such as abalone, shrimp, and lobster, leftover cooked fish, or mussels or clams, are equally delicious when prepared with care.

1½ pounds lump crabmeat

¾ pound stale white bread, crusts removed and cubed (about 8 cups)

3 cups warm water

3 tablespoons vegetable oil or butter

1 medium onion, finely chopped

1 red bell pepper, diced

3 medium carrots, peeled and coarsely grated

3 cloves garlic, finely minced

1 teaspoon ground cumin

1 teaspoon dried oregano

1 teaspoon sweet paprika

Salt and freshly ground black pepper, to taste

2 cups milk

¼ cup heavy cream

½ cup dry white wine

2 tablespoons Salsa de Ají Colorado a la Chilena (p. 66) or ground fresh chili paste, such as sambal oelek or Moroccan harissa sauce

⅔ cup freshly grated Parmesan cheese

Preheat the oven to 375F (190C). Pick carefully through the crabmeat to remove any remaining cartilage.

In a big bowl, soak the bread in the water 20 minutes. Press the water out with your hands, and crumble the bread to a smooth consistency. Set aside.

Heat the oil in a medium skillet over medium heat. Add the onion and bell pepper, and sauté until soft but not brown, about 3 minutes. Add the carrots, garlic, cumin, oregano, paprika, salt and black pepper. Sauté 1 minute, reduce the heat, and add the bread, milk, cream, and wine. Cook, stirring constantly, 5 minutes more. Stir in the crabmeat, and turn off the heat. If the mixture is too dry, add a little more milk; it should be moist, but not runny. Season generously with salt, pepper, and salsa de ají.

Divide the crab mixture into 8 individual gratin dishes or one large gratin dish. Sprinkle the cheese on top, and bake 20 to 25 minutes, or until the cheese is nicely brown. Serve immediately.

The drive along the narrow, winding coastal road between San Antonio and Valparaiso is a rather nerve-wracking experience. This is especially true during the summer months, when about half the population of Santiago tries to escape the heat. Everyone is looking for solace along the breezy seashore and sandy beaches. For the country folk and fishing families, it's the busiest time of the year. From early dawn to sundown, they all flock along the main road, setting up little stands to sell their wares—everything from beach umbrellas to silly hats to beautiful Romaine lettuces, the specialty of the region. I always keep my eyes open for the large-bodied crabs that the kids sell, holding them up high on a piece of string. They are a handful to clean but the effort is more than worth it! For the busy home cook, I recommend buying the crabmeat, cleaned and ready to use.

Sea Bass and Shrimp Marinated in Lime Juice

Cebiche de Corvina

Makes 6 servings

Chile's northern regions, the Tarapaca and Antofagasta, are strongly influenced by neighboring Peru and Bolivia. This is not surprising because most of the region was annexed by Chile in the late 1890s, during the war of the Pacific.

The charming coastal towns of Arica and Iquique provide the most important commercial sector of the region—fishing. But the tourists come for the miles of unspoiled white beaches, the eternal summer temperatures, and the important archaeological sites along the former Inca road.

Excellent seafood was a valid reason for me to check the area out! Among the more traditional preparations, I preferred the region's specialty of seviche. This is a Peruvian-inspired dish of the freshest, raw seafood that is "cooked" in the juice of local fragrant limes (limón de Pica) and flavored with bold herbs and chiles. The secret is to not overcook the delicate fish, which will result in an overly tart and mushy consistency. For seafood lovers, this is the best way of enjoying the pure, crisp flavors of the ocean.

1½ **pounds very fresh sea bass, scrod, red snapper or other white,
    firm-fleshed fish fillet, cut into ½-inch cubes**
½ **pound raw, small shrimp, peeled**
1½ **cups freshly squeezed lime juice**
1 **small clove garlic, finely minced**
Salt, to taste
1 **serrano chile, seeded and finely chopped, or to taste**

2 celery ribs, thinly sliced
¹/₂ red onion, thinly sliced
1 tablespoon minced fresh cilantro
1 tablespoon vegetable oil
4 cold cooked sweet potatoes or white potatoes, thinly sliced
    (optional)

Place the fish and shrimp in a glass bowl. Add the lime juice, garlic, salt, and chile. Mix to combine, cover, and refrigerate 2 hours.

Stir in the celery, onion, cilantro, and oil; refrigerate 30 minutes more. Serve at once, nicely displayed on a plate, and accompanied by the sliced potatoes, if using.

Seafood Seviche

Cebiche de Gambas y Ostiones

Makes 4 servings

The first condition to a wonderful seviche is, of course, the freshness of the fish or shellfish. If that's a problem, poach the fish or shellfish slightly. It won't be the same, but it'll still taste good. Juicy fragrant limes are preferable, but I've come across delicate seviches marinated in lemon and bitter Seville oranges. There are countless variations of seviche; the only limitations are the cook's inspiration and the fish's availability.

> **1 pound very fresh bay scallops or small peeled raw shrimp**
> **1 cup freshly squeezed lime juice**
> **1 to 2 jalapeño or serrano chiles, seeded and finely minced, or to taste**
> **Salt, to taste**
> **½ red onion, cut into ¼-inch dice**
> **½ red bell pepper, cut into ¼-inch dice**
> **1 tablespoon finely minced fresh cilantro**
> **2 ripe Haas avocados**
> **Lettuce leaves**

Place the scallops in a glass dish. Add the lime juice, chile peppers, and salt. Cover, and refrigerate about 2 hours.

Stir in the onion, bell pepper and cilantro; combine. Refrigerate 30 minutes more.

Just before serving, peel the avocados, remove the pits, and cut into ¼-inch dice. Stir into the seafood mixture. Line individual plates with the lettuce leaves, and spoon the seviche over top. Serve at once.

Variation

Cut the avocados in half, remove the pits, and peel. Spoon the seafood into the avocado shells.

The north of Chile is an intriguing land of extremes that can only be described in superlatives. Most of this region is covered by the driest, most barren desert in the world: the infamous Atacama. The desert valley is dissected by deep canyons with walls rising toward the impressive Andes Mountains, whose peaks reach more than six thousand meters (twenty thousand feet). Yet the desert holds many wonders, such as the haunting Valley of the Moon, a place without a hint of organic life to be found. The desert is also home to some of the oldest mummies from pre-Inca Indian groups and rock paintings that are more than seven thousand years old. Don't miss the fascinating geyser show at El Tatio. Every morning, more than a hundred geysers throw their columns of steam high into the Andean air in an aerial ballet.

In the nineteenth century, the region made its fortune during the saltpeter boom; but only ghost towns have survived the collapse of the saltpeter market that occurred at the end of World War I. Visit Chuquicamata, one of the world's largest open-pit copper mine, for an experience you'll never forget.

Seafood Pie with Corn Topping

Pastel de Choclo a la Chilota

Makes 6 servings

This wonderful variation on a popular national dish was created in the aquatic world of Chiloé. Fish and seafood are plentiful in those generous waters and make a delicious base for this corn-topped pie.

FILLING

1 cup dry white wine

1 cup water

3 pounds mussels, debearded

3 pounds clams

3 tablespoons butter or vegetable oil

5-inch link of chorizo, coarsely chopped

¾ cup finely chopped onion

3 scallions, minced

1 teaspoon sweet paprika

Pinch of cayenne pepper

2 tablespoons all-purpose flour

1 tablespoon finely minced fresh parsley

CORN TOPPING

11 cups fresh or frozen corn kernels

¾ cup milk

12 large basil leaves

4 tablespoons butter

1 teaspoon salt, or to taste

½ teaspoon freshly ground black pepper, or to taste

1 large egg, lightly beaten

ASSEMBLY

12 medium-size shrimp, peeled

12 to 16 bay scallops or 6 sea scallops

12 green olives

In a large pot, combine the white wine and water and bring to a rapid boil over high heat. Add the mussels; cover, and steam, stirring once or twice, until they are wide open, 3 to 5 minutes. With a slotted spoon, remove the mussels to a colander, and reserve. Add the clams to the cooking liquid, and steam in the same manner until open. Remove with the slotted spoon to the colander, and let cool. Strain the poaching liquid, and reserve. When the mussels and clams are cool enough to handle, remove the meat from the shells, and set aside. Discard any that do not open.

Melt 3 tablespoons of butter in a medium saucepan over medium heat. Add the chorizo, onion, and scallions; sauté over medium heat, stirring occasionally, 3 to 4 minutes. Season with paprika and cayenne. Sprinkle the flour over the mixture, and gradually stir in 1½ cups of the poaching liquid. Bring to a boil, and cook, stirring, until thickened, 2 minutes. Add the parsley, and taste for seasoning. You won't need any salt, as the poaching liquid will be quite salty from the seafood.

To make the corn topping, puree the corn kernels, in batches, with the milk and the basil in a blender or food processor. For a smooth, pastry-like texture press the mixture through a sieve, if you'd like. Melt 4 tablespoons of butter over medium heat in a large skillet. Add the corn purée, salt, and black pepper. While stirring constantly with a wooden spoon, add the egg. Cook, stirring constantly, over low heat until the mixture thickens slightly, 3 to 4 minutes. Taste for seasoning, and adjust as necessary.

Preheat the oven to 375F(190C). Divide the mussels, clams, shrimp, and scallops among six 2-cup earthenware dishes. Ladle the chorizo sauce over the seafood and place 2 olives in each dish. Cover each dish with the corn mixture. (The dish can be prepared in advance up to this point. Refrigerate until ready to serve or overnight.)

Bake 25 to 35 minutes, or until the topping is lightly browned. Serve immediately with a pungent Chilean salsa on the side.

Rice with Razor Clams and Spicy Sausage

Arroz con Machas y Longaniza

Makes 4 servings

Rice, introduced by the Spanish, was cultivated in the northern regions of Chile and became the base of many popular dishes such as arroz con pollo, arroz con lentejas, and arroz con machas (rice with chicken, lentils, and razor clams). The razor clams, dear to the Mapuche Indians, and the tasty longaniza (pork sausage), a specialty of the city of Chillán, are the main flavorings in this recipe. For the authentic version, you'll have to come to Chile, but I can assure you that this adapted version is just as tasty!

> 3 dozen razor clams, cherrystone or littleneck clams, or mussels
> 4 cups water
> ¼ cup vegetable or olive oil
> 1 (3-inch) link chorizo or other spicy pork sausage, sliced
> ½ cup finely chopped onion
> ¼ red bell pepper, cut into fine strips
> ¼ carrot, coarsely grated
> 2 cloves garlic, finely minced
> 1 teaspoon sweet paprika
> 2 cups long-grain rice
> Salt and freshly ground black pepper, to taste
> 2 tablespoons minced cilantro

Place cleaned clams in a tall soup pot with a tight-fitting lid. Add the water, cover, and cook over high heat until the clams just open, 3 to 5 minutes. Remove the pan from the heat and allow the shellfish to cool enough to handle. Take the meat out of the shells, discarding any clams that haven't opened. Strain the broth, and reserve and keep warm.

Heat the oil in a large skillet. Add the chorizo, onion, and bell pepper; sauté, stirring frequently, 5 minutes. Add the carrot, garlic, and paprika; cook 1 minute. Add the rice, and sauté, stirring, until the rice absorbs the oil, 2 minutes. Pour 3 cups of reserved broth over the rice; cover, and cook over medium heat or until the rice is tender, 20 to 25 minutes.

Add the clams and ½ cup of the reserved broth; season with salt and black pepper. Simmer uncovered until most of the liquid is absorbed, 1 to 2 minutes. Garnish with the cilantro, and serve at once.

If fresh shellfish isn't available, you can still prepare a wonderful dish using frozen shellfish and bottled clam juice for the broth.

Fillet of Sole with Seafood Velouté Sauce

Lenguado con Salsa Margarita

Makes 4 servings

In the beginning of the twentieth century, upper-class Chilean families often had a French chef in the house. Soufflés, consommés, Bavarian creams, and the whole repertoire of French sauces made their entree in the Chilean culinary world.

The very popular salsa Margarita, a rich seafood velouté sauce, was here to stay. Unfortunately, it seems that a few techniques got lost in the translation. Too often, a starchy, rather tasteless imitation is served. When this velvety sauce is correctly prepared, it is a real delicacy, especially when made with exquisite Chilean seafood, such as sea urchins, razor clams, abalone, shrimp, and langostinos. It's the ideal accompaniment for about any poached, steamed, or pan-fried fish.

In this recipe, I chose delicate sole fillets. I like them lightly sautéed in butter, but you can poach the fish for a lighter version. Serve with a generous serving of mashed potatoes or crispy French fries and a green salad.

16 small raw shrimp or unpeeled cooked shrimp
1 dozen razor or littleneck clams, scrubbed
¾ cup dry white wine
¾ cup water
1 celery rib, 3 parsley sprigs, and 3 oregano sprigs, tied together
    with kitchen string
1 dozen small mussels, debearded
4½ tablespoons butter
1½ tablespoons all-purpose flour
Salt and freshly ground black pepper, to taste
Pinch cayenne pepper
¼ cup heavy cream
Squeeze of fresh lemon juice, or to taste
8 sole fillets (about 2 pounds)

Peel the shrimp. Place the shrimp peels and clams in a medium saucepan. Add the wine, water, and herb bundle; cover tightly, and cook over high heat until the clams open, 4 to 6 minutes. Using a slotted spoon, remove the shrimp peels and clams, and set them aside. Discard any clams that haven't opened.

In the same cooking liquid, steam the mussels over high heat until they open, about 3 minutes. (If using raw shrimp, cook them with the mussels until pink.) Using a slotted spoon, remove the mussels, and set them aside. Discard any that haven't opened. Remove the clams and mussels from their shells. Reserve the broth.

Strain the shellfish broth through cheesecloth or a paper coffee filter into a medium saucepan. Bring to a boil. Melt 1½ tablespoons of the butter in another medium saucepan. Whisk in the flour, and cook over medium heat for 1 minute. Add 1¼ cups of the hot broth, and bring the sauce to a boil, whisking constantly. Reduce the heat to low, and simmer, stirring occasionally, 10 minutes. Season with salt, black pepper, and cayenne. Add the cream, quickly bring to a boil, and remove from the heat. Add the lemon juice and the clams and mussels; keep warm.

Meanwhile, in a large skillet over high heat melt the remaining 3 tablespoons of butter until foaming. Add the sole and season with salt and black pepper. Sauté, turning once, 2 to 3 minutes on a side.

Arrange the sole on individual warm plates, and spoon the seafood sauce over it. A safe way to reheat the sauce and fish is to run each plate under a hot broiler for a few seconds.

If you'd like to poach the sole instead of pan-frying it, do so after removing the clams and mussels from their shells. Season the sole with salt and black pepper, and poach in the flavorful shellfish broth over low heat until just done, about 5 minutes. Reserve the broth. Keep the sole warm while you prepare the sauce.

Salmon Steaks with Hazelnut Butter and Capers

Salmon a la Mantequilla Negra con Alcaparras

Makes 4 servings

The southern Lake District and the island of Chiloé seem to be the ideal places for large-scale salmon farming, one of Chile's big export products. The Pacific Chinook salmon (appreciated for its richness) and the smaller Coho or silver salmon are raised in the lakes and in offshore sea farms.

Chileans prefer their fish rather simply prepared and for good reason. Salmon is really at its best freshly broiled or hot smoked, a specialty of the south. I do not think that Chilean attempts to imitate the cold-smoked, Nova Scotia–style salmon have been very successful.

This classic combination of nut brown butter and tart little capers, a specialty of Spain, is popular in the better seafood restaurants. It's indeed a perfect match for many broiled or pan-fried fish fillets.

> **9 tablespoons butter or 1 tablespoon oil and 8 tablespoons butter**
> **4 salmon steaks (about 8 ounces each)**
> **Salt and freshly ground black pepper, to taste**
> **2 tablespoons capers, drained**
> **Fresh lemon wedges, garnish**

Heat 1 tablespoon of the butter or the oil in a nonstick skillet over medium heat. Add the salmon, and cook, turning once, 5 minutes on a side. The flesh should be slightly undercooked and moist in the center. Remove the steaks to a warm platter. Wipe the pan out with a paper towel.

Gently heat the remaining 8 tablespoons of butter in the same skillet over medium heat until the butter turns a nice hazelnut color. Remove from the heat, and add the capers. Pour the butter sauce over the salmon, garnish with the lemon wedges, and serve at once.

Swordfish en Escabeche

Escabeche de Pescado

Makes 4 servings

The traditional *en escabeche* (pickling) is still a popular way of preparing and preserving fish. The first choice for pickling would be a meaty, oily fish such as kingfish, sardines, herring, mackerel, and the famous pejerreyes. These small, silver fish are a variety of smelt found in rivers, lakes, and ocean. The tiny ones are lightly floured and fried up crisp and crunchy; they're a real delicacy. The bigger ones are pickled. Firm-fleshed swordfish and shark are good substitutes. Serve as a wonderful appetizer or light meal accompanied with a potato salad.

> 1½ **cups white vinegar**
> ¾ **cup water**
> 1 **teaspoon whole peppercorns**
> 4 **bay leaves**
> ½ **teaspoon salt**
> 4 **swordfish or shark steaks, rinsed and dried (5 to 6 ounces each)**
> **Salt and freshly ground black pepper, to taste**
> **All-purpose flour for dredging**
> **About** ½ **cup of vegetable oil**
> 1 **large onion, halved and thinly sliced**
> 1 **carrot, peeled and thinly sliced**
> ½ **red bell pepper, thinly sliced**
> 1 **serrano or jalapeño chile, halved and seeded**

Bring the vinegar, water, peppercorns, bay leaves, and salt to a boil in a non-aluminum saucepan. Let cool.

Season the fish steaks with salt and pepper, and dredge in the flour, shaking off the excess. Heat the oil in a large skillet over medium-high heat.

Add the fish, and fry until brown on both sides, turning once, 3 to 5 minutes. Drain on paper towels.

Arrange half of the sliced vegetables in a shallow earthenware dish. Place the fish fillets on top, and cover with the remaining vegetables. Pour the pickling liquid over the fish; cover the dish, and refrigerate overnight or up to 24 hours.

Crispy Fried Fish Fillets

Congrio Frito

Makes 4 servings

The long-bodied congrio is considered a real delicacy in Chile. The flesh is white and meaty and has a delicate flavor. They are often mistaken for eels, because their long, eel-like body and their name means "eel" in Spanish. They are native to the cold Chilean waters, although they are sometimes fished along the Peruvian coast.

Congrio is not available in the United States, but monkfish, Chilean sea bass, cod, red snapper, or any firm-fleshed, nonoily fish makes a perfect substitute.

Deep-frying is also an excellent method for cooking whole fish, as it guarantees moist and delicate meat. To ensure a crispy crust, Chilean cooks often fry the fish twice. Accompany this Chilean dish with Ensalada a la Chilena (p. 72) a tomato and onion salad, some mixed greens, and a generous serving of mashed potatoes or Arroz Graneado (p. 214).

> **4 (about 1-inch-thick) pieces boneless, skinless monkfish, cod, or
>   other white fish or 4 (about 1½ pound) whole red snappers,
>   ready to cook**
> **Salt and freshly ground black pepper, to taste**
> **2 cups all-purpose flour**
> **4 cups (approximately) vegetable oil**
> **½ teaspoon dried oregano (optional)**
> **Lemon wedges**

Rinse the fish and pat dry with paper towels. Season with salt and black pepper on both sides. Place the flour in a shallow bowl and mix in the oregano. Dredge the fish in the flour and shake off the excess.

Heat the oil in a large sauté pan or wok to 350F(175C), or until a bread cube turns brown in 65 seconds. Add the fish, in batches, and fry until light brown on both sides, 2 to 3 minutes a side. Keep the oil hot.

Drain the fish on paper towels, and dredge once more in the flour, shaking off the excess. Fry the fish, in batches, a second time until crispy and golden brown on both sides, 2 to 3 minutes a side. Drain on paper towels and serve at once. Garnish with lemon wedges.

Baked Sea Bass, Creole Style

Corvina a la Criolla

Makes 4 servings

*B*aking whole fish or fish fillets on a bed of aromatic vegetables is one of the easiest and most attractive ways of preparing fish. No wonder it is a favorite dish throughout the Caribbean and Central and South America.

The Chilean sea bass has become a popular item on many restaurant menus throughout the United States. And its sweet, delicate meat makes it a perfect match for many styles of preparation.

1 (about 4-pound) or 2 (2- to 2½-lb.) whole sea bass or
red snapper, ready to cook
Salt and freshly ground black pepper, to taste
¼ cup freshly squeezed lemon juice
3 tablespoons vegetable oil
1 onion, halved and thinly sliced
½ green bell pepper, thinly sliced
2 tomatoes, sliced
1 teaspoon dried oregano
2 tablespoons finely minced cilantro

Preheat the oven to 350F(175C).

Rinse the fish and pat dry with paper towels. Season with salt and black pepper inside and out, and drizzle the lemon juice evenly over the fish.

Heat the oil in a medium skillet over medium heat. Add the onion and sauté until softened but not brown, 4 minutes.

Arrange the onion, bell pepper and tomatoes on the bottom of a large ovenproof platter. Season with salt and black pepper. Place the fish on top of the vegetables, and sprinkle with the oregano and cilantro. Bake 20 to 35 minutes, depending on the thickness of the fish, or until it feels firm to the touch and almost flakes.

Grilled Sea Bass with Cheese, Oregano, and Chorizo

Cancato de Corvina

Makes 4 servings

I actually discovered this dish by following my nose! Irresistibly intrigued by aromas reminiscent of pizza and grilled fish, we entered a tiny restaurant. We were greeted with *"Pasa no mas, la cocina esta abierta"* ("Come right in, the kitchen is open"), which led us to believe we were in the right place. And there it was, a huge fish grilled over smothering charcoal with all my favorite pizza toppings: cheese, spicy sausage, and tomatoes seasoned with garlic and oregano. An odd combination that, surprisingly, tasted great.

The origin of the name cancato—from the Indian word *canca,* meaning "grilled" or *cancay,* meaning "grilling or toasting"—makes me believe that it's a dish with history. Cancato is a specialty of southern Chile. It's usually prepared with a big fish; but I've found it more practical to use smaller fish, because they don't fall apart and are easier to serve. Sometimes the fish is folded in half to enclose the filling, but traditionally, it's grilled open-faced. Both versions are delicious and recommended for your next cookout. Serve it with a variety of Chilean salads.

> 4 (1-pound) whole small sea bass or red snappers
> Salt and freshly ground black pepper, to taste
> 4 ounces Spanish chorizo, thinly sliced
> 3 tomatoes, peeled and sliced
> 1/2 pound Gouda cheese, thinly sliced
> 3 cloves garlic, finely minced
> 1 tablespoon dried oregano
> 4 tablespoons butter, melted
> Small bunch parsley
> 1/2 cup white wine

Prepare the coals for grilling.

Cut each fish along the sides, detaching the bones from the flesh, leaving the sides attached at the back. Carefully open the fish like a book. Discard the bones.

Place the fish on a fine meshed grill, skin side down. Season with salt and black pepper. Arrange the chorizo, tomatoes, and cheese evenly over each fish. Sprinkle with the garlic and oregano. Drizzle with the melted butter.

Grill the fish until the cheese starts to melt, 10 to 15 minutes. Brush the fish a few times with the parsley sprigs dipped in white wine to give the dish a special touch. Serve at once.

El Curanto: The Chilean Clambake

Chile has its own version of the traditional New England clambake. It is an ancient specialty of the indigenous tribes living along the rich coastlines in the south of the country. It's in fact a truly archaic way of cooking, often attributed to the Polynesians. Yet cooking meat and/or seafood over hot stones piled in a large pit has been done in many parts of the world, probably since the beginnings of time.

A variation found in the Chilean desert in the north, known as *huatía,* consists of mostly meats and vegetables, much like the Peruvian *pachamanca;* whereas the inhabitants of the eastern islands prefer the richness of the ocean.

In the fascinating aquatic world of the islands of Chiloé, the curanto is prepared as a communal celebration of the Chilotes' ancient traditions. Traditions that have been faithfully preserved, largely because of this region's geographic isolation. The best time to visit Chiloé is in February during *la semana costumbrista,* a weeklong celebration of the islands' rich folklore.

As part of this celebration, a large pit—about 5 feet across and 2 feet deep—is dug and is partly filled with stones. A wood fire is kept going for a few hours to heat the stones thoroughly. The ashes are brushed aside, and the hot stones are covered with *nalca* (large seaweed leaves), or the more convenient aluminum foil. And cases of food are delivered to the site: A curanto is made for nothing less then a crowd!

The stones are covered with ears of corn, tons of clams, all kinds of seafood and fish, the indispensable potatoes, seasonal vegetables, chicken legs, spicy pork sausages, and pork chops. All kept separate by layers of seaweed or cabbage leaves. This gargantuan heap of food is then covered with layers of leaves and damp burlap to trap the steam. The food is left to cook for about one hour.

Traditionally, dense breads made with mashed potatoes and flour (*chapaleles*), sometimes with pork cracklings added (*milcaos*), are steamed as well. The curanto is part of an experience rich in folklore, an almost mystical celebration. But I do not think that it can be considered a gastronomical delight!

Clambake in a Pot

Curanto en Olla

Makes 8 to 10 servings

A simple home version of the traditional clambake has been invented over the years. The *pulmay* (clambake in a pot) is a rich concoction that certainly offers several possibilities to please a demanding palate. When prepared with a wide variety of seafood, a few chorizos for flavor, vegetables such as fennel or cabbage, and a generous amount of a crisp white wine, the dish becomes a true delicacy. Small lobsters, shrimp, and squid can also be added.

½ cup vegetable oil
1 onion, coarsely chopped
1 red bell pepper, cut into big pieces
4 chicken legs, halved
1 pound pork butt, cut into 1-inch pieces
4 ounces chorizo sausage, thickly sliced
1 tablespoon hot red pepper flakes
10 small potatoes
3 cups chicken broth
2 fennel bulbs with some green attached, sliced, or cabbage leaves
3 pounds mussels
3 pounds clams
5 pieces of sea bass, red snapper, cod, or other firm-fleshed fish
1 (750-milliliter) bottle Chilean sauvignon blanc
Crusty bread
Pebre Chileno (p. 65)

Heat the oil in a stock pot over medium-high heat. Add the onion and bell pepper, and sauté for a few minutes. Add the chicken and pork, and sauté until light brown.

Stir in the sausage, red pepper flakes, potatoes, and broth. Cover with a layer of fennel. Arrange the seafood on top in several layers, ending with the sea bass. Pour the wine over all, and cover with the remaining fennel. Place a heavy plate on top to keep all the ingredients in the broth. Cover, and cook over medium heat, until the potatoes are soft, 30 to 45 minutes.

Serve the seafood, meat, and vegetables in deep plates, swimming in the flavorful broth. Pass crusty bread and Chilean Pebre at the table.

Poached Trout with Green Herb Salsa

Truchas en Salsa Verde

Makes 4 servings

The south is home to a great variety of rivers, streams, and lakes, all cold, clean, and fast flowing. It's the favorite hiding place for *trucha*. The trout caught in these waters is plump, sweet, and quite delicious. In this recipe, the trout (rainbow or salmon trout or the tail end of a salmon) is poached in a delicately seasoned water and served lukewarm or cold, accompanied by a boldly flavored green salsa.

½ **onion, sliced**
1 **leek, trimmed and sliced**
1 **carrot, peeled and sliced**
1 **small bunch fresh parsley**
1 **tablespoon whole black peppercorns**
Salt, to taste
4 **(about 1 pound) rainbow or salmon trout, ready to cook, or**
     1 **(3- to 4-lb.) piece of salmon, tail end if possible**
Cucumber slices
Lemon slices
Lettuce leaves
2 **cups Salsa Verde (p. 64)**

Place the onion, leek, carrot, parsley, and peppercorns in a saucepan large enough to hold the fish. Add water to cover the vegetables by 2 inches. Season generously with salt. Bring to a boil, reduce the heat, and simmer 15 minutes. Add the fish, and simmer over low heat until the fish just begins to flake. For every 1 inch of thickness, measured at the thickest point, allow 10 minutes of cooking time.

Carefully transfer the cooked fish to a rack and let cool to lukewarm. Peel off the skin, and arrange the fish on a decorative platter. Garnish with the cucumber, lemon slices, and lettuce. Serve the Salsa Verde on the side.

Vegetables

Moving to Chile was a big step, but starting a new life in the deep Chilean countryside turned out to be an unforgettable and unique experience.

The imposing Andean heights rise up immediately behind the house. We're miles away from civilization and surrounded by endless orchards. This is the country of the proud countryman and his *señora*, who takes care of the entire household, her children, a menagerie of animals, and the indispensable vegetable garden.

In Chile, the central part of the country is blessed with a sunny climate, mild winters, and plenty of life-giving water. The slowly melting snow cascades down from the mountains and is ingeniously channeled to irrigate the land. In contrast, the north is covered by one of the driest deserts of the world, the Atacama.

I immediately felt a strong attraction to this country, the pristine natural beauty, the unspoiled products offered by a generous land, and the unpretentious, wonderful foods prepared with them.

The recipes I gathered from the country folk shine because of their simplicity and honesty. Best of all, these foods will make you feel good. Like all people living in close contact with nature, rural Chileans have a diet that seems to follow the guidelines suggested by the modern medical community.

Out of pure necessity—as there isn't a shop around for miles—and out of a romantic urge to get closer to nature, we adapted our life and eating habits to those of our new homeland. A sailor and boat person at one time, a city dweller at other times, I had only vague notions of how to make a living on the land. Nevertheless, I nurtured ambitious plans for my vegetable garden, wanting a little bit of almost everything. We purchased a few hens and a rooster.

The first month we attacked the garden with the zeal of young lovers. I adored the perfect eggs I found every morning and was delighted by the tender seedlings that finally appeared.

The second and third months, I feared I would lose the battle against the crawling weeds. The garden still looked like a wilderness. I spent my time chasing the chickens out of the vegetable patches and keeping my dog from running after the chickens. (Although the day they picked my first ripe strawberries, they almost ended up in the cooking pot!) But nature prevailed and finally everything settled. We savored the fruits (and vegetables) of our hard labor with respect and gratitude. I'll never look at a tomato or a tender bunch of lettuce with the same eyes again. I am sure that every gardener knows what I mean.

Fortunately, I wasn't alone in my venture; my assistant, Maria Angelica, soon turned out to be a bottomless source of wisdom (and my salvation). She can't read or write, but she recognizes the song of every bird and no plant or herb has secrets for her. She knows how to cure my baby's upset stomach and the dog's sore throat. She digs, plants, and soothes. She actually loves the taste of the earth so much that she sometimes eats a piece of it. One day, she made me plant a row of tall sunflowers bordering our field of watermelons. "You have to be aware of the evil eye," she told me. "One malevolent look and the whole field will dry out. But now, if someone walks by, his eye will be caught by the proud sunflowers without even noticing your melons!" I never questioned her words. The truth is that the whole summer long, we enjoyed huge sweet watermelons and gorgeous flower arrangements on the table.

Cheesy Zucchini Gratin with Tomatoes

Budín de Zapallos con Tomate

Makes 4 appetizer servings or 6 side dish servings

I have never seen a plant as generous and forgiving as the zucchini. Even badly cared for or grown in poor weather conditions, the beautiful yellow flowers greet you every morning. The whole summer long, you can pick the green vegetables. They grow so profusely, you hardly know what to do with them!

In Chile, we have a whole repertoire of zucchini dishes; we stuff the larger ones with rice, meat, or cheese; and we make soups, stews (*guisos*), and salads with the young ones. I particularly like them in this casserole—a custard-like, cheesy gratin that can be prepared with many vegetables, such as spinach, eggplant, cauliflower, green beans, and Swiss chard. This tasty, satisfying dish can easily be served as a course by itself, as the Chileans do, but it also makes a great accompaniment to any roasted or grilled meat or poultry.

3 tablespoons vegetable oil or butter

1½ cups finely chopped onions

2 cloves garlic, finely minced

3 large zucchini, cut into ¼-inch dice (about 8 cups) or 8 cups
   green beans or other vegetable

Salt and freshly ground black pepper, to taste

2 cups diced day-old white bread, crusts removed

1 cup milk, warmed

½ cup grated Gouda or Swiss cheese

2 eggs, lightly beaten

Pinch of freshly grated nutmeg

1 large tomato, peeled and sliced

¼ cup freshly grated Parmesan cheese

Preheat the oven to 375F (190C). Butter a medium baking dish. Heat the oil in a medium saucepan over medium heat. Add the onions, and sauté until softened but not brown, 5 minutes. Add the garlic and zucchini, and cook, covered, until the vegetables are soft, 15 to 20 minutes. Season with salt and black pepper.

Meanwhile, soak the bread in the warm milk.

When the vegetables are soft, add the soaked bread and Gouda cheese; cook, stirring constantly, 5 minutes more. Remove from the heat, stir in the eggs and nutmeg, and combine well. The mixture should be thick and moist.

Spoon the vegetable mixture into the prepared baking dish; arrange the tomato slices on top, and sprinkle with the Parmesan cheese. (The recipe can be prepared ahead of time up to this point. Refrigerate for several hours or overnight, and bake just before serving.)

Bake the casserole 20 to 25 minutes, or until the cheese is melted and brown. Serve at once.

Spicy Potato and Tomato Casserole

Picante de Papas

Makes 4 servings

In the northern provinces, people like their food *picante*, as do their Peruvian neighbors. In this popular recipe, the Andean staples potatoes and tomatoes are turned into a delicious casserole that's enlivened by the fragrant fire of fresh chiles. It's important to know the power of the chiles you're using. You can make this dish as *picante* as you desire by increasing the number of chiles. Serve as an accompaniment to roast meats or poultry.

> 3 tablespoons vegetable oil
> 1 medium onion, thinly sliced
> 1 clove garlic, minced
> Salt, to taste
> 5 medium potatoes, cooked, pared, and sliced (about
>   1½ pounds)
> 4 tomatoes, peeled and sliced
> 2 serrano or jalapeño chiles, seeded and finely minced,
>   or to taste
> 2 tablespoons freshly grated Parmesan cheese
> ¼ cup grated Gouda cheese
> 1 cup half-and-half or whole milk

Preheat the oven to 400F(205C). Oil a medium earthenware or glass baking dish.

In a small skillet, heat 2 tablespoons of the oil over medium heat. Add the onion, and sauté, stirring occasionally, until softened but not brown, 5 minutes. Add the garlic, and cook 1 minute more. Season with salt.

Scatter half of the sautéed onion on the bottom of the prepared dish. Cover with half of the potatoes and half of the tomatoes; salt lightly. Sprinkle half of the chiles and half of the cheeses on top. Repeat the layers, ending with the cheeses. Pour the half-and-half evenly over the vegetables. Bake 35 to 40 minutes, or until the half-and-half has been absorbed and the cheese is brown. Serve at once.

Corn, the Grain of the Americas

Long before Columbus and his crew set foot on the shores of Central and South America, corn was already being cultivated, dried, ground, and used in refined and elaborate dishes.

In Central America it is called elote (from the Nahuatl word *elotl*). The British call it maize (from the West Indian Tahina word *mahis*). In Chile we know corn as choclo (from the Quechua word *chocello*). This truly indigenous American grain was and still is an important sustenance crop for humans and animals.

Corn is plentiful in Chile and is often planted in backyards for the family's consumption. Fresh, the kernels are paired with the other indigenous staples: tomatoes, pumpkins, beans, and chiles. When the mostly meatless New World expanded its diet with cattle, pigs, and poultry, other favorites were born including hearty stews and the national specialty of Pastel de Choclo, an oniony meat and olive mixture topped with a sweet corn purée (p. 130). And this is only the beginning of a long list of recipes that feature the magic grain in all its aspects, from dried and ground to toasted, grilled, and fermented kernels. Corn is part of a long and passionate love affair that the world outside the Americas doesn't seem to understand.

Seasoned Fresh Corn Steamed in Corn Husks

Humitas

Makes 4 or 5 servings

Chilean's passion for corn comes out in myriad tasty dishes. My favorites are these delicately flavored little corn packages steamed in the husks. They strongly resemble Mexican tamales made with *masa harina*, which is made from dried corn. I prefer the Chilean version, based on fresh corn, because it is creamier, moister, and lighter than tamales.

For more than nine thousand years, native Indians have been repeating the same action, enclosing the seasoned corn into neat little bundles made from the husks. Through the ages, tasty humitas have become a true national summer favorite.

The assembly might be a little tricky at first but practice soon makes perfect. Serve with Ensalada a la Chilena (p. 72) as the Chileans do.

> **14 to 16 large fresh ears of corn in the husks**
> **10 large fresh basil leaves**
> **½ serrano or jalapeño chile, seeded and finely chopped**
> **3 tablespoons lard or butter**
> **2¼ cups finely chopped onions**
> **¼ green bell pepper, minced**
> **1 teaspoon sweet paprika**
> **1½ tablespoons salt, or to taste**

Carefully peel the husks off the corn without tearing them. Set aside the softer, pliable inner leaves. Using a sharp knife, cut the kernels from each cob, not too close to the cob. With the back of the knife, scrape off any remaining pulp and milk. You should have about 9 cups.

Purée the corn, basil, and chile, in batches, in a blender or food processor until smooth.

Heat the lard in a heavy saucepan over low heat. Add the onions, bell pepper, paprika, and salt, and cook over low heat until soft, 10 minutes. Combine the corn purée with the onion mixture; cook, stirring occasionally, for 10 to 15 minutes more. The mixture should be moist but not runny. Taste for seasoning.

To assemble the humitas, place 2 soft, inner leaves side by side, one overlapping the other by about ½ inch. Place 3 to 4 tablespoons of the corn mixture in the center (remember that the corn mixture will expand during cooking). Fold the bottom edge of the husks over the filling, fold in the sides, and finally fold the top edge to make a tight package. Tie with a strip of corn husk. Repeat until all the filling is used up.

Bring a big pot of salted water to a boil. Carefully place all the humitas flat in the water; they should be completely covered. Simmer over low heat, 40 minutes. Let cool a few minutes, and serve.

Leftover humitas reheat well in a 375F(190C) oven; heat about 20 minutes. Chileans sometimes reheat them in the hot ashes of a wood stove or barbecue, which imparts a delicious smoky flavor to the tasty packages.

Bean and Corn Stew with Basil and Paprika Oil

Porotos Granados con Masa Morra

Makes 6 servings

F ew countries sell fresh, mature shelling beans; the bulk of the harvest is usually dried and stored for winter. In Chile, this situation is slightly different. In early summer woven baskets filled with fresh ivory, white, or red-speckled beans still in their pods appear in the farmers markets, and they are awaited with great pleasure. In the United States, with a little luck, you might find tender green lima beans, young fava beans, and the French flageolets. Fresh shelling beans are lighter in texture than the dried ones, and they make delicious stews, soups, and salads.

This Chilean bean casserole is truly a wonderful dish, making great use of all the indigenous ingredients: beans, corn, pumpkin, and herbs. This chunky, nutritious casserole is often served topped with *color chilena* (hot lard or oil flavored with sweet paprika and garlic) for extra color and zest. The dish makes a tasty meal all by itself, but meat lovers will appreciate some spicy grilled sausages or lamb chops. Accompany the casserole and grilled sausages with a Chilean salad, end your meal with a slice of summer-sweet watermelon, and you'll experience a Sunday feast in the way we celebrate it in the Chilean countryside.

> 2½ to 3 pounds fresh shelling beans, such as kidney, pinto, or black-eyed peas, in pods (about 3 cups shelled)
> ¾ pound pumpkin, cut into ½-inch cubes
> 1 chicken bouillon cube, crumbled
> 1 tablespoon vegetable oil
> 4 slices smoked bacon, finely diced, or 2 ounces spicy chorizo, crumbled

1½ cups finely chopped onions
½ red or green bell pepper, diced
1 carrot, coarsely grated
Salt and freshly ground black pepper, to taste
2 cups fresh or frozen corn kernels
10 large fresh basil leaves
2 tablespoons minced fresh basil
Paprika Oil (p. 235)

Shell the beans, rinse under cold running water, and drain.

Place the beans in a Dutch oven, and cover with 1½ inches hot water. Add the pumpkin and bouillon cube, and bring to a boil over high heat. Reduce the heat to low, cover, and simmer until the beans are tender, 1 hour. (Cooking times vary according to size and type of beans used.) The pumpkin will dissolve somewhat and thicken the mixture.

Meanwhile, heat the oil in a small skillet over medium heat. Add the bacon and sauté 2 minutes. Add the onions, bell pepper, and carrot. Cook, stirring frequently, 5 minutes. Season with salt and black pepper to taste. Add the onion mixture to the beans, and simmer 15 minutes.

To prepare the corn mixture, reserve ½ cup of the whole corn kernels. Purée the remaining corn with the whole basil leaves in a blender. If the mixture is very dry, add a ladle of the bean cooking liquid. Season the purée with salt. Add the purée to the bean mixture and simmer, stirring frequently, 15 minutes more. The corn purée will thicken the stew; add more water if necessary. The bean mixture should be moist without being soupy. Taste, and adjust the seasoning. (The recipe can be prepared in advance up to this point; refrigerated. Reheat in individual earthenware bowls in a 375F (190C) oven for about 20 minutes, or until piping hot.)

To serve Chilean style, serve the stew in earthenware bowls; top each bowl with 1 tablespoon Paprika Oil and some minced basil. Serve at once.

Pilar's Baby Lima Bean Casserole

Porotos Granados de la Señora Pilar

Makes 4 servings

I came across many tasty variations of this wonderful fresh bean dish, and just when I had made up my mind which one to put in this book, my friend Pilar told me, "You haven't tried my recipe yet, *unos porotos a chuparse los dedos* ["some beans to lick your fingers"]. I don't use bacon or onions, the dish is softer, more delicate, and just as delicious." She was right.

You can use any fresh shelling beans, but the tender lima beans that come to market in the United States in late spring make this dish a real treat, especially when served with Pierna de Cordero Mechada (roasted leg of lamb, page 144), Chilean style.

> **2 pounds fresh baby lima beans in the pod (about 3 cups shelled)**
> **3 tablespoons lard or vegetable oil**
> **1 large ripe tomato, peeled, seeded, and coarsely chopped**
> **3 large fresh basil leaves, chopped**
> **About 4 cups of chicken broth**
> **½ pound pumpkin, cut into ¼-inch cubes**
> **Salt, to taste**
> **1½ cups fresh or frozen corn kernels**
> **½ red bell pepper, seeded and very finely diced**
> **1 tablespoon finely minced fresh basil**

Shell the lima beans, rinse, and drain.

Heat 1 tablespoon of the lard in a Dutch oven over medium heat. Add the tomato and chopped basil; cook 3 minutes. Add the beans and add enough chicken broth to cover by 1 inch. Bring to a boil, reduce the heat to low, and simmer covered, 20 minutes. Add the pumpkin; simmer until the beans are very tender but still holding their shape, 20 to 30 minutes. (Cooking times will vary according to age and size of beans.) Season generously with salt.

Meanwhile, purée the corn with a generous cup of the bean cooking liquid in a blender or food processor. Press the purée through a sieve; only the milky part will be used. Discard the solids.

Stir the corn milk into the beans, and cook, stirring with a wooden spoon, until thickened, 3 to 4 minutes. Taste, and adjust the seasoning.

Heat the remaining 2 tablespoons of lard in a small pan over medium heat. Add the bell pepper, and sauté until tender, about 3 minutes. Season with salt.

Ladle the lima beans into individual earthenware bowls, and top with the bell pepper oil and a sprinkle of minced basil.

Baked Stuffed Tomatoes with Rice and Herbs

Tomates Rellenos de la Señora Chita Ponce

Makes 6 servings

Chile's Central Valley is blessed with endless warm, dry summers, much like the French Provence. Juicy vine-ripened tomatoes are abundant, and many of us can just step outside in the backyard and pick a few to slice for supper. A luxury indeed.

The following original recipe was given to me by an excellent and enthusiastic cook, Señora Chita Ponce. Her tomatoes are stuffed with an herbed rice mixture and baked. They make a fine and elegant accompaniment to any roasted meat, poultry, or even fish.

> 6 firm, ripe beefsteak tomatoes
> 4 tablespoons butter or 2 tablespoons olive oil and 2 tablespoons
>   butter
> ½ cup finely chopped onion
> 2 large cloves garlic, finely minced
> 2½ cups cooked long-grain rice (1 cup raw)
> 5 tablespoons finely minced fresh parsley
> 5 large basil leaves, finely minced
> ½ teaspoon minced fresh oregano or ¼ teaspoon dried
> Salt and freshly ground black pepper, to taste
> ¾ cup water
> 2 basil leaves
> ½ cup freshly grated Parmesan cheese

Preheat the oven to 350F (175C). Generously butter a glass or enameled baking dish just large enough to hold the tomatoes snugly.

Cut a thin slice off the stem end of each tomato, and reserve. Holding each tomato upside down in the palm of your hand, discard as much of the seeds as possible with your finger. Using a small spoon, scoop out the pulp. Coarsely chop the pulp and reserved tomato tops; set aside. Sprinkle the scooped-out tomatoes with salt and place upside down on a plate to drain.

Heat 2 tablespoons of the butter in a saucepan over medium heat. Add the onion, and sauté about 3 minutes. Add the garlic, and cook until translucent but not brown, 1 minute more. Add 1 cup of the tomato pulp, the rice, and minced herbs. Simmer, stirring, until the rice absorbs most of the juices, 4 to 5 minutes. Season generously with salt and black pepper.

Mix the remaining tomato pulp with the water; add the basil leaves, salt, and black pepper. Purée in a blender until smooth.

Fill the tomatoes with the herbed rice, sprinkle with cheese, and place in prepared pan. Pour puréed sauce around the tomatoes, and dot with the remaining 2 tablespoons butter. Bake 20 to 25 minutes, or until the cheese is nicely browned.

Chilean Rice

Arroz Graneado

Makes 4 servings

Ever since the Spanish settlers introduced rice, Chile has produced this versatile grain in the northern provinces. It soon became a staple in the people's diet.

Chileans like their rice *graneado,* meaning the rice grains are fluffy, separated; and delicately flavored with onion, bell pepper, or carrot. To prevent the grains from clinging together, the rice is rinsed under cold running water before cooking. I try to stay away from converted rice, which has been soaked and pressure steamed; the procedure reduces the surface starch but eliminates most of the flavor as well.

> 1½ cups long-grain rice
> 2 tablespoons lard or vegetable oil
> 3 tablespoons very finely chopped onion or scallions
> 1½ tablespoons very finely diced red bell pepper
> 1½ tablespoons finely diced or grated carrot
> 2¼ cups hot water
> 1½ teaspoons salt, or to taste
> 1 tablespoon finely minced fresh parsley or cilantro
>   (optional)

Rinse the rice thoroughly under cold running water and drain.

Heat the lard in a heavy saucepan over medium heat. Add the onion, bell pepper, and carrot; sauté, stirring, 2 minutes. Add the rice, and cook until the rice has absorbed the flavorful oil, 1 minute. Pour in the hot water, and add the salt and parsley.

Bring to a boil, reduce the heat to low, cover, and simmer 15 to 20 minutes. Do not stir, and cook the rice as slowly as possible. Use a heat diffuser, if you have one. The rice is done when the water has been completely absorbed and the rice is tender. Fluff the rice with a fork and serve at once.

Potatoes and Pumpkin with Polenta

Papas con Chuchoca o Polenta

Makes 4 servings

In the late twentieth century, the humble potato has moved to center stage in the trendy North American culinary scene; whereas in southern Chile, it never left its privileged position to begin with. The Chilotes, the inhabitants of Chiloé, an intriguing aquatic world of islands and canals, love their potatoes. A day without some kind of potato, whether in a stew, simply boiled, mashed, or kneaded into a dense bread, is simply unthinkable!

This recipe combines creamy potatoes, sweet pumpkin, and polenta in a surprising and tasty side dish that's perfect served with a luxurious roast or grilled chicken.

> 2 tablespoons vegetable oil
> 1 cup finely chopped onion
> 1 clove garlic, finely minced
> 1/2 teaspoon sweet paprika
> 1 1/2 pounds medium potatoes, peeled and cut into 1/4-inch cubes
>   (4 or 5)
> 1/2 pound pumpkin, peeled and cut into 1/4-inch cubes
> 2 cups chicken broth
> Salt and freshly ground black pepper, to taste
> 1/2 cup instant polenta or chuchoca (see "Chuchoca or Polenta?"
>   p. 123)
> 1/2 cup hot water
> 1 tablespoon finely minced fresh parsley or cilantro

Heat the oil in a medium Dutch oven over medium heat. Add the onion, and sauté 2 minutes. Add the garlic and paprika, and cook, stirring frequently, or until the onion is softened but not brown, 2 minutes more.

Add the potatoes, pumpkin, chicken broth, salt, and black pepper. Bring to a boil, reduce the heat to low, and simmer covered until the potatoes are soft and most of the liquid has evaporated, 25 to 30 minutes.

Dissolve the polenta in the water, and add to the potatoes. Simmer, stirring occasionally, until slightly thickened, 10 minutes. Taste and adjust the seasonings. Serve at once, sprinkled with the parsley.

Hot Mashed Potatoes

Puré Picante

Makes 4 servings

In pre-Hispanic times, the potato (*Solanum tuberosum*) grew in various valleys along the Pacific coast, from Peru and Colombia to the canals and islands of Chiloé in the south. The story goes that a frail Spaniard, Jerónimo Cardán, carried the tuber from Chiloé back to his homeland and to Italy in the sixteenth century, 200 years before Frenchman Antoine Augustin Parmentier finally popularized the nutritious and versatile spud on a big scale.

Although potato recipes are abundant, creamy mashed potatoes seem to be an all-time, universal favorite. Chilean cooks like to whip a zesty hot chile sauce into the potatoes to make them even better. These are great with grilled sausages or pork chops. The quality of your hot sauce is, of course, of the utmost importance; if you'd like to make your own, try Salsa de Ají Colorado a la Chilena (p. 66).

> 2½ pounds baking potatoes, peeled and cut into pieces
> ⅓ cup milk, warmed
> 3 tablespoons mild vegetable oil
> 2 tablespoons butter
> Salt, to taste
> 2½ tablespoons Salsa de Ají Colorado a la Chilena or ground chile
>   paste, such as the sambal oelek or harissa sauce

Place the potatoes in a large saucepan, cover with salted cold water, and bring to a boil over high heat. Reduce the heat to medium, and cook until tender, 15 to 20 minutes. Drain.

Press the potatoes through a food mill or crush with a potato masher. Return potatoes to the pan; add the warm milk, oil, butter, salt, and salsa de ají, and mix to combine. Serve at once.

Legumes

Maybe the happiest culinary discovery I've made during my stay in Chile is the many heartwarming, full-flavored dishes based on legumes.

I've always been attracted to the corner of the market where huge bins and sacks are stacked, exposing the most wonderful collection of legumes in all shapes and deep earthy tones. As a child I played with the little organic pearls; later on, I stored them in glass jars, neatly displayed on my kitchen shelves for the pure pleasure of the eye.

In Chile, I finally learned how to cook and appreciate legumes. In Central and South America, rice and beans are practically a trademark dish. What would Mexico be without the refried beans, the Caribbean without its rice and pigeon peas, Nicaragua without some kind of *gallo pinto* (red beans and rice), Cuba devoid of its *frijoles negros* (black beans)? Many of these ethnic dishes have been incorporated in the ever-evolving American cuisine. Once a humble peasant staple, legumes have been adopted by many top chefs all over the United States, and their popularity has skyrocketed ever since. And for a good reason: Legumes have everything to seduce a health-conscious consumer. They are rich in vegetable protein; have no cholesterol and little fat; and are rich in complex carbohydrates, minerals, vitamins, and fiber.

But there's more to a bean than the sole promise that it is good for you! I can guarantee you that a perfectly cooked bowl of beans, fully flavored, mashed thick with just the right scattering of little vegetables to make the texture interesting, can appeal to the most critical food lover.

In Chile, I've found a wealth of inspiring recipes that intrigued the gourmet in me and seduced the gourmand. Here, it goes far beyond the typical side dish of rice and beans, rice and chickpeas, and rice and lentils. In Chile, the legume is found in luxurious soups, stick-to-the-ribs stews, soulful vegetable guisos, satisfying salads, and even sweet purées. Seldom have I visited a country where cooks prepare their beloved legumes with so much caring and dedication.

Since pre-Colombian times, the Mapuche Indians understood that beans have a natural affinity with corn, pumpkin, and even the leafy Swiss chard. Often, legumes are enriched with a flavorful sofrito—a fried onion, bell pepper, and carrot mixture spiced with the traditional trio of cumin, sweet paprika, and oregano. Or the legumes may be cooked with an extra piece of salt pork or spicy sausage (a tribute to the Spanish settlers), which elevates the dish to a real culinary experience. Some recipes play with cream, milk, and cheese (ingredients dear to the French cuisine) and are finished in the oven to obtain a heavenly cheesy crust.

But let's not overlook what is most important: the art of cooking the perfect beans, chickpeas, or lentils so that they're creamy and soft, without being mushy, and hold on to their shape.

Cooking Legumes

- Legumes cannot be hurried. An overnight soaking is essential for beans and dried peas to completely rehydrate them. This step will also considerably reduce their cooking time. (Lentils don't need to be soaked, although a few hours' soaking won't hurt them.) Soak the legumes in a big bowl (they swell considerably) covered by 2 inches of cold water and place in a cool spot or even in the refrigerator (to prevent fermentation). In Chile, cooks change and discard the soaking liquid, to eliminate possible toxic preservatives and some of the oligosaccharides, which can make beans hard to digest. Unfortunately, the quick-soaking method—often found on packages of beans—works well for only very fresh dried beans. So play it safe, and soak them overnight.

- Choose legumes from the most recent harvest, if possible. Their freshness influences not only their quality but also their cooking time. The fresher the bean, the quicker the cooking.

Cooking Legumes (*cont.*)

- Cook legumes in plenty of fresh cool water and simmer as slowly and patiently as possible, so that each one is tender and creamy without falling apart. For the same reason, do not stir during cooking, but simply give the pot a good shake. A slow cooker is ideal for cooking beans. Leave them on low heat for twelve hours or overnight, making sure there is enough liquid in the pot so the beans won't scorch. A pressure cooker can help reduce the cooking time, but once the flavoring ingredients are added, the beans need a slow simmer in an uncovered pan, so the juices can evaporate, concentrating all the flavors into a thick, creamy mixture.

- Add salt at the end of the cooking to prevent the skins from becoming tough. (For lentils and chickpeas, however, you can safely add salt at the start.) Chilean cooks often soak and cook their legumes in rainwater to prevent tough beans. Indeed, it has been shown that water with a high calcium content slows down the cooking process. As a result, the beans need a much longer cooking time and may begin to fall apart without ever becoming tender. When rainwater isn't available, use bottled water that is low in calcium.

- Acidic ingredients, such as tomatoes and vinegar, should be added only at the end of the cooking time for all types of legumes. Acid will double the cooking time.

- Keep your pretty jars filled with legumes on the windowsill as kitchen ornaments, but buy fresh ones for cooking. Legumes should be stored in airtight containers in a cool and dark place. In Chile, housewives stick a few dried hot chiles or a whole bulb of garlic in the bean jar. They say this keeps the bugs away.

- Cooked legumes improve in flavor and texture if refrigerated overnight. They tend to absorb liquid during storage, so a little extra water or milk will be needed when you reheat them.

Lentils and Rice with Sofrito and Spicy Sausage

Lentejas con Arroz y Chorizo

Makes 4 to 6 servings

Paging through old cookbooks from Chilean convents, I came across intriguing and elaborate legume dishes that are often enriched with cream, cheeses, or sausages. I can't help but feel that somehow these still-popular recipes for dishes such as Sister Clara's lentils or the convent's bean dish connect us with the long-forgotten occupants in the missions. The nuns certainly didn't (and neither do we) deny themselves the pleasures of a well-furnished table.

As early as the seventeenth century, various Spanish religious orders followed the conquistadores to Chile, and left their indelible marks not only in spiritual matters but also in the very worldly culinary area.

The hardworking nuns were once famous for the production of sweets and candies, but they also introduced new cooking techniques and savory ingredients.

This country favorite is a perfect example: a soulful, nourishing, and tasty pot of creamy lentils and rice flavored with a pungent mixture of vegetables, spices, and chorizo.

> 1½ **cups lentils**
> 4 **cups water**
> **Salt, to taste**
> 1 **tablespoon lard or vegetable oil**
> 1½-**inch link chorizo or other Spanish-type spicy sausage, diced**
> ½ **cup finely chopped onion**
> ½ **carrot, peeled and coarsely grated**

½ **serrano or jalapeño chile, finely minced**

2 **cloves garlic, finely minced**

1 **teaspoon sweet paprika**

½ **teaspoon ground cumin**

1 **teaspoon dried oregano**

½ **cup long grain rice**

1 **tablespoon finely minced fresh parsley**

2 **hard-cooked eggs (optional), finely chopped**

Pick through the lentils, and remove any small stones or other foreign objects. Rinse the lentils, and place them in a heavy saucepan. Add the water, and bring to a boil. Reduce the heat, and simmer covered until soft but still holding their shape, 15 to 25 minutes. (Cooking times vary according to size and age of the lentils.) Season with salt.

Meanwhile, heat the lard in a small skillet over medium heat. Add the sausage, onion, and carrot, and cook 3 minutes. Add the garlic, chile, paprika, cumin, and oregano; season with salt and cook 1 minute. Stir the onion mixture into the lentils with the rice, and simmer partly covered until the rice is tender and the lentils very soft, 15 to 20 minutes. The dish should be moist but not soupy.

Just before serving, correct the seasonings; the dish should be highly seasoned. Serve in earthenware bowls or deep plates, sprinkled with the parsley and hard-cooked egg.

Choosing Legumes

Legumes come in all shapes, sizes, and colors. Because of their rising popularity, many heirloom varieties are now widely available in the United States. Today's beans are fresh and of good quality.

In Chile, the most commonly used bean is the mendez or the coscoron, a small white bean that resembles the cannellini. Cranberry beans, Great Northern, and white kidney beans are good substitutes. Chilean cooks also use frutilla (strawberry-colored, red-speckled beans), tortola o el burrito (small, gray turtle beans) brown, red, and black- and red-eyed legumes—all beautiful and slightly different in flavor! The only variety that has never won much popularity is the black bean, which is usually exported or given as feed to the animals.

Chilean lentils, like the common green or brown varieties in the United States, are a touch bigger than the exquisite French lentils from Le Puy in Auvergne.

The earthy tasting chickpea (garbanzo bean) is another favorite. In Chile, most chickpeas require long soaking and cooking, a necessary step to remove their tough outer skin. Nowadays, the chickpeas are of a superior quality and come in a peeled version, which cooks to tenderness in less than an hour. Cooking times, however, vary greatly, according to the quality, the place of origin, and the age of the legume.

In the recipes in this book, only dried legumes can be used, certainly not the canned ones. We can't begin with compromising the star ingredient. But don't worry, legumes are easy to prepare; they can be time-consuming, yes, but the actual hands-on working time is really minimal. Legumes take perfectly good care of themselves.

In Chile, wholesome, cold-weather legume dishes are served as a first course, often followed by a main meat course. But all of the recipes make wonderful side dishes (served in smaller portions). I've even found them to be satisfying and filling enough to be served as a meal, perhaps accompanied by a bowl of fresh greens.

The Witch's Bean Cuisine

In the deep rural areas, some women are still cooking their beans in a magical, ageless way. A heavy kettle filled with beans, herbs, and flavorful broths or other concoctions is boiled for no longer than 10 minutes over a wood stove. The bubbling hot kettle is then covered and placed inside a wooden box, which is thoroughly insulated on the inside to prevent the slightest bit of air from reaching the hot kettle. (Today's cook uses thick layers of paper and pieces of old mattresses as insulation.) A few oratories are whispered, and the cook warns all that no one is allowed to even come close to the box, not until twelve hours later. The box is dismantled before the eyes of an enchanted and hungry audience, and a pot of perfectly cooked beans appears. Not surprising it's called *la cocina bruja* ("the witch's cooking"); it's the Chilean housewife's clever version of the modern slow cooker.

La Doña Chita's Creamy Lentils with Bacon

Lentejas de la Doña Chita Ponce

Makes 6 servings

In the pure Chilean culinary tradition, homey and comforting legume dishes are served on their own as a first course and are followed by a more substantial meat course. I've found myself serving this utterly satisfying pot of creamy lentils all by itself, simply accompanied by a bowl of mixed greens for a light midday or evening meal. I can guarantee you that paired with some grilled pork sausages, lamb chops, or even a roasted pheasant, these lentils will steal the show.

If you have a choice, use the small French lentils from Le Puy. Lentils are the most user-friendly of all the legumes; they don't need to be soaked, and the cooking time is relatively short.

> 2½ cups lentils
> 2 chicken bouillon cubes
> 2 tablespoons butter
> 3 ounces smoked bacon, cut into small pieces
> 1 cup minced onion
> 1½ teaspoons dried oregano
> Salt and freshly ground black pepper, to taste
> ¾ to 1 cup milk
> 2 tablespoons finely minced fresh parsley or cilantro
> ¼ cup freshly grated Parmesan cheese
> 1 hard-cooked egg, sliced

Pick through the lentils and remove any small stones or other foreign objects. Rinse the lentils, and place in a heavy saucepan. Add enough water to cover by 1 inch, and bring to a boil over high heat. Crumble the bouillon cubes into the pan, reduce the heat, and simmer covered 10 minutes.

Meanwhile, heat 1 tablespoon of the butter in a small skillet over medium heat. Add the bacon and onion, and sauté over medium heat until the onions are translucent but not brown, 5 minutes. Season with the oregano, salt, and black pepper. Stir the onion mixture into the lentils, cover, and simmer until the lentils feel soft but still hold their shape, 15 to 25 minutes more. (Cooking times vary according to size and age of the lentils.)

Add the ¾ cup of the milk and the remaining 1 tablespoon of butter to the lentils, and simmer, stirring frequently, 7 minutes. Taste for seasonings, and adjust as needed. If the mixture is too dry, add more milk; the mixture should be moist and creamy. (The recipe can be made ahead up to this point. Refrigerate. Add a little more milk or water, if necessary, before reheating.)

Serve the lentils warm in an earthenware bowl or deep plate. Sprinkle with the parsley, Parmesan cheese, and egg.

Well-Matched Pairs

Legumes paired with cereals have been a staple of the human diet for at least seven thousand years all over the world. Suddenly, they've become fashionable again. Now scientists have reiterated what folk wisdom, mostly accumulated through intuition, knew all along.

Legumes are convenient, they dry naturally, and store well. For centuries, they have been praised for their versatility and for being a cheap yet highly nutritious source of protein and fiber. Country people instinctively knew which ingredients to combine with legumes to maximize the nutritional value, long before their diets received the approval of modern science.

When legumes are combined with other specific protein foods, the amino acids complement each other, producing a highly nutritional diet. This is exactly what occurs in traditional dishes, such as legumes with rice, corn, or other grains; with small amounts of sausages or other meats; and with eggs or cheese.

Baked Beans with Pumpkin and Bell Peppers

Porotos con Pimentón al Horno

Makes 4 servings

Chileans are passionate about their beans. Winter or summer, rich or poor, from the country folks to the urban Santiaguinos, everyone has a soft spot for a satisfying bowl of beans.

In the United States, beans and their siblings have been steadily climbing the social ladder. We have seen the humble bean paired with the most luxurious, from lobster and calamari to foie gras, confit of duck, and braised rabbit in whimsical and daring creations. But seldom are these dishes up to the Chilean standard of creamy, properly cooked beans. All too often do the beans reach our plates undercooked and under seasoned. The reason is simple: beans don't tolerate shortcuts or compromises. No canned substitutes, no quick-soaking, or cooking miracles but only a lovingly, slow, and patient cooking process leads to success (however pretty the presentation or lavish the accompaniment).

> 1½ cups dried white beans, Great Northern beans, white kidney beans, cranberry beans, or black-eyed peas
> ½ pound pumpkin, cut into ½-inch cubes
> 2 small red bell peppers, thinly sliced
> Salt and freshly black ground, to taste
> 2½ tablespoons lard or butter
> ½ cup finely chopped onion
> 2 large cloves garlic, finely minced
> 1 teaspoon sweet paprika
> ½ teaspoon dried oregano
> ½ cup freshly grated Parmesan cheese

¼ cup fresh bread crumbs
3 tablespoons whole milk or heavy cream
1 tablespoon butter

Pick through the beans and remove any small stones or other foreign objects. Rinse the beans, and place in a large bowl. Add about 2 quarts cold water and soak overnight in a cool place.

Drain the beans and place in a heavy pot. Add enough water to cover by 1½ inches. Bring to a boil over high heat, reduce the heat, and simmer covered 1 hour. Add the pumpkin and bell peppers; simmer until the beans are soft but still holding their shape, 25 to 40 minutes more. (Cooking times vary according to the size and age of the beans.) Season generously with salt to bring out all the flavors.

Press half of the bean mixture through a food mill or purée in a blender or food processor until smooth. Set aside.

Preheat the oven to 375F (190C).

In a small skillet, melt the lard over low heat. Add the onion, and cook until soft but not brown, 5 to 7 minutes. Add the garlic, paprika, salt, black pepper, and oregano. Stir the onion mixture into the whole beans along with the puréed beans, ¼ cup of the Parmesan cheese, the bread crumbs, and milk. Cook, stirring constantly, 5 minutes; the mixture should be moist and creamy. Taste for seasonings, and adjust as needed.

Pour the beans into a large ovenproof earthenware dish. Dot with the butter, and sprinkle with the remaining ¼ cup Parmesan cheese. Bake 15 to 20 minutes, or until the cheese is nicely brown. Serve at once.

Hearty Bean and Vegetable Stew with Pasta

Porotos con Rienda

Makes 4 or 5 servings

During the chilly winter months, nothing seems to soothe and nourish the hungry Chilean horseman better than a huge plate of tasty beans cooked with long strips of pasta that are affectionately called *rienda,* referring to the reins of his bridle. The rural horsemen definitely favors beans above any lentil or chickpea concoction. And I've observed, more than once, how they, discreetly, mash the beans into the flavorful broth with the backs of their spoons before bringing it to their mouths, their eyes half-closed in pure contentment.

The addition of the complementary source of protein, the pasta, turns this dish into a complete, satisfying meal. A fresh green salad is all it needs. Well, for me at least . . . For the Chilean countryman, this is just the beginning, he'll happily continue with a hearty stew such as a carbonada or a cazuela.

2 cups dried white beans, Great Northern beans, white kidney
     beans, cranberry beans, or black-eyed peas
½ pound pumpkin, cut into ½-inch cubes
1 chicken bouillon cube, crumbled
Salt and freshly ground black pepper, to taste
2 tablespoons lard or vegetable oil
3-inch link chorizo or other spicy Spanish sausage, diced, or 3
     ounces smoked bacon, cut into small pieces
1 cup finely chopped onion
2 cloves garlic, finely minced
½ carrot, peeled and coarsely grated

3 tablespoons diced red bell pepper

1 teaspoon sweet paprika

1 teaspoon dried oregano

4 ounces spaghetti, broken into thirds

Pick through the beans, and remove any small stones or other foreign objects. Rinse the beans, and place in a large bowl. Add about 2 quarts cold water, and soak overnight in a cool place.

Drain the beans, and place in a heavy pot. Add enough water to cover by 2 inches. Bring to a boil over high heat, reduce the heat, and simmer covered 30 minutes. Add the pumpkin and bouillon cube; cook until the beans are tender but still hold their shape, 45 to 60 minutes more. (Cooking times vary according to size and age of the beans.) Salt the dish generously.

Meanwhile, heat the lard in a small skillet over medium heat. Add the sausage, and cook 3 minutes. Add the onion, garlic, carrot, bell pepper, paprika, oregano, and black pepper. Cook, stirring constantly, 5 minutes.

Stir the sausage mixture into the beans, and cook covered 15 minutes. Taste for seasonings, and adjust if needed. The dish should be quite soupy; add more water if it seems too dry.

Add the spaghetti and cook, stirring frequently, until the pasta is just tender to the bite, 10 to 15 minutes. Add more water if necessary; this dish should be moist, almost soupy. Spoon the beans into deep soup plates and serve at once.

Creamy Skinned Beans with Paprika Oil

Porotos Pelados

Makes 4 to 6 servings

This is without a doubt the ultimate bean preparation. Every single bean is patiently dismantled of its peel. The innocent-looking skin, which causes so many disgraceful side effects, has completely discredited the beneficial and gastronomic qualities of beans. Next, the naked bean is cooked to creamy perfection along with an array of vegetables. The dish is served topped with rust-colored paprika oil.

Following ageless native traditions, my assistant, Angelica, cooks the beans in wood ashes (lye) for a few minutes and then washes and rubs them forever until the last bean is hulled, leaving her hands tingling from the cold water but feeling soft as silk. (Remember that wood ashes were once used as soaps and detergents.) Nowadays, the wood ashes are often replaced by a pinch of baking soda. It works fine but Angelica's method is by far superior. I must warn you, either way it's a long and tedious process. And if you are one of those people who needs to juggle time just to get dinner on the table, abstain. This may well bring you to the verge of a nervous breakdown!

> 2 cups dried white beans, Great Northern beans, white kidney
>   beans, cranberry beans, or black-eyed peas
> 1 teaspoon baking soda
> 1 chicken bouillon cube, crumbled
> Salt, to taste
> 3 tablespoons lard or vegetable oil
> ½ cup finely chopped onion
> 3 tablespoons red bell pepper
> ¼ carrot, peeled and very finely diced

¼ carrot, peeled and coarsely grated
1 clove garlic, finely minced
½ cup long-grain rice
Paprika Oil (p. 235)

Pick through the beans, and remove any small stones or other foreign objects. Rinse the beans, and place in a large bowl. Add about 2 quarts of cold water, and soak overnight in a cool place.

Drain the beans, and place in a heavy pot. Add enough water to cover the beans by 1 inch, and bring to a boil over high heat. Add the baking soda, and boil 1 minute. Drain, and rinse the beans under cold running water. Hold the beans in a bowl of cold water, while you peel them by rubbing them between your palms.

Return the beans to the pot. Add enough hot water to cover by 1½ inches. Add the bouillon cube and salt. Bring to a boil over high heat, reduce the heat, and simmer covered until the beans are soft but still hold their shape, 15 minutes.

Meanwhile, heat the lard in a small skillet over medium heat. Add the onion, bell pepper, diced and grated carrot, and minced garlic; sauté over medium heat until softened and fragrant but not brown, 5 minutes. Season with salt.

Add the onion mixture and the rice to the beans; simmer covered until the rice is tender, 20 minutes. Add more water if necessary; the dish should be almost soupy. Taste and adjust the seasonings.

Meanwhile, make the Paprika Oil.

To serve, spoon the beans into earthenware bowls or deep plates, and drizzle with the hot Paprika Oil.

Hearty Chickpea and Swiss Chard Stew

Guiso de Garbanzos con Acelga

Makes 6 servings

The combination of the earthy-tasting chickpeas with the leafy Swiss chard is a happy one that probably finds its roots in Middle Eastern cookery from the Moorish occupation of Spain. Chilean cuisine is specked with Arabic influences, such as the use of certain spices, fried pumpkin pancakes, dense breads, and a long list of traditional sweets. There still exists an important and thriving Middle Eastern population within the Chilean society, favoring continuing culinary interaction.

> 2 cups chickpeas (peeled variety)
> 5 cups cold water
> Salt, to taste
> 1 bay leaf
> 2 tablespoons lard or vegetable oil
> 1 cup finely chopped onion
> 2 large cloves garlic, finely minced
> 1 carrot, peeled and coarsely grated
> 1 teaspoon dried cumin
> Freshly ground black pepper, to taste
> 1 (about 6-oz.) bunch Swiss chard, leaves only, or spinach, finely
>   shredded
> 2 tablespoons finely minced fresh parsley
> Paprika Oil (opposite) or ¼ cup freshly grated Parmesan cheese

Pick through the chickpeas, and remove any small stones or other foreign objects. Rinse the chickpeas and place in a large bowl. Add about 2 quarts cold water and soak overnight in a cool place.

Drain the chickpeas, and place in a heavy pot. Add the water, salt, and bay leaf. Bring to a boil over high heat. Skim off any foam that rises to the surface. Reduce the heat, and simmer partly covered until tender, 50 minutes to 1½ hours. (Cooking times vary according to the size and age of the chickpeas.)

Transfer 2 cups of the cooked chickpeas and 1 cup of the cooking liquid to a food processor or blender, and purée until smooth. Set aside.

Heat the lard in a small skillet over medium heat. Add the onion, and sauté 3 minutes. Add the garlic, carrot, cumin, salt, and pepper, and sauté 2 minutes more.

Stir the onion mixture, Swiss chard, and parsley into the whole chickpeas. The mixture should be very soupy; add ½ to 1 cup of warm water, if necessary. Cook covered over medium heat until the Swiss chard is tender, 10 to 15 minutes. Add the puréed chickpeas and cook, stirring, until lightly thickened and creamy, 3 to 4 minutes. Taste and adjust the seasonings.

Serve the hot stew in individual earthenware bowls or deep plates. Drizzle each portion with hot Paprika Oil or sprinkle with Parmesan.

Paprika Oil

¼ cup lard or vegetable oil
1 clove garlic, crushed
½ tablespoon sweet paprika

Heat the lard in a small pan over medium heat. Add the garlic, and sauté until light brown, 1 minute. Discard the garlic. Remove from the heat, and stir in the paprika.

Creamy Baked Chickpea and Crispy Bacon Pie

Garbanzos al Horno

Makes 6 servings

This wonderful original recipe was found in a shoebox filled with old, yellowed newspaper clippings. My friend Pilar, a busy professional and mother, has been an avid recipe collector since she was a teenager, patiently waiting for that magic moment in her life when she would actually be cooking some of the tantalizing recipes she so eagerly saved.

This luxurious chickpea pastel (pie), flavored with crispy bacon strips and zesty fresh chiles originated in the mind of a wonderful cook who's name has been lost with time but whose creation will delight many generations to come.

2 cups dried chickpeas (peeled variety)
3 cups cold water
Salt and freshly ground black pepper, to taste
2½ tablespoons butter
1 cup finely chopped onion
2 cloves garlic, finely minced
1 serrano or jalapeño chile, seeded and finely minced
1 teaspoon dried cumin
1½ cups heavy cream
4 ounces smoked bacon, cut into small strips and sautéed until crisp
1 large egg

Pick through the chickpeas, and remove any small stones or other foreign objects. Rinse the peas, and place in a large bowl. Add about 2 quarts cold water, and soak overnight in a cool place.

Drain the chickpeas, and place in a heavy pot. Add the water and salt. Bring to a boil over high heat; skim off any foam that rises to the surface. Reduce the heat, and simmer covered, until tender, 50 minutes to 1½ hours. (Cooking times vary according to the size and age of the chickpeas.) Transfer half of the cooked chickpeas and the cooking liquid to a food processor or blender, and purée until smooth. Return the purée to the pot with the whole chickpeas.

Preheat the oven to 375F (190C). Butter a deep 1½ quart earthenware or glass baking dish.

Melt 1½ tablespoons of the butter in a small skillet over medium heat. Add the onion, and sauté 3 minutes. Add the garlic, chile, cumin, salt, and pepper; sauté until the onion is softened and fragrant but not brown, 4 minutes.

Stir the onion mixture and ½ cup of the cream into the chickpea mixture. Cook, stirring constantly, over low heat until slightly thickened, 3 minutes. Taste for seasonings, and adjust as needed.

Spoon one-third of the chickpea mixture into the prepared dish. Add another layer of one-third of the chickpea mixture. Add half of the bacon, then the remaining bacon, and finally the remaining chickpea mixture. In a small bowl, whisk the egg with the remaining 1 cup of cream, remaining ½ tablespoon of butter, salt, and pepper. Pour the egg mixture over the chickpeas. Bake 20 to 25 minutes, or until the custard-like topping sets and is lightly brown. Serve at once.

The Mapuche of Southern Chile

The southern Lake District and volcanic region has turned into a popular destination for tourists hungry for the purity, beauty, and peace offered by this untouched land.

In the smaller villages, I have been struck more than once by the unique sight of the latest-model Range Rover parked next to a Mapuche oxen wagon with its sturdy, leather-bound stone wheels. Both people, living centuries apart, buy groceries in the same little store.

The Mapuche ("the people of the land") are the direct descendants of pre-Colombian peoples and constitute one of the few original ethnic groups remaining in the modern world. On the threshold of the twenty-first century, the Mapuches cling tightly to their true heritage, despite foreign influences and discrimination. Their ancestors' complex pre-Hispanic culture formed an important part of Chile's broad cultural and culinary heritage.

Since ancient times, the Mapuche diet has been based on vegetables, fruits, nuts, and herbs (both cultivated and gathered). The popular staples of the Chilean diet (and of all the Americas for that matter) are corn, potatoes, beans, chiles, and pumpkins, all of which were cultivated by the Mapuches, who lived along the rivers and in swamps.

A daily staple was and still is the potato. The Mapuche like their potatoes cooked in a vegetable broth, buried in hot ashes, and even fermented. They never forget to respect the tuber's connection with the spiritual realm, even the manner of preparation is important. Potatoes are generally cooked in a closed cooking utensil, symbolizing a cosmic totality.

We can easily trace many popular Chilean dishes to Mapuche influences, including the vast array of satisfying vegetable-filled broths (guisos), fermented fruit juices (chichas), and the use of cereals (such as mote). Mote is corn or wheat kernels cooked in water and ashes, peeled, and served in vegetable stew or desserts like the popular Mote con Huesillos (p. 276.)

The ocean has always offered an inestimable source of protein; seafood, fish, and seaweed were abundant. For the Mapuche, the consumption of meat is associated with ritual festivities and offerings, which explains the many dishes and odd drinks based on blood.

The Mapuches are great consumers of pine nuts, the fruits of the native *Araucaria* trees. Pine nuts are stored underground during the long winters, and provide the Mapuches with a vital source of nutrition. The nuts are toasted and made into flour or boiled and fermented to make their favorite drink, *chicha*, or *muday*. Their sacred *Araucaria* trees are some of the oldest pine trees original to the South American continent; they have a life span of more than fifteen hundred years. Entering some of these dense natural forests is like entering a cathedral. An ongoing tragedy concerns precisely the last vestiges of the once immense native forests, which often belong to the Indians. The forests have been devastated at an alarming rate.

Sweet Endings

Postres

Sitting around the remnants of what once was an elegantly dressed table, and enjoying a refreshing after-dinner drink, I asked my Chilean friends to name some of their favorite *postres* (desserts). A little startled by my question, they named the usual fruit desserts one can find on every typical restaurant menu: Papayas al Jugo (poached papayas), Higos con Nueces al Almibar (poached figs filled with walnuts), Panqueques Celestino (crepes filled with a rich caramel), and the beloved ice cream.

Hardly satisfied by their answers, I asked again: "But your mother never prepared you special sweet treats?" "My mother, not exactly, but my grandmother . . . " Another joins in, "At one time we had a nanny, she would make these incredible . . . " I knew there was more to come. What followed was a heated debate and an avalanche of exotic-sounding dishes, beginning with Turrón de Vino, Crema de Lúcuma, Espuma de Manzanas y Membrillo, and Chirimoya Alegre.

Invariably, the favorites are leche asada and leche nevada, the Chilean versions of flan and floating island. When I told my friends that these desserts were not any more authentic Chilean than a pair of jeans, I immediately set off a storm of indignant protests and more discussion.

I came to the conclusion that Chileans have an incurable sweet tooth, but that they prefer to eat fruit—fresh or dried—after their meal. Understandable, if you consider that few countries in the world have such a rich selection from which to choose.

There are a large variety of exotic tropical fruits such as papayas, cherimoyas, guavas, mangoes, kiwifruits, pepinos, pineapples, bananas, and citrus fruits besides the usual selection of apricots, peaches, plums, strawberries, cherries, apples, and pears.

The long, hot summers tempt one to consume loads of ice cream. Unfortunately, most ice creams are produced on an industrial scale and present little of interest; but you can still find delicious ice creams prepared by skilled craftsmen in most big cities.

Slowly but surely the afternoon arrives and with it the long-awaited 5 o'clock *onces,* the time for a sweet snack, a few pastries, a plate of cookies, or a slice of kuchen (the German-style cakes popular in the south), accompanied by a cup of tea or coffee. A true revelation is the huge variety of the traditional colonial sweets, *los dulces chilenos,* which are cherished as a national treasure and are still prepared according to ancient recipes.

In the countryside, popular treats are Mote con Huesillos (p. 276; poached dried peaches with puffed wheat) or Sopaipillas Pasadas con Chancaca (p. 274) As the name sopaipilla suggests, these fried cakes, as do most of the traditional Chilean pastries and confections, have a strong Moorish influence. At one time Arab, Jew, and Christian co-existed in Spain, and all left their culinary mark. With the Spanish rulers, sugarcane entered the New World.

In the wake of the Spanish conquistadores came several religious orders that settled in the New World by the end of the seventeenth century. Honoring their centuries-old tradition of producing and selling sweets, the agile Catholic nuns soon conquered the Chilean market with their delectable sweets, known as *alfajores, principes, rosquillas, hojuelas, chilenitos, cocadas, empolvados*. And to this very day, *los dulces chilenos* are made by both religious orders and lay pastry bakers, according to the same ancient recipes. Some sweets are typical of a certain region, such as los dulces de la Ligua (La Ligua is the region in which the first Chilean sugar producers started), los dulces de Curicaví, los suspiros de Monja (a specialty of Chillán), and las tortas Curicanas montero (pride of the city of Curicó).

But not to worry, wherever you travel along Route 5, *the* highway in Chile, you can stock up on sweets. Often, friendly women, nicely dressed in white, line up along the highway, waving frantically with a white flag to catch your attention to let you know that they have homemade treats to sell. In the town of Melipilla, these women are known as *las palomas de Melipilla*—the (white) doves of Melipilla—and they're quite a sight!

Taking into consideration the incredibly rich Chilean repertoire of sweets, it's hard to understand why most Latin American restaurants in the United States seem to lack originality and inspiration in their dessert offerings. It's unforgivable indeed. Most of the recipes in this chapter were inspired by tradition, but others reflect modern food trends. So whether you're looking for something classic or cutting edge, these desserts are sure to satisfy—and to surprise—just about any American sweet tooth.

Basic Egg Pastry for Chilean Sweets

Masa Amarilla para Dulces Chilenos

Makes about 18 (4-inch) rounds

The traditional sweet repertoire of many South American countries, Spain's wicked legacy, amazes by the sheer respect it shows to tradition and the desire to keep the centuries-old recipes alive and thriving. This miraculous survival is, in great part, the result of the zealous but obstinate dedication of the Catholic orders who, in the old days, adopted sweet making as a craft. They steadfastly baked their treats, a major gloria de Dios, using ancient recipes. These recipes were devoutly shared with generations of young girls, who were educated by the nuns.

To say that someone cooks *de mano de monja,* "with the gifted hands of a nun," is still the highest praise a cook can get. Most dulces Chilenos have a pastry rich in egg yolks and lard. A sure indication of their Christian background, because both Jewish and Arab communities were forbidden to eat pork.

I've come across countless variations of this popular pastry. In the old days, when sugar was scarce and expensive, honey was used instead. This recipe has been updated, using sugar and butter instead of honey and lard. The result is much like a crisp, thin cookie, the ideal partner for the popular *manjar*, a thick, tasty caramel filling.

> 1 cup all-purpose flour
> Pinch salt
> 2 tablespoons butter, melted and left to cool
> 2 tablespoons cold water
> 1 tablespoon white wine vinegar
> 1 tablespoon brandy or rum
> 4 large egg yolks

Preheat the oven to 375F (190C). Lightly flour a baking sheet.

Sift the flour onto a work surface. Make a well in the center; add the remaining ingredients, and work together with your fingertips until well mixed. Gradually draw in the flour and knead until the dough is satiny and quite elastic, about 5 minutes.

On a lightly floured work surface, roll out the dough to a ⅛-inch thickness. Cut the dough out into rounds (2½ inches for hojarascas and 6 to 8 inches for tortas), rectangles (for lanchitas), or ovals (for chilenitos). Prick the dough with a fork (to help keep them flat) and transfer to the prepared pan. Bake about 5 minutes, or until light golden brown. Transfer the pastries to a wire rack; cool completely before filling and decorating.

Filling Dulces Chilenos

Dulces Chilenos are mostly filled with *manjar*, which is sometimes enriched with chopped walnuts, chopped almonds, or orange zest; dulce de alcayote con nueces (a rich preserve made with a special pumpkin and walnuts mixture); huevo mol (an egg yolk candy), or lúcuma purée (p. 281). The more sophisticated versions are rolled in finely chopped nuts or covered with *betún*, an Italian meringue that's left to dry in the oven.

These traditional Chilean sweets are actually very simple, so the quality of the ingredients and the skill with which they are made are instantly discernible. This is why, even though they are made commercially nowadays, traditional methods are still closely observed. These popular sweets keep well; but it's always a good idea to check the dates, if you buy them from one of the many street vendors.

Chilean Pastry

Chilenitos

Makes 10 to 12 pastries

This is my favorite dulce Chileno. In this interesting recipe, the pastry is flavored with orange zest and juice and encased in Italian meringue. Chilenitos are wonderful filled with the flavored manjar. For a less sweet version (these pastries are sweet), omit the meringue.

PASTRY
1 cup all-purpose flour
½ teaspoon baking powder
Pinch salt
½ tablespoon finely minced orange zest
4 to 5 tablespoons freshly squeezed orange juice
2 large egg yolks

ITALIAN MERINGUE
½ cup water
1 cup sugar
4 large egg whites
Pinch salt
4 tablespoons powdered sugar

ASSEMBLY
1½ cups Manjar Casero de Don Pablo (p. 252)
Powdered sugar for sprinkling

To make pastry: Preheat the oven to 375F (190C). Lightly flour a baking sheet.

Sift the flour, baking powder, and salt onto a work surface. Make a well in the center, add the remaining pastry ingredients, work together with your fingertips until well combined. Gradually draw in the flour and knead to a smooth, but rather dry dough, about 5 minutes.

On a lightly floured work surface, roll out the dough to a ⅛-inch thickness. Cut the dough out into rounds with a 2½-inch round cutter. Prick the rounds with a fork, and place them in the prepared pan. Repeat with any leftover dough. Bake about 5 minutes, or until the pastries start to brown around the edges. Transfer to a wire rack, and cool completely before filling. Leave the oven on.

To prepare the meringue: Place the water and sugar in a small saucepan. Bring to a boil over medium heat, stirring frequently. When the mixture comes to a boil, cease stirring, and continue to cook until it reaches 248F (120C) on a candy thermometer, 3 to 5 minutes.

Meanwhile, beat the egg whites with the salt until stiff peaks form. Continue to beat while pouring the hot sugar syrup into the egg whites in a thin stream. Beat until cold. Carefully fold in the powdered sugar by hand.

To assemble: Place a heaping tablespoon of Manjar Casero de Don Pablo in the center of a pastry round, and cover with another round without pressing them together. Using a small spatula, cover the sides and the tops of the pastries with the meringue. Smooth out and arrange the pastries on a rack. Sprinkle with some powdered sugar. Place in the the lower third of the oven, and bake 2 minutes. Turn off the heat, and leave the pastries 30 minutes. Transfer the rack to the upper third of the oven, and leave 30 minutes more so the meringue can harden and dry. The meringue topping should remain as white as snow.

Manjar

Manjar, which is nothing more than milk and sugar cooked down to a rich, gooey caramel paste, has the power to provoke passionate discussions to defend the sweet's many qualities. When a Chilean's taste buds happen to be enthralled by an exquisite flavor, he'll describe the taste sensation as *un verdadero manjar,* "nothing less than a true delicacy."

Since colonial times, manjar has been the backbone of traditional Chilean pastries known as *los dulces chilenos.* It is literally the cement that glues the complicated pastries together. Kids are crazy about it and smear the sweet spread thick on their toast and sandwiches, much like peanut butter in the United States.

I have to admit, used with discretion, because it is so decadently sweet, manjar has its charms. Homemade manjar (manjar casero), often prepared with fresh cow's milk, offers a rich and delicate flavor, definitely a far cry from the commercialized brands that are available in all supermarkets.

Making manjar is time-consuming and tricky and is thus a dying occupation, even in the Chilean countryside. But since I set about this quest of saving the forgotten flavors of the past, I did come up with a wonderful and easy-to-follow recipe. All you need is a little time and lots of patience.

Soft Meringue Flavored with Honey

Turrón de Miel de Abejas

Makes 6 servings

Adelicious variation and an always welcome idea for a unique and original low-fat dessert.

> **6 tablespoons honey**
> **6 tablespoons white wine**
> **4 large egg whites, at room temperature**
> **Pinch salt or cream of tartar**
> **½ cup toasted almond slivers**

In a small nonreactive saucepan, bring the honey and wine slowly to a boil, stirring frequently. Simmer without stirring until the mixture becomes syrupy and reaches the soft ball stage or 248F (120C) on a candy thermometer, 5 to 7 minutes.

Meanwhile, in the bowl of an electric mixer, beat the egg whites with the salt until soft peaks form. Continue beating while pouring the hot syrup, in a thin stream, into the egg whites. Beat until cool and shiny. Spoon the soft honey meringue into tall decorative glasses and garnish with the slivered almonds.

Flavored and Light-Colored Milk Spread

Manjar Blanco con Nueces

Makes about 3 cups

Manjar blanco is, as the name indicates, light in color and is usually enriched with eggs. This recipe is actually a shortcut, making use of two popular convenience foods—canned sweetened condensed milk and canned evaporated milk. Here I've suggested different aromas for the manjar. This delicate confection makes a unique and delicious dessert when served with discretion. But it's also the best filling for traditional Chilean pastries and for almost everything from pancakes to cakes!

1 (14-oz.) can sweetened condensed milk
1 (12-oz.) can evaporated milk
2 large eggs
½ teaspoon pure vanilla extract
**¾ cup finely ground toasted walnuts or almonds, 1 ripe cherimoya,
    peeled, seeded, and cut into small pieces, or 1 cup black
    sapote or unsweetened chestnut purée**
Pinch salt
Whipped cream and plain cookies, to serve

Combine the sweetened condensed and evaporated milks in a large heavy saucepan. Bring the milk mixture to a simmer over medium heat and cook, stirring constantly, until the mixture is thick and golden, and the bottom of the pan can be seen when the spoon is drawn across it, 15 to 20 minutes. Remove from the heat and continue stirring for 1 minute; reserve.

Separate the eggs and whip the egg yolks in a bowl until foamy. Fold the yolks gradually into the milk mixture, and return to the heat. Cook, stirring constantly, 3 minutes. Remove from the heat and stir in the vanilla. If you're flavoring the manjar with ground nuts, add them, and combine well. (The other flavors are added later.) Allow the manjar to cool about 10 minutes.

Meanwhile, beat the egg whites with a pinch of salt in a medium bowl until stiff but not dry. Fold into the manjar. Return the mixture to the heat, and cook, stirring constantly, until it thickens once more, 2 to 3 minutes. Remove from the heat, and beat the mixture for a few minutes longer to guarantee a satiny, shiny consistency. If you're flavoring the manjar with cherimoya, sapote, or chestnuts, stir it into the mixture now to combine. Spoon the delicately flavored manjar into individual serving dishes or tall wineglasses. It's heavenly rich; a small amount is enough. Refrigerate until chilled, and serve with a dollop of whipped cream and a plate of cookies. Manjar can be covered and refrigerated up to 2 months.

Homemade Caramelized Milk Spread

Manjar Casero de Don Pablo

Makes about 2½ cups

Manjar is known as *dulce de leche* in Spain and Paraguay, adored as *arequipe* in Colombia, prepared with goat's milk and dark brown sugar as the Peruvian *natillas piuranas*, and wrapped in small wooden boxes in Mexico under the name *cajeta de celaya*. It is the most popular sweet in Chile. This rich caramel paste is wonderful as a filling for pancakes, angel food and pound cakes, and layered tarts made with meringue or puff pastry.

> **8 cups whole milk**
> **5 cups sugar**
> **¼ teaspoon baking soda**
> **1 cinnamon stick and/or 1 vanilla bean, split lengthwise**

In a 6-quart copper or other heavy saucepan, bring all the ingredients slowly to a boil, stirring frequently with a wooden spoon by tracing a figure eight in the pot. Once the mixture comes to a boil and all the sugar has dissolved, reduce the heat to very low, and cook the mixture, stirring occasionally, until most of the liquid has evaporated and the mixture begins to thicken, 1½ to 2 hours. Be on your guard constantly, milk boils over very quickly!

Discard the cinnamon stick. Continue to cook, stirring constantly, while the mixture is thickening and turns an amber caramel color. When the mixture is so thick that the bottom of the pan can be seen when the spoon is drawn across it, or when a spoonful placed on a cool plate retains its shape and is no longer runny, take the pan off the heat. Continue stirring for a few minutes longer, to ensure a satiny and smooth texture. Turn the manjar into a serving bowl, and allow to cool at room temperature. Manjar can be covered and refrigerated up to 3 months.

Making Manjar

I had the good fortune to come across old-time pastry chef Don Juan Pablo Asenjo (p. 254) who told me the following rules for making manjar.

- An even heat distribution is of the greatest importance. Copper pots are preferred, but any heavy saucepan will do, as long as it's not aluminum.

- The pan must be twice as big as the quantity of milk and sugar used. This to avoid major spills when the milk rises and foams. And it will spill all over the stove like an angry volcano, if you're not careful.

- Once the milk mixture is simmering, keep the heat down to a minimum. If you have trouble keeping the heat low enough, place the saucepan on a heat diffuser; some cooks even use a fan to blow cool air over the saucepan.

- It's a good idea to have a pitcher of cold milk next to the stove. If the milk mixture threatens to boil over, quickly add a little cold milk.

- A pinch of baking soda helps the manjar turn to a nice amber caramel color (don't use it if you want to keep the manjar light).

- Manjar has a reputation of being very tricky! Only one person should stir the pot, patiently tracing a figure eight, or so he told me.

Portrait of a Traditional Pastry Baker: Don Juan Pablo, Rebel with a Sweet Cause

For over a century now, the provincial town of Cúrico brings to the mind of most Chileans visions of sweet layered tarts filled with manjar and rolled in a crispy coating of chopped nuts. Las tortas Curicanas Montero have restored and satisfied many travelers heading south, be it by train, bus, car, or on horseback.

It all started in 1891 when the gifted Doña Cristobalina Montero decided to sell the fine pastries she prepared according to centuries-old recipes. That she also had a nose for business besides sweets was rapidly proven, as the astute woman started to present her sweets to the first hungry travelers who arrived in the newly built railroad station of Cúrico. She happened to be in the right place at the right time.

Now, more than a hundred years later, her great-grandson Don Juan Pablo Asenjo continues the tradition. The bakery, at Prat 659, is almost a relic and is filled with museum pieces. The delicate pastries are still baked in the old adobe ovens, fueled with wood, requiring baking skills that border on magic.

I was in awe when one of the pastry chefs shuffled around some of the coals, when he noticed that the left corner of the eighteen by twenty-two-foot oven was getting too hot. And believe it or not, the paper-thin pastries came out cooked to perfection. This under the watchful eye of Osbaldo Candia, the oldest pastry chef working in Chile, with fifty-eight years of experience to his credit. The man is a living legend and a bottomless source of the most incredible stories.

He tells about a time when everything had to be done by hand and required artful skills, a time when obtaining a steady supply of farm eggs was the biggest nightmare. He recalls flour that felt soft as silk, of honey that replaced the expensive sugar, and of tasty lard (now mostly replaced by margarine).

What never changes is the stubborn dedication with which Don Juan Pablo runs the family business. This generous and passionate man writes poetry and retires for days on end in the Andes Mountains, in the sole company of his horse; he is a great defender of all good things past. Yet his interest in cooking and baking came to him out of pure necessity.

At the age of thirteen, this rebellious boy left his maternal home on a horse and wandered through the Cordillera all the way to Argentina. He got to know the rough country well, but eventually the memory of his mother's cooking and an empty stomach brought him back home. He had to promise his desperate mother never to leave again. A promise he kept—but on one condition: that she would reveal all her culinary secrets to him. From there the step into his great-grandmother's footsteps was only natural.

In 1995, he decided to give Doña Cristobalina's tarts a worldly reputation and set about to bake the biggest torta Curicana ever prepared, an endeavor that gained him a honorable mention in the *Guinness Book of Records*. The monster tart weighed forty-six thousand pounds, was thirty feet wide and sixteen inches high. More than five hundred thousand Chileans from all over the country had to help eat it. But a difficult goal was accomplished: the tortas Montero and the whole gamut of traditional Chilean pastries retained their place and respect in this competitive world.

It takes men like Don Juan Pablo, of an almost lost age, to give Chile its unique and so-charming character.

Celestino's Crepes Filled with Manjar

Panqueques Celestinos

Makes 4 servings

Chileans have a real passion for manjar, which is basically sweetened milk cooked down to a rich caramel. Manjar makes a wonderful filling for delicate, paper-thin French-style crepes. Wherever you travel in this stretched-out country, you'll find Celestino's pancakes on the menu of the more traditional restaurants and *picadas*. They're easy to put together at home and make an elegant dessert.

> 1 cup milk
> 2 large eggs
> 1 teaspoon pure vanilla extract
> Pinch salt
> ¾ cup all-purpose flour
> 2 tablespoons butter, plus additional butter or oil for cooking
> 1 cup Manjar Casero de Don Pablo (p. 252)
> Powdered sugar

In a medium bowl, whisk the milk and eggs until combined. Add the vanilla and salt. Stir in the flour, a little at the time, until well combined. Let the batter rest about 30 minutes.

Melt 2 tablespoons of butter in an 8-inch nonstick skillet over medium heat. Stir into the batter. Heat a little more butter or oil in the skillet. Pour a scant ⅓ cup batter into the pan. Tilt the pan slightly to cover the entire surface of the pan with a thin layer of batter. Cook over medium heat until light brown on the bottom. Turn the crepe with a spatula and brown the other side. Repeat until all the batter is used. There should be at least 8 crepes. Stack the crepes on a plate until ready to serve.

Preheat the broiler.

Spread each crepe with 1 to 2 tablespoons of manjar and roll tightly or fold in quarters. Place the crepes on a baking sheet and sprinkle generously with powdered sugar. Broil for a few minutes or until the sugar lightly caramelizes. Serve at once.

Wine-Flavored Soft Meringue with Crème Anglaise

Turrón de Vino

Makes 6 servings

Though this dessert is considerably different from the traditional Spanish hard *turrón*, made with nuts, honey, and aromatic spices, both are clearly a legacy from ancient and cultured forebears with a well-developed sweet tooth.

Most Spanish-influenced sweets seem to rely heavily on eggs rather than on the rich butter and cream of the French and Viennese pastries. Meringues of all guises, soft or hard, as a base or as an airy covering, floating in milk or whipped into flans, are turned into true masterpieces.

This recipe is an intriguing example. The soft meringue is perfumed with red wine and aromatic spices and served with a rich vanilla sauce. It makes an original and elegant dessert.

CRÈME ANGLAISE
1½ cups milk
½ cup heavy cream
½ vanilla bean, split lengthwise, or 1 teaspoon pure vanilla extract
4 large egg yolks
½ cup sugar

MERINGUE
½ cup red wine
1 whole clove
¼ teaspoon ground cinnamon
1-inch piece lemon zest
¾ cup sugar
3 large egg whites, at room temperature
Pinch salt or cream of tartar
6 walnut halves, garnish

To prepare the Crème Anglaise: In a medium saucepan, heat the milk, cream, and vanilla until hot. Discard the vanilla bean. Beat the egg yolks and sugar in a medium bowl until light and foamy, about 3 minutes. Starting with a few tablespoons, gradually stir in the hot milk.

Return the mixture to the saucepan and cook over medium heat, stirring constantly with a wooden spoon, until the custard starts to thicken slightly. Do not let the custard come to a boil or it will curdle. Pour the custard into a heatproof bowl to cool completely, and refrigerate until ready to use.

To prepare the meringue: In a small nonreactive saucepan, bring the wine, spices, and sugar slowly to a boil over medium heat, stirring with a wooden spoon. Simmer until the mixture becomes syrupy and reaches the soft ball stage or 248F(120C) on a candy thermometer, about 10 minutes. Discard the clove and the lemon zest.

Meanwhile, in the bowl of an electric mixer, beat the egg whites with the salt until soft peaks form. Continue beating while pouring the hot syrup, in a thin stream, into the egg whites. Beat until cool and shiny.

To serve, spoon the custard onto 6 individual plates. Divide the meringue evenly over the custard, using a large spoon. Garnish each with a walnut half.

Easy Apple and Walnut Pudding

Pastel de Manzanas de María

Makes 6 servings

A sea of apple trees: A whole valley covered with snowy white spring blossoms turns into a bounty of red, orange, and green apples by the end of the hot Chilean summer. La Señora Maria, the cook at the ranch, preserves, purées, and bakes to her heart's content. And there are always takers for her goodies. The children are especially fond of this tasty and easy pudding served still warm with a generous scoop of vanilla ice cream.

> **6 large apples, peeled, cored, and coarsely grated**
> **1 (14-oz.) can sweetened condensed milk**
> **1 teaspoon pure vanilla extract**
> **½ cup coarsely chopped walnuts**
> **3 large eggs, separated**
> **2 tablespoons cornstarch**
> **Pinch cream of tartar or salt**
> **3 tablespoons sugar**

Preheat the oven to 375F (190C). Butter a medium baking dish.

Combine the apples, milk, vanilla, walnuts, egg yolks, and cornstarch in a medium bowl. Pour the apple mixture into the prepared dish. Bake 40 to 45 minutes, or until the batter is set and is light brown.

Meanwhile, beat the egg whites with the cream of tartar until soft peaks form. Gradually add the sugar and continue beating until stiff peaks form. Cover the apples with the meringue and return to the hot oven for 5 minutes more, or until the meringue is light brown. Serve the pudding lukewarm or cold.

Christmas the Chilean Way

Once the pages of the calendar have been turned to December, Chileans impatiently start the countdown. The notion that the end of the year is in sight, seems to trigger some of the most hectic, chaotic times in the country. In this part of the world this period coincides with the end of the academic year, the beginning of a two-month break for students, a general exodus to the beaches, and a true holiday shopping frenzy. It's impossible to book a meeting in Santiago, the lines in the post offices and supermarkets are horrendous, and bus and train employees seem to be tremendously overwhelmed by the onslaught of work.

The sweltering summer heat doesn't seem to interfere one bit with the Chileans' zeal to celebrate Christmas in all its glory. Since it's predominately a Christian nation, Chile does recognize the religious context of the holiday. But in my opinion, Chileans adopted most of the Western customs in a somewhat corny way. I'll never get used to the sweaty Santa Claus parked on every street corner, the fake Christmas trees covered with packages of white cotton, and the imported songs coming from every shopping mall speaker, all while the outdoor temperature is about to top 90F (32C).

Chileans are notorious for being late, and this busy time is no exception. You would be surprised how many people still have to run out in the late afternoon of December 24 to buy some Christmas presents or even a tree! But all this is easily forgotten, because it's all done with a big heart and the best of intentions. And that's how a lot of things are done in Chile. They also have a well-earned reputation of being very generous with the needy and the less fortunate.

Chileans are family people, and the kids are king. Christmas is their holiday. People do send out tons of cards, buy too many presents, and travel hundreds of miles to spend time with their loved ones—even at the risk of a nervous breakdown!

Grandmother Clara's Christmas Cake

Pan de Pascua de la Mami Clara

Makes 1 (9-inch) cake

*I*nseparable from the Chilean Christmas is *pan de pascua*, a rich cakelike bread loaded with nuts, raisins, candied fruits, and aromatic spices. Much like the Mexican *rosca de reyes*, the Italian *panettone*, and the English fruitcake, this rich, fruity confection keeps well, a guarantee that you'll always have something on hand to offer during the holiday season.

This recipe was given to me by Sonia Torres Díaz, who, in the footsteps of her grandmother Mami Clara, dedicates herself to the creation of traditional sweets, based on the authentic recipes of her gifted grandma who studied a long time ago with the nuns.

If you ever drive southward along Route 5, make sure to stop in the village of Teno and sample some of these delectable sweets in Sonia's own pastry shop, which she affectionately calls *Salon de Te, Mami Clara.*

3 cups, plus 2 tablespoons all-purpose flour
1½ teaspoons baking powder
Pinch salt
1 teaspoon ground anise seeds
1 teaspoon ground cinnamon
¼ teaspoon ground cloves
1½ sticks (¾ cup) butter, at room temperature
½ cup packed dark brown sugar or light, unsulfured molasses
⅓ cup granulated sugar, plus additional for sprinkling
5 large eggs
1 cup milk
1 cup mixed candied fruits

½ cup coarsely chopped walnuts
¼ cup coarsely chopped almonds
1 cup raisins
½ cup Cascara de Naranja Confitada (p. 264)

Preheat the oven to 300F(150C). Line the bottom of a 9-inch springform pan with a double layer of buttered parchment paper, and generously butter the sides of the pan.

In a large bowl, sift 3 cups of the flour with the baking powder. Add the salt and spices; mix to combine. In a second large bowl, beat the butter with the sugars until light and fluffy. Add 4 of the eggs, one at a time, beating well after each addition. Using a wooden spoon, stir in the flour mixture in batches, alternating with the milk, to make a smooth, thick batter. Stir vigorously a few times to lighten the batter. Dust the candied fruits and nuts with the remaining 2 tablespoons of flour, and stir into the batter.

Spoon the batter into the prepared pan. Bake 45 minutes. Beat the remaining egg, brush the top of the cake with the egg, and sprinkle lightly with granulated sugar. Bake a total of 2 to 2½ hours, or until a knife inserted in the center comes out clean. If the cake starts to brown too quickly, cover loosely with foil.

Cool the cake in the pan; then turn out, and peel off the paper. Store covered in a brown paper bag in a cool, dry place. Let the cake age for at least 1 day before slicing it. It will keep 2 to 3 weeks in a dry spot.

Candied Orange Peel

Cascara de Naranja Confitada

Makes 1 cup

"Making your own candied orange peel is really very easy and satisfying," confides Sonia, a dark-haired young woman with surprisingly clear blue eyes. She seems to have inherited more than just recipes from her grandmother—her gifted hands to prepare sweets and a fiercely independent nature that allow her to run her business all by herself.

> **2 large untreated thick-skinned oranges**
> **3¼ cups water**
> **¼ cup sugar**

With a vegetable peeler or a zester, cut strips of zest from the orange rind, leaving the bitter white pith behind. Slice the zest into thin julienne.

In a small saucepan, bring 1 cup of the water to a boil. Add the orange zest, and boil about 3 minutes. Drain and repeat the boiling for a total of three times, changing the water each time. Drain.

In the same saucepan, dissolve the sugar in the remaining ¼ cup water. Bring the sugar mixture to a boil, and add the orange zest. Simmer over low heat until all the liquid has evaporated, and the zest is covered with the thick syrup, 8 to 10 minutes. Be careful not to caramelize the sugar. Transfer the zest to a rack or a lightly oiled baking sheet. Let cool, and store in an airtight container until ready to use.

The German Influence

When I opened my eyes at 5:30 A.M., awakened by a herd of noisy cows passing underneath my window, for a moment I thought I was in Germany. The lush, green, rolling hills, the typical wood and stone farmhouses, even the cuckoo clock on the wall added to my confusion. But no, I was in a *hospedaje* (a bed and breakfast) facing Lake Llanquihue with its breathtaking view of the snow-topped Vulcano Osorno.

Our hostess, la Señora Hellen, a talkative small woman, surprised us with a breakfast fit for a king: a basket of fresh biscuits, homemade jams, cheese, ham, coffee, and a jug of fresh, creamy warm milk from her cows. She moved from kitchen to the living room like a busy bee, all the while recounting to us the story of her family. It was a tale of hard labor, perseverance, joy, sorrow, and finally success.

"Nowadays, many of us are turning to the increasing tourism in the region to make a living. All my kids are grown and on their own now, so I decided to open my house as a bed and breakfast. I had to find someone to eat my breads, jams, and cakes." She laughed as she brought us more coffee and a sumptuous coffeecake loaded with black cherries from her orchard. (See Lemon Cake Topped with Dark Cherries, p. 268.)

Mami Clara's Rich Walnut Tart

Kuchen de Nueces de la Mami Clara

Makes 8 to 12 servings

This is by far the most exquisite walnut tart I've ever tasted. It's so decadent that it's an ideal companion for an afternoon cup of tea. In homage of fall, I love to serve a small wedge of this tart as a dessert, graced by some fresh figs, grapes, or sliced flavorful pears. Walnuts are plentiful in Chile, but toasted almonds or even toasted peanuts make an equally delicious tart.

PASTRY

1½ cups all-purpose flour

1 teaspoon baking powder

½ teaspoon salt

4 tablespoons butter, at room temperature

1 large egg yolk

⅓ to ½ cup ice-cold water

FILLING

2 cups finely ground walnuts

1 (14-oz.) sweetened condensed milk

3 tablespoons butter, melted

1 egg white

TOPPING

½ cup whipping cream, chilled

1 tablespoon powdered sugar

10 complete walnut halves

To make the pastry in a food processor: Place the flour, baking powder, salt, butter, and egg yolk into the bowl of the food processor. Pulse a few times until the mixture has a coarse texture. Add the water, a little at the time, and pulse just enough to hold the dough together and form a ball. Wrap the dough in plastic wrap, and refrigerate 1 hour.

To make the pastry by hand: Sift the flour with the baking powder onto the work surface. Make a well in the center. Add the salt, butter, egg yolk, and ⅓ cup of the water. With your fingertips, blend the flour into the other ingredients. Add more water if it's too dry. Work quickly to make a soft non-sticky dough. Do not overknead or the crust will be tough. Wrap the dough in plastic wrap, and refrigerate 1 hour.

Preheat the oven to 400F (205C).

To prepare the filling: In a medium bowl, stir together the walnuts, milk, and butter with a wooden spoon. Beat the egg white in a small bowl until stiff peaks form. Carefully fold the egg white into the walnut mixture.

On a lightly floured work surface, roll the dough into a thin 12-inch round. Line a 10-inch tart pan with a removable bottom with the dough. Trim and crimp the edges. Prick a few holes into the bottom with a fork. Fill the pie crust evenly with the walnut mixture.

Bake 20 to 30 minutes, or until the custard is brown and puffs up slightly. Let cool on a rack before topping.

To top the tart: In a medium bowl, beat the whipping cream with the powdered sugar until stiff peaks form. Spoon the whipped cream into a pastry bag fitted with a star tube. Pipe 10 rosettes evenly around the border and 1 large rosette in the center of the tart. Put a walnut half on each small rosette.

Lemon Cake Topped with Dark Cherries

Kuchen de Guindas

Makes 6 servings

The adventurous traveler is naturally drawn toward the spectacular region of lakes and volcanoes in the southern part of Chile. It was in this area that many German and eastern European immigrants settled during the late nineteenth century. They made an undeniable and lasting imprint on the Chilean society, noticeable in architecture and farming techniques. They also greatly contributed to the successful tourist development in this part of the country.

On a culinary level, the influence is perhaps the most obvious. Indeed, German specialities—like cured and smoked hams, various sausages (especially the frankfurter or hot dog), pâtés, breads, and pastries—have become staples in the Chilean diet. The kuchen, the cakelike pastries filled with pastry cream or fruit, have conquered the Chilean markets as far north as Santiago.

This cake tastes delicious with some whipped cream, served on the side.

CAKE
1 stick (½ cup) butter, at room temperature
1¼ cups sugar
3 eggs, separated
1 tablespoon grated lemon zest
3 cups all-purpose flour
2 teaspoons baking powder
1 cup milk
Pinch salt

FRUIT TOPPING
1 (15-oz.) can (2 cups) dark sweet cherries in heavy syrup
1 tablespoon cornstarch
¼ cup freshly squeezed lemon juice
2 tablespoons kirsh or other cherry-flavored liquor, or to taste

Preheat the oven to 375F (190C). Coat the inside of a 9-inch springform pan with butter and line the bottom with buttered parchment paper.

In the bowl of an electric mixer, beat the butter and sugar, until the mixture is light and fluffy, about 4 minutes. Beat in the egg yolks, one at a time, then add the lemon zest.

Sift the flour with the baking powder in a small bowl. Stir the flour mixture into the butter mixture, ¼ cup at a time, alternating with the milk.

In another, clean bowl, beat the egg whites with the salt until soft peaks form. Carefully fold the egg whites into the batter.

Pour the batter into the prepared pan. Bake 25 to 30 minutes in the middle of the oven, or until a knife inserted in the center comes out clean. Allow the cake to cool 10 minutes before removing from the pan. Place the cake on a plate.

Meanwhile, prepare the fruit topping. Drain the cherries and reserve 1 cup of the syrup. In a small saucepan, bring the reserved syrup to a boil. Dissolve the cornstarch in the lemon juice and stir into the boiling syrup with a wooden spoon. Cook, stirring constantly, until the sauce has thickened. Remove from the heat. Add the kirsh.

Arrange the black cherries evenly on top of the warm cake. Pour the thickened syrup over the fruit. Cool before serving.

Chilean-Style Cheesecake

Kuchen de Quesillo

Makes 10 servings

To be correct we should say *German-style cheese tart* prepared with the popular Chilean fresh cheese called *quesillo*, which is a silky, refreshing cheese made from cow's milk. For this recipe, a mixture of ricotta and heavy cream results in an equally delicious, not too sweet tart. I love to serve this cake topped with a raspberry or blackberry sauce.

CRUST

2 cups all-purpose flour

Pinch salt

½ teaspoon baking powder

¼ cup sugar

1 stick (½ cup) butter, cut into small pieces

1 large egg, lightly beaten

About 1 tablespoon cold water

FILLING

1½ cups whole milk ricotta mixed with ½ cup heavy cream

1 cup powdered sugar, plus additional for dusting

4 eggs

1 tablespoon finely minced lemon zest

3 tablespoons cornstarch

¾ cup raisins or currants, soaked in hot water or rum 15 minutes, drained

To prepare the crust: Sift the flour, salt, and baking powder onto a work surface. Make a well in the center and add the granulated sugar and butter. Working quickly and using your fingertips, rub the butter into the flour mixture until it forms coarse crumbs. Add the egg and 1 tablespoon cold water. Mix quickly; if it's too dry, add a little more water. Gather the dough into a ball, and knead lightly with the palm of your hand for a few minutes until it feels soft and no longer sticky. Wrap the dough tightly in plastic wrap and refrigerate at least 30 minutes.

Preheat the oven to 375F(190C). Generously butter a 9-inch spring-form pan or deep pie plate.

To prepare the filling: Place the ricotta mixture in a blender, and blend until smooth. Pour the mixture into a bowl. Add the powdered sugar and the eggs, one at a time, and whisk to combine. Stir in the lemon zest, cornstarch, and raisins.

Roll out the dough into a large enough circle to fit the pan. Line the prepared pan with the dough and chill 15 minutes.

Pour the cheese mixture into the crust; it should reach the top of the pan.

To finish: Bake in the lower third of the oven 50 to 60 minutes, until the filling is set. If top browns too quickly, cover loosely with foil. Allow the cake to cool on a wire rack before removing from the pan. Serve lukewarm or chilled, dusted with powdered sugar.

Fried Bow-Tie Pastries

Calzones Rotos

Makes about 20 pastries

*T*hese lemon-scented fried pastries, affectionately named Calzones Rotos (old, torn underpants) are a favorite afternoon snack in the Chilean countryside. Like most of the traditional desserts, they can be traced to the Spanish settlers.

I love to serve these tasty treats as an accompaniment to poached pears or peaches. To make it a truly irresistible dessert, add a scoop of vanilla ice cream to each plate.

> 2½ to 3 cups all-purpose flour
> 1½ teaspoons baking powder
> ¼ cup sugar
> 1 tablespoon finely minced lemon zest
> 2 egg yolks
> 2 tablespoons butter, at room temperature
> 1 cup milk
> Vegetable oil for deep-frying
> Powdered sugar

Sift the flour with the baking powder into a large bowl. Stir in the sugar and lemon zest. Make a well in the center. Add the egg yolks, butter, and milk. Gradually work the flour into the liquid ingredients until you have a soft, nonsticky dough that holds together. Do not overwork the dough, or it will become tough. Cover, and let stand 30 minutes at room temperature.

Roll the dough out on a lightly floured surface to a ⅛-inch thickness. Using a square cutter or a sharp knife, cut the dough into 1½-inch squares.

Make a slit on the diagonal in the center of each square. Carefully pull one side of the square through the opening to get a twisted bow tie look. Place the pastries on a baking sheet. Cover lightly and refrigerate up to 1 day.

Preheat the oven to 250F (122C). Line a baking sheet with paper towels.

Heat 2 inches of oil in a heavy medium saucepan or wok to 375F (190C). Add 4 pastries and cook until deep golden brown, turning occasionally, about 1 minute. Using a slotted spoon, transfer the pastries to the paper towels to drain. Keep the pastries warm in the oven while frying the rest, in batches. Sprinkle the pastries generously with powdered sugar and serve at once.

Pumpkin Fritters Dipped in Spiced Syrup

Sopaipillas Pasadas con Chancaca

Makes 4 servings

Where I live, in the heart of the Chilean countryside, winter smells like damp earth, wood fires, and these flat crispy pumpkin fritters.

In the Central Valley, winter is short and easily forgotten. But in the country, it can hit hard, especially when it starts to rain and a dampness settles in the poorly insulated houses. This is the time when the countrywoman mixes the cooked pumpkin with flour, and in the palms of her calloused hands, pats little pancakes that she'll fry in rendered pork fat. Crusty on the outside, soft and a little spongy on the inside—just as they should be—they are eaten out of hand as a snack. For a special occasion, they are soaked in a flavorful syrup, made with chancaca (a by-product of sugar making) and perfumed with cloves, cinnamon, and orange zest. I like them a lot with blackberry jam, maple syrup, and honey.

In Chile, rain invariably brings these fritters to mind. Even in the trendy capital, Santiago, the tasty fritters are a popular street fare. At various strategic points, street vendors fry them to order, tempting more than one passerby. Most supermarkets sell them, neatly packaged and ready to fry. Needless to say, they are not as good as the ones my gentle neighbor brings me every time I hear the raindrops hit the roof.

In the southern windswept regions and in Chiloé, I came across an interesting version made with boiled potatoes. But, then *everything* is made with potatoes in that part of the world.

½ **pound pumpkin, cut into** ½**-inch cubes**
1½ **cups water**
Salt, to taste

2 cups all-purpose flour
1 teaspoon baking powder
1 large egg yolk
2 tablespoons melted lard or vegetable oil, plus extra for deep-frying
Powdered sugar or Chancaca Syrup (p. 278)

In a small saucepan, bring the pumpkin, water, and salt to a boil over high heat. Reduce the heat and simmer covered until fork tender, 20 to 30 minutes. Drain, reserving the cooking liquid. Mash the pumpkin with a fork in a small bowl.

Sift the flour and the baking powder into a bowl. Add the egg yolk, pumpkin, and 2 tablespoons melted lard. Dissolve ½ teaspoon salt in 2 tablespoons of the reserved cooking liquid. Add the flour mixture; stir to combine with a wooden spoon, adding more flour or liquid, until you obtain a soft but smooth dough.

On a lightly floured surface, roll the dough out to a ¼-inch thickness. Cut out rounds using a 2-inch cutter. Prick holes in each round with a fork for even rising. Gather the leftover dough, roll, and cut into rounds.

Preheat the oven to 250F (122C). Line a baking sheet with paper towels.

Heat about 2 inches of lard in a deep skillet or wok to 425F(220C). Fry 2 to 3 fritters, at a time, flipping them over with a slotted spoon, until puffed and golden brown, about 30 seconds on a side. Drain on paper towels and keep warm in the oven. Serve the crispy hot pumpkin fritters sprinkled with powdered sugar or place them in a deep serving platter and drizzle warm Chancaca Syrup over them.

Remember that with all frying the secret lies in keeping a high and steady temperature. Not too hot or the food burns, not too low or the food will be greasy.

Poached Dried Peaches and Puffed Wheat Drink

Mote con Huesillos

Makes 8 servings

The very first time I tasted Mote con Huesillos, I was sitting in a plastic chair under a bright orange awning in the famous handicraft market of Chillán. We were desperately looking for some solace against the burning summer sun. A dark-eyed lady served us tall glasses, filled to the rim with chewy, nutty cooked wheat berries (the mote), poached dried peaches (the huesillos), and plenty of cool juice. An odd drink, but it is tasty and refreshing.

Mote con Huesillos is as Chilean as the *huaso* (the proud horseman), and its preparation can be traced back to the pre-Colombian native populations. Wherever you travel along Route 5, you'll see plenty of signs advertising this drink. I urge you to try one, it's one of the most refreshing, nutritious, and healthiest snacks I have come across in this country.

> 1 pound dried peaches (about 16)
> 1 cup whole wheat berries (see Mote, p. 279), soaked overnight in
>   cold water and drained
> Pinch salt
> 2 cups sugar
> 2 cinnamon sticks
> 2 cloves
> 1 (4-inch) piece orange zest

Place the peaches in a large bowl and cover with 6 cups of hot water. Cover and steep at least 12 hours or overnight.

Bring the wheat berries and 4 cups of salted water to a boil in a medium saucepan over high heat. Reduce the heat and simmer uncovered, stirring occasionally, until the wheat berries are tender, 50 to 60 minutes. Drain, and rinse the wheat berries under cold running water. Set aside to cool.

Transfer the peaches and their liquid to a large saucepan. Add the sugar, cinnamon, cloves, orange zest, and an additional 6 cups of water. Bring to a boil, reduce the heat, and simmer partially covered until the fruit is soft, about 1 hour. Let the peaches cool in the poaching liquid, and refrigerate until ready to serve.

Fill 8 tall glasses with 2 to 3 tablespoons of cooked wheat berries, 2 peach halves, and plenty of the flavorful poaching syrup; give each guest a long spoon.

Variation

Use other dried fruits, such as apricots, prunes, or sour cherries. I have gone against tradition and used poached *fresh* summer fruits—such as plums, peaches, and apricots—along with a little white wine in the poaching liquid. I serve this version with the cooked wheat berries and plenty of cold juice. In southern Chile, locals use dried sour cherries and mote de maíz. (p. 279), which is soothing and refreshing on a hot summer day.

Cane Syrup

Sirup de Chancaca

Makes about 1 cup

In South America, *chancaca*, obtained from the first cooking of the sugarcane, is a relatively unrefined dark sugar and is sold in solid cakes or lumps. From the time sugarcane was introduced by Europeans to the New World, the strong molasses-like flavor of chancaca and its dark caramel color made it a popular ingredient in most of the traditional desserts and pastries.

In the early days sugar, imported from Peru, was scarce and extremely expensive. It was often replaced by the abundant honey or the refined *miel de palma*, a syrup extracted from the Chilean palm tree. The Peruvian chancaca is still prized for its excellence and constitutes the main ingredient in the creation of traditional Peruvian sweets and pastries.

In the United States, I substitute dark brown sugar or molasses; they, just like the original chancaca, pair beautifully with spices like cinnamon, cloves, and fruity zests. The syrup keeps well and lends an exotic twist to pancakes, waffles, French toast, and doughnuts.

> 1 cup dark brown sugar, chancaca, or light unsulfured molasses
> ½ cup granulated sugar
> ¾ cup water
> 1 whole clove
> 1 cinnamon stick or 1 vanilla bean, split lengthwise
> 1 (4-inch) piece of orange or lemon zest

In a small saucepan, combine all the ingredients. Simmer over low heat, stirring frequently, until the sauce becomes syrupy, 15 to 20 minutes. Discard the clove, cinnamon stick, and zest. Syrup can be covered and stored in the refrigerator up 3 months.

Mote

As the name indicates, mote ("grain peeled with ashes") refers to whole wheat kernels (*mote de trigo*) or corn kernels (*mote de maiz*) that have been boiled with wood ashes (lye) until the husks loosen and the kernels swell and turn golden. The mote is then thoroughly washed, boiled, and left to dry in the air before storing. Nowadays, in every street market and supermarket, processed and precooked mote is available.

In the United States, look for whole wheat kernels (for mote de trigo) or dried hominy (for mote de maiz), both are available in most health food stores and specialty gourmet shops. Both need to be soaked overnight before cooking.

In the Chilean countryside, mote is frequently used as a nutritious ingredient in many savory vegetable stews and salads.

Chilean Fruits

Few countries produce such a bounty of extravagant, curious, and old-fashioned fruits as Chile.

The northern third of the country is covered by the Atacama, one of the most arid and hostile deserts of the world. Yet, miraculously, here and there, one can find small green pockets, fertile oases, such as the valley of Pica. This prodigious garden has been cultivated since pre-Colombian times, and relies on ingenious subterranean canals. Pica is known for its wonderful tropical fruits, such as mangoes, guavas, pomelos (a grapefruit-type fruit as big as a football), oranges, and a small, extremely fragrant lime (el limón de Pica).

In El Norte Chico, a touch farther south, the dynamic combination of a subtropical climate and life-giving Andean snowmelt water, produces a wealth of exotic fruits such as papayas, cherimoyas, lúcumas, pineapples, oranges, lemons, pepinos, and prickly pears.

The Central Valley, the area from Los Andes, just eighty kilometers north of the capital to some five-hundred kilometers south, produces the bulk of the out-of-season fresh produce, known in the United States as winter fruit. The fertile soil and mild, almost frost-free climate of this region has made Chile one of the world's important exporters of apples, pears, strawberries, peaches, kiwifruits, plums, quinces, cherries, and apricots.

Exotic Fruits

Cherimoyas (from the Quechua dialect, *chiri* meaning "fresh" and *mayu*, meaning "globe or circumference") are prized as a national treasure in Chile. The fruit grows in the warm valleys north of Santiago. The fragrant and refreshing pearlike, grainy flesh makes the cherimoya (custard apple) an ideal ending to a rich meal. Cherimoyas are studded with shiny black seeds that are easy to remove. Cherimoyas are available in the United States in specialty stores. Choose unblemished fruit. It is more than likely that the cherimoya will be unripe; just leave it a few days to ripen at room temperature until it feels squeezably soft to the touch and a floral scent permeates the skin.

Kiwifruit, egg-shaped fuzzy brown fruits, originated in China but were commercialized on a big scale in New Zealand. Nowadays, kiwifruit is grown successfully in Chile and exported with the other winter fruits to the United States (since our seasons are reversed). Kiwifruit are loaded with vitamin C, store well, and look stunning in fruit salads and fruit tarts.

Lúcuma is a native of the sunny valleys north of Santiago. This oval-shaped fruit with golden flesh has a creamy, pudding-like consistency and a mild flavor suggestive of dates and butterscotch. Lúcuma is usually mashed and pressed through a strainer or sieve and mixed with pastry cream, whipped cream, or manjar and used as a filling for pastries, custards, and layered tarts. It makes the most luxurious ice cream. In Chile, pureed lúcuma is also sold canned and frozen. We can only hope it will be available in the United States one day. In most recipes, black sapote—a tropical fruit grown in Florida and available in specialty stores—can be substituted. Black sapotes have a similar custard-like consistency and flavor. They must be fully ripe and seeded before being mashed.

Murtilla is an indigenous berry grown in the southern regions of Chile. Its juicy flesh tastes like a cross between sour cherries and a granada apple. The murtilla was crowned "the queen of all fruits" by the Spanish conquistadores.

Nísperos (medlars) are small, round orange fruits that look like apricots but have nothing in common flavor-wise. The spicy flesh of the fruit feels hard even when ripe, so medlars are left to rot slightly before being turned into jelly and jam. Medlars are usually found in old-fashioned gardens, and they have become rare in the United States.

Pepinos (melon pears) are handsome pear-shaped fruits with smooth green skins streaked with purple when fully ripe. The juicy flesh tastes like an acidic, perfumed melon. The fruit is often eaten fresh in the same way as melon. They complement any fruit salad, make great juices, and are interesting poached. They are available in the United States in specialty stores and by mail order.

Persimmons (kaqui or maqui in Chile) originated in Asia but are common in Chilean gardens. The bright orange fruits are eye-catching in the fall. They grace the branches long after the leaves have fallen. When unripe, the flesh is cottony and extremely tart, but it ripens to a sweet, slightly gelatinous pulp. Persimmons can be eaten plain, but I love to add them to fruit salads and mousses.

Tunas (prickly pears) are originally native to the American Southwest, but the fruit appears in many Chilean markets. Its pulp is rather bland and studded with seeds; but simmered with sugar, it turns into a gorgeous orange-red purée, ideal for flavoring ices, juices, jams, and custards.

Cherimoya, Chilean Style

Chirimoya Alegre

Makes 4 to 6 servings

This strange, plump round fruit, covered with scalelike green skin, hides the most delicious juicy white pulp.

Chileans like cherimoyas nicely chilled and marinated in orange juice; the juice prevents the flesh from turning dark and lends a complementing tartness. Often soft meringue is piped on top, which I find too sweet to my taste; but a few tablespoons of Grand Marnier added at the end seems to work magic.

If you grew up with the usual apples and pears, as I did in Belgium, and you've never tasted cherimoyas, I urge you to do so. You'll experience an exuberant burst of floral, honeyed flavors, like nothing you've ever tasted before.

1 cup freshly squeezed orange juice
1 tablespoon sugar or to taste
1 large or 2 smaller ripe cherimoyas
2 tablespoons Grand Marnier, or to taste (optional)

Combine orange juice and sugar in a bowl. Peel the cherimoya, cut the flesh into big cubes, and discard the black seeds. Add to the orange juice mixture; stir together gently. Cover and refrigerate up to 2 hours. Before serving, sprinkle the Grand Marnier over the fruit. Spoon the fruit and juice into decorative large glasses or bowls.

Apple and Quince Flan Caramel

Espuma de Manzanas y Membrillo

Makes 6 servings

Let me introduce you to an old-fashioned espuma. Part flan, part soufflé, this airy and fruity dessert is simply delicious. What is the secret ingredient? The hard-to-come-by, but oh-so-heavenly fragrant quince (p. 294). If your quest for quinces is unsuccessful, substitute ripe apricots, a ripe guava, peaches, or even berries. To turn this homey and healthy dessert into a luscious one, serve with a generous portion of Crème Anglaise (p. 258) or a scoop of vanilla ice cream.

4 large apples, peeled, cored, and finely diced
1 quince, peeled, cored, and finely diced
3 to 4 ripe apricots or 1 guava or 2 peaches or $\frac{1}{2}$ cup berries
$\frac{1}{2}$ cup plus 3 tablespoons water
$1\frac{1}{2}$ cups sugar
2 tablespoons butter, at room temperature
1 teaspoon pure vanilla extract
3 eggs, separated
$\frac{1}{2}$ cup plain cookies, crushed to a fine powder with a rolling pin
Pinch salt

Place the apples and quince in a large saucepan with $\frac{1}{2}$ cup of the water; bring to a boil. Reduce the heat and cook covered, stirring occasionally, until the fruit is very soft, 10 to 15 minutes. Add $\frac{1}{4}$ cup of the sugar, and cook, stirring constantly with a wooden spoon, over medium heat to reduce the liquid slightly, about 2 minutes. Set aside.

In a small bowl, whisk the butter with $\frac{1}{4}$ cup of the sugar until fluffy. Add the vanilla, and whisk in the egg yolks, one at a time. Add the cookies. Stir this mixture into the fruit, and combine well. Let cool.

Preheat the oven to 375F (190C).

Meanwhile, to prepare the caramel, combine the remaining 1 cup of sugar and 3 tablespoons of water in a heavy saucepan. Cook over high heat, stirring, until the sugar is dissolved. Cook, without stirring, until the syrup caramelizes and turns a medium-dark amber, about 4 minutes. To stop the cooking, immerse the bottom of the pan immediately into cold water. Divide the caramel quickly among six 1-cup custard cups, or ramekins, swirling the cups to evenly coat the bottoms. Set aside.

Beat the egg whites with the salt in a medium bowl until stiff but not dry.

Add one-third of the beaten egg whites to the fruit mixture and mix well. Gently fold in the remaining whites. Divide the mixture evenly into the caramel-coated cups.

Place the ramekins in a roasting pan and add enough hot water to come halfway up the sides of the pan. Bake in the center of the oven 35 to 40 minutes, or until the custard is set. Remove the ramekins from the water bath and let sit about 15 minutes before unmolding. Serve warm, lukewarm, or chilled.

Poached Summer Fruits

Fruta en Almibar

Makes 4 to 6 servings

*S*low cooking in a flavorful broth brings out the best of many fruits. If you have a surplus of ripe fruit on hand, poaching is the answer and is certainly a clever way of preserving the fruit before it gets overripe and utterly useless.

Where I live, most fruit is sun ripened and best eaten fresh out of hand; but in the bigger cities we also have our share of disappointing peaches, rock-hard plums, and make-believe apricots. Again, poaching them is the best idea I have to offer. If you're using unripe fruit, the cooking time will be longer.

1½ quarts water
3 cups sugar
Juice of 1 lemon or lime
1 cinnamon stick
½ vanilla bean, split lengthwise
4 ripe peaches or nectarines
8 ripe plums
8 ripe apricots

In a large saucepan, bring the water and sugar slowly to a boil, stirring occasionally, over medium heat. Reduce the heat, and add the lemon juice, cinnamon, and vanilla. Simmer 20 minutes. Discard the cinnamon and vanilla.

Drop the peaches and the plums into the poaching liquid, and simmer 5 minutes. Add the apricots, and cook until all the fruit is tender but still holding their shape, 10 to 15 minutes. Allow fruit to cool in the poaching liquid; then transfer to a bowl. Reduce the juice over high heat until syrupy, about 15 minutes. Pour over the poached fruit. Set aside to cool. Cover and refrigerate until ready to serve.

Variation

Poached Papayas
Papayas al Jugo

One of the most popular ways to end a meal in Chile is with a serving of preserved papayas in syrup, with or without a dollop of whipped cream.

The Chilean papaya is smaller, yellower, and more fragrant than the tropical variety. They're excellent for poaching. Chilean papayas grow profusely in El Norte Chico, the sun-drenched valleys around La Serena. But I've come across various sturdy-looking trees farther south along the seaside. In many of the tiny, forgotten villages, the women make a living by preserving the papayas and preparing an aromatic, honeylike syrup called miel de papayas. As always, I was curious and bombarded the women with questions.

This is what they told me: It is best to rinse the ripe papayas thoroughly and soak them a few hours in cold water. They will swell slightly to facilitate peeling, which is usually done with a razor blade, but a sharp paring knife will also do the trick. Halve the papayas, and scoop out the tiny black seeds. Place the seeds and peels in a saucepan, cover with 2 inches of water, and cook 20 minutes. Drain, and measure the juice. Add ½ cup of sugar for each cup of juice. Bring this syrup to a boil. Reduce the heat, add the papayas, and poach over very low heat, 40 to 60 minutes (depending on variety, size, and ripeness). Allow the fruit to cool in the heavy syrup, and refrigerate until ready to serve.

In the United States, look for the small elongated papayas with rosy flesh. Fully ripened, they're best eaten fresh with a sprinkle of lime juice. But to my taste, papayas gain in fragrance (and lose that peculiar taste that turns some people off) by being poached. Use slightly underripe fruit for poaching.

Strawberry, Kiwifruit, and Orange Salad

Ensalada de Frutillas, Kiwi, y Naranjas

Makes 4 servings

Fresh fruit salad combinations are endless, limited only by your imagination. But some fruits seem to be made for each other. The sweet ruby red strawberries, the national pride of the Chileans, and the tart bright green kiwifruit, also a big export product, make a great pair.

> ¼ **cup white dessert wine**
> ¼ **cup sugar**
> **Juice of 1 orange**
> **4 ripe kiwifruits, peeled and thinly sliced**
> **1 pint fresh strawberries, hulled and halved**
> **Fresh mint leaves, garnish**

A few hours before serving, combine the wine and the sugar in a small bowl. Add the orange juice, kiwifruits, and strawberries; stir carefully to combine, and refrigerate. Serve in tall glasses or decorative bowls, and garnish with mint leaves.

Sliced Bananas with Maple Syrup

Plátanos con Miel de Palma

Makes 4 servings

Whenever you're invited to a generous table, like that of my mother-in-law, you'll end the meal with a little dessert. Often it's a simple offering, such as a piece of fresh fruit, but always nicely presented. A popular combination is a sliced banana drizzled with the genuine *miel de palma*, a delicate syrup extracted from the native Chilean palm tree, much in the same manner as maple syrup is produced in the United States.

> **4 ripe bananas**
> **4 tablespoons maple syrup**
> **2 tablespoons finely chopped toasted walnuts (optional)**

Slice the bananas diagonally and arrange on individual plates. Drizzle 1 tablespoon of syrup on top of each banana, and sprinkle with the nuts. Serve at once.

Poached Figs with Walnuts

Higos con Nueces al Almibar

Makes 4 servings

*I*n Chile, most old-fashioned colonial houses are blessed with wonderful back-yards. There you'll find a wealth of old fruit trees such as figs, peaches, per-simmons, quinces, medlars, cherries, and the ubiquitous grapevines for the shady area. Unfortunately, the country's accelerated entry into the modern age, a fran-tic uncontrolled urban growth is encroaching on these miniature Gardens of Eden, which will soon be a nostalgic memory.

In the countryside, however, where I live, we're still resisting progress and are blessed with a prodigious variety of fruits. At harvest time, the kitchen is bustling with activity. Most fruit is dried, stored in alcohol, or preserved—making use of traditional recipes—to brighten the long winter months with sweet treats. Plump poached figs, studded with walnuts, are one of my favorites. In Chile, these sweet treats are often served with a dollop of whipped cream.

> **4 cups water or unsweetened apple juice**
> **2 cups sugar**
> **½ vanilla bean, split lengthwise**
> **16 plump fresh figs**
> **16 walnut halves**

In a large and wide saucepan, bring the water, sugar, and vanilla slowly to a boil over medium heat. Reduce the heat, and simmer 10 minutes.

Using a sharp paring knife, make a small incision in each fig, and push 1 walnut half inside.

Place the figs, stems up, in one layer in the saucepan. Simmer over very low heat until soft but still holding their shape, 45 to 60 minutes. Allow the figs to cool in the poaching liquid. Refrigerate until ready to serve.

About Ruins and Forgotten Gardens

At the end of my little street stand two abandoned houses. They seem to exert a strong attraction to me, because I often find myself prying a way through the thorny blackberry bushes, which have invaded what once was a lovely garden.

I know by now to take a basket with me, as the abandoned garden hides many secrets. On a recent trip in late fall, I came back with the last ripe figs of the season, a bouquet of white roses, and a huge *alcayote*, sort of spaghetti squash that we turned into a sweet jam mixed with walnuts. But a strong, floral vanilla scent led me to the back of the garden where I discovered bright yellow and greenish quinces.

Quince Paste

Dulce de Membrillo

Makes about 1½ pounds

Sweet and fragrant quince paste is a pricey and popular confection in many parts of the world, especially in Hispanic and Latin American countries. It is a traditional companion to soft and hard cheeses.

Quinces are high in natural pectin, which makes them particularly well suited for making jams and jellies. They are widely appreciated for their tart spiciness and intoxicating aroma and perfume. They smell exactly like they taste. Actually, as quinces keep well, I usually let them linger in a bowl on the dining table so they will infuse the whole room with their floral scent.

Preparing quince paste is a true work of love; you will be stirring constantly and patiently for a little bit more than an hour.

3 pounds partly unripe quinces
1 cup sugar for each cup of pureed quinces
½ cup water

Lightly oil an 8 × 4-inch loaf pan with a flavorless oil, such as safflower or almond oil, or line with parchment paper.

Rinse the quinces thoroughly under cold running water. Dry with a towel, and rub the fuzzy layer off the skin. Quarter the quinces, discarding any blemished parts. If you don't have an old-fashioned food mill but do have a blender or food processor, peel and core the quinces, and wrap the peels, stems, and cores in a piece of cheesecloth.

Place the unpeeled, quartered quinces (or peeled fruit with the cheesecloth pouch) in a large saucepan, and cover with about ½ inch of cold water.

Bring to a boil, reduce the heat, and simmer until the fruit is very soft but still holding its shape, 20 to 25 minutes. Drain, and discard the cheesecloth pouch if you have used one. Press the unpeeled quinces through a food mill (the fine mesh will retain the peels and other impurities) or purée the peeled fruit in a blender or food processor.

Measure the purée. For each cup of purée, add 1 cup of sugar. In a large, heavy saucepan, heat the sugar and ½ cup of water, stirring occasionally, over low heat until all the sugar is dissolved. Bring to a boil, and boil, without stirring, about 5 minutes. Remove from the heat and add the quince purée, stirring vigorously to combine. Return to the heat, and cook, stirring constantly, over medium heat until the mixture is thick and the bottom of the pan can be seen when the spoon is drawn across it, 50 to 60 minutes. The longer the mixture is cooked, the denser the paste will be, but be careful not to let the quince paste stick to the bottom and scorch. Transfer the hot quince paste to the prepared pan, and let cool. Leave the paste out at room temperature for a few days to dry, before unmolding and storing it in an airtight container. Slice the fragrant quince paste into thin slices and serve with cheese.

It would be a shame to discard the perfumed poaching liquid. Reduce it by one-third and add sugar to taste. Quince juice is wonderful and refreshing.

Quinces and Figs

Quinces are covered with a fuzzy skin, feel brick hard, and have to be cooked to reveal their hidden beauty. From a grainy-textured, hard-and-tart fruit they turn into a soft, heavenly perfumed delicacy of a glorious rose or gold color when cooked. Being the ancestral companions of apples, quinces added to an ordinary apple compote, a pie filling, or apple jelly, work magic.

In Chile we have two types of quinces: the common and most fragrant *membrillo acido* and the peculiar *membrillo lúcuma*, which is usually peeled and eaten out of hand.

In the United States, the captivating golden quinces have become an oddity, a pricey rarity on an exclusive restaurant menu. Once common in American orchards, quinces fell out of favor in the late 1900s. Now, it is one of the country's least grown fruit trees. You'll have to look in Latino or Korean markets or specialty food stores. Most American-grown quinces come from California and are available from September through November, whereas most of the imported ones are from Chile.

Figs, plump and luscious, are just as hard to come by in the United States. The main reason is that the delicate fruits have to be picked ripe and don't travel well. But thanks to technical improvements in packing and transport, there is still hope. Look for plump, heavy figs and let them ripen at room temperature until soft and yielding to the touch. Fully ripe figs will show cracks in the skin and look bruised. Figs are rich in iron, potassium, magnesium, copper, and phosphorus. They contain a high amount of dietary fiber and lots of calcium.

In the Chilean countryside, fig trees are bathed in an air of mystery and wonder. Not surprisingly, because fig trees bear one to three crops each year. The fruits of the first crop are called brebas in Chile and are usually greenish in color and large. The fruits of next crops are small, purple-brown, and sweet.

Chile's Glorious Fruits of the Vine

Although Chile keeps a low profile on a culinary level, its growing and ambitious viticulture is causing waves on the international fine wine scene. Not surprising, if we consider that Chile benefits from unique natural conditions and a sound experience based on some of the oldest winemaking traditions of the Americas.

Around 1550, Spanish missionaries planted the first vines to make wine for the celebration of Mass—this was done almost two hundred years before vines were planted in California. These were the origins of what is known as the país grape, a tasty and productive black grape closely related to the Californian mission grape and the Argentinian *criolla*. The rustic país is still widely planted and is responsible for the bulk of the domestic table wine.

During colonial times, the vineyards flourished in the exceptional climatic and geographical conditions. They produced too well, according to the Spanish rulers who imposed serious restrictions, fearing competition; but the restrictions were easily forgotten. In the eighteenth century, Chilean wines were exported to Peru and as far as Mexico.

The nineteenth century brought independence and a serious turning point in the country's viticulture. Some visionary, wealthy aristocrats with a thirst for fine French wines brought over an impressive amount of noble vine cuttings from France. We're talking about cabernet sauvignon, cot, merlot, pinot noir, sauvignon, semillon, and riesling—the same varieties that account for Chile's excellent wines today.

In 1877, the first Chilean wines produced from these noble vines were exported to Europe; their producers hoped to conquer the overseas market. And they did; the cabernet sauvignon was on top and gained a fine reputation and won prizes in several European exhibitions.

For the Chileans, the timing couldn't have been better. Shortly thereafter, the dreaded phylloxera beetle nearly destroyed the vineyards in France, Italy, and Germany. The only salvation for the desperate European wine growers was to graft their own vines on the tougher, resistant American stocks.

Chile has been saved from this deadly blight. Its isolation, its natural barriers—the imposing Andes in the east, the Atacama desert in the north, and the Pacific Ocean west—have been effective protectors. Chileans love to boast about being the only country in the world where the original pre-phylloxera clones still exist; it is amazing but true.

During the same difficult times, an important number of French winemakers who were suddenly unemployed emigrated to Chile, that far-off promised wine paradise. The French winemakers introduced new wine-making techniques and built wine cellars. Many of the cellars still exist today and can be visited at some of the most prestigious wineries, which were established during that period. The wineries of Cousiño Macul, Concha y Toro, Santa Rita, Santa Carolina, and others are all located close to the capital.

In the second part of the twentieth century, the Chilean wine industry suffered a long period of stagnation caused by political instability, market isolation, strict government regulations, dated equipment and technology, and the decline of the local market (owing to the ever-rising popularity of beer and soft drinks). Above all there was a growing discrepancy between the local demand for heavy, aged wines with little of the fruit flavor left and an evolving international taste for easy-drinking, fruity, refreshing wines. This culminated in the crisis of the 1970s. Some serious changes were needed.

Spaniard Miguel Torres Carbó, from Bodegas Torres in Spain, is often cited as the trendsetter. In 1978, he invested in a vineyard in the area of Curicó, introducing new machinery and top-of-the-line technology and causing a small revolution in the wine-making industry. He was soon followed by the other Chilean wineries. The rest is history. The 1980s saw a steady revival, which evolved into *the* great wine success story of the late twentieth century.

In 1997, Chile became the third largest exporter of wines to the United States, following France and Italy. Most Chilean wine costs under $10 a bottle. Every year the list of Chilean wines—published by the *Wine Spectator*—that score at least in the 80s (out of 100 for the perfect wine) is growing.

The 1997 annual roundup of Chilean wines published by *The Wine Spectator* was the biggest ever: there were nearly 250 wines, and an impressive sixteen wines qualified as "Best Values." In the European market, they're also a strong value. At the International Wine Challenge in London (June 1998), the Chilean wines distinguished themselves with four gold medals, forty-six silver medals, and ninety-eight bronze medals.

These are the well-earned fruits of an enormous effort. The country has invested heavily in new vineyards; modern equipment; and the know-how of talented local and foreign oenologists, who are the new heroes of the wine scene. Myriad small enterprises are popping up in the Central Valley, the so-called boutique wineries that are dedicated almost exclusively to exportation.

It's hardly surprising that this new Wine El Dorado interests eager foreign investors, who are attracted to the country's exceptional climate, rich lands at good prices, low labor costs, and increasing international demand. Well-known names such as Torres (Spain) and Château Lafitte in Viña Los Vascos have been present for years in Chile and have recently been joined followed by Mondavi (associated with Errazuriz), Agustin Huneeus (Veramonte Wineries in the Casablanca Valley), Kendall Jackson (the Viña Calina line), Beringer (Viña Tarapaca), Grand Marnier (Casa Lapostolle) and Pernod Ricard (Viña Terra Andina). Bruno Prat, owner of Bordeaux's Cos D'Estournel teamed up with Paul Pontallier, winemaker of Château Margaux to create Viña Aquitania. One of the latest joint ventures is between Mouton-Rothschild and Concha y Toro. All are hoping for a piece of Chile's promising wine future.

It seems to me, however, that Chile's wine industry finds itself at the fork of two diverging paths. For the past decades, the country has presented itself on the international market as a source of easy-drinking varietal wines at very reasonable prices. Young, fruity, uncomplicated wines, (mostly Californian-style) that are great with food.

Yet, recently, the quality of several red and white wines has been increasing steadily. Ambitious winemakers are anxious to get rid of the bargain label and are striving hard to take Chilean wines beyond the best buy into the best wine category.

Some hope to create their own unique style of lively, premium-quality wines. While others (especially the established houses and the French-financed wineries) clearly hope to produce distinctive, age-worthy wines that are able to compete with the grand dames of the international wine scene. Consequently, prices are escalating with the improving quality. This is precisely the tricky point.

On the one hand, there is a serious danger of overproduction, pulled by an ever-increasing international demand, that results in one-dimensional wines with little structure and thin fruit—an often heard criticism. But on the other hand, when quality is delivered, there seems to be an even louder outcry (with the wine journalists leading the way) that Chilean wines are becoming too expensive! All too often, consumers abroad expect to pay the lowest prices when they see a Chilean label, when we all know that for that price nobody in the world can afford to produce rich, concentrated wines.

I'm quite confident, though, that the country's unique and wonderful wine potential and the enthusiastic and highly qualified winemakers will continue to amaze and delight the many happy wine drinkers all over the world.

Chile's Recipe for Success

Chile presents a unique situation. The wine-growing area is concentrated mainly in the Central Valley, 250 miles of fertile land wedged between the striking snow-capped Andean Mountains and the cooling Pacific Ocean. Its natural beauty and diversity evokes a cross between the Napa Valley, the Mediterranean countries, and the Garden of Eden.

Owing to its unique physical isolation and a steady, dry climate, most insects, mildew, and rot—real nightmares in other wine-growing regions—are practically nonexistent in Chile. Fewer pesticides are necessary, scoring the Chilean wines among the most organic and ecological in the world.

In Chile, most wine grapevines are growing on their own root stock, whereas in the United States and most European countries grape varieties must be grafted on special disease-resistant North American root stock. So far, Chile has been spared from the dreaded phylloxera beetle; however, various growers are playing it safe by planting resistant root stocks. The question of whether fruit from ungrafted vines produces better-quality wines remains a point of disagreement. But what certainly makes a difference is that ungrafted vines produce three to four times longer than the grafted stock.

The Central Valley stands out for its unique, ideal climate. Winters are mostly frost-free, and the summers are long and dry; and the region that would be a desert by nature is blessed by a valuable source of water, Andean snowmelt, which guarantees a mostly consistent crop. This is true even during the drought years, like 1997. Several winemakers, however, curtail this generously flowing water; vines that suffer produce a higher fruit concentration.

Indeed, vintages in Chile are rather consistent and do not vary dramatically from year to year. It is rather the drastic change in vinification and aging techniques from the past decade that accounts for most of the ever-improving quality of the Chilean wines.

This fascinating country presents one more particularity that's highly welcomed by the winemakers. The eternal snowcap of the Andes and the cold Humboldt current produce dramatic differences in temperature between the hot summer days and the cool nights. This thermal gap results in a slow, gradual maturation, increasing the aromatic potential of the grapes and of most other fruits grown in the area.

But according to Angel Germade Barros, general manager of the Torres wineries in Curicó, Chile's major advantage lies in its soil, *El vino se hace en la tierra y no en la bodega.* ("The wine is made in the soil, not in the wine cellar.") He makes his point by comparing the results the Torres winery obtains in Spain, in California, and in Chile. Contrary to what some might think, it's not a rich soil that produces premium wines but rather poor soil.

To conclude on a general note, you'll all remember the theories concerning the French paradox that made waves in the 1990s. The findings, so happily accepted by wine lovers, proved that a moderate amount of red wine a day reduces the risks of cardiovascular disease. Studies published in 1998 by Dr. Alan Grozier of the University of Glasgow show that of sixty-five red wines tested from all over the world, the highest amounts of flavonoids (an important antioxidant) were present in the Chilean cabernet sauvignons.

The Principle Wine Regions

Regional characters are only slowly emerging. In Chile, most wines are still blends of grapes from different regions. The different valleys that encompass the whole of the wine-growing area, are made up of unique and specific microclimates and soil. In recent years, local winemakers have been making a serious effort to plant varieties in suitable areas and to develop vineyards that reflect the specific qualities of the site, resulting in better-quality of the wines.

In 1996, a new appellation law was enforced in Chile. Its purpose is to establish viticultural zones and set norms for its uses, regulating label descriptions as strictly as California does. In Chile, however, the provenance is certainly not a guarantee for quality, the winery is the determining factor. There are three major wine-growing regions: the Aconcagua Region, the Central Valley, and the Southern Region; each is divided into subregions.

REGION	SUBREGION	ZONE
Aconcagua	Aconcagua Valley	
	Casablanca Valley	
Central Valley	Maipo Valley	
	Rapel Valley	Cachapoal Valley
		Colchagua Valley
	Curicó Valley	Teno Valley
		Lontué Valley
	Maule Valley	Claro Valley
		Loncomilla Valley
		Tutuven Valley
Southern	Itata Valley	
	Bio-Bio Valley	

The highest concentration of vineyards is found in the Maule Valley (30 percent), followed by Curicó (17.5 percent), Rapel (16.2 percent), and Maipo (8.9 percent).

The Maipo Valley has the oldest viticultural tradition in the country and has proven to be extremely suitable for producing cabernet sauvignon. Some of the most remarkable cabernets are made by Cousiño-Macul, Concha y Toro, Viña Santa Rita, Santa Carolina, Viña Aquitania (labeled Domaine Paul Bruno), Viña Undurraga, Canepa, Tarapaca, Carmen, and Caliterra.

But let's not forget the other beautiful cabernets: Errazuriz Panquehue from the Aconcagua Valley; Los Vascos, Montgras, and Viu Manent in Colchagua; Casa Donoso, Viña Segú Ollé Maule; Casa Lapostolle in Rapel; Montes, Echeverria, Veramonte, and Viña Torres in the Curicó Region; Viña Calina, Terra Andina, and Bel Arbor in the Central Valley; and Stonelake in Lontué. This list is incomplete and grows every year (based on the *Wine Spectator* and *Decanter*).

The latest newcomer on the scene is the emerging Casablanca Valley, located on the coastal plain and clearly influenced by a cool maritime breeze that tempers thermal conditions. Whereas years ago nobody would ever have considered planting vines in this region, Californian, French, and domestic wineries are pushing to explore this new potential.

The Casablanca Valley is now one of the country's most promising areas for white grapes, and some extraordinary chardonnays and sauvignon blancs are being produced. Most of these vineyards are owned by Concha y Toro, Viña Carmen, California's Franciscan Winery, Viña Casablanca, Caliterra, Veramonte, Casa Lapostolle, Errazuriz, and Santa Rita.

The south is home to most of Chile's newest estate bottlers, such as Viña Porta and Terranoble.

The Style of the Chilean Wines

The tiny raisin seeds that the Spanish conquistadores brought from the Canary Islands or Spain and dropped in the Chilean fertile soil were the forebears of the robust país grapes. This variety still accounts for most of Chile's present-day production of local table wine.

However, the noble vine cuttings that Don Silvestre Ochagavia and some of his friends brought back from Bordeaux in 1850 were responsible for today's successful Chilean wines.

In the past twenty years the style of wine-making has changed dramatically in Chile. For years, the Chileans themselves favored heavy, full-bodied red wines mostly aged in casks of raulí, an indigenous redwood that imparted an odd, sometimes off-putting flavor to the wine, hopelessly masking its natural fruit. However, the expanding export market was pleading for lighter, fruitier, fresher, unblended wines (varietals), en vogue in the United States and in Europe.

Adapting to international demand meant heavy investments in new equipment, stainless-steel fermentation tanks, and small wooden casks, made out of French or American oak to replace the raulí.

But while the move away from the traditional Chilean style is accelerating, there seems to be no agreement on which road to take. Some winemakers clearly go for the young, fruity, easy drinking (California-style), and moderately priced varietals, targeting their biggest client, the United States. The more traditional French-inspired wineries are marketing more assertive, somewhat austere wines with more complexity for aging. These are wines for the serious wine drinkers, who are willing to pay extra for better quality.

Many wineries play it safe by producing two types of wine. A perfect example is the biggest winery in Chile, Viña Concha y Toro (including the Walnut Crest brand), responsible for more than 50 percent of all of Chile's wine export to the United States. They produce a classic, top cabernet sauvignon, Don Melchor (the first Chilean wine scoring ninety-one points out of one hundred on the *Wine Spectator* list for its 1993 vintage), while successfully launching a new line of fruity varietals under the name Trio.

The Reds

Cabernet sauvignon grapes account for 47 percent of the total acres of noble grape varieties planted in Chile. This variety has always brought the highest prices among Chilean wines, and still does. Chilean cabernets are elegant wines of delicacy and harmony. These qualities are even more highlighted in the *reservas* and *gran reservas,* wines with mellowed tannin and a deep, earthy complexity. Cabernet sauvignon winemakers place strict oak and bottle aging requirements on their wines. For a list of some of the wineries producing cabernet sauvignon, see page 302.

Generally speaking, the vast majority of the Chilean wines are not made for aging, but are made to drink young. They are soft, fruity wines that are medium bodied with balanced tannins. The premium cabernet sauvignons are the exception to the rule. The winemakers generally recommend an aging period of six to seven years.

Merlot accounts for 10.3 percent of the vines. Although not new in Chile's vineyards, merlot only recently emerged as Chile's potential varietal trump card. It proved to be a strong value on the European market and following the recent merlot-mania it is also popular in the United States. In 1997, merlot accounted for most of the new vineyards. Bursting with color and clearly defined fruit, these easy-drinking wines complement many of the dishes from the colorful international array that defines today's gastronomy. The wine's attraction lies in its opulence of fruit. The merlots are at their best young and even served slightly chilled. The oak-aged merlots have potential for improving with age.

Some excellent merlots come from the Maipo Valley (Cousiño-Macul, Viña Gracia, Santa Rita, Tarapaca, Santa Carolina, Alameda, La Playa), the Cachapoal Valley (Viña La Rosa, Viña Porta, Villard), the Aconcagua Valley (Errazuriz), the Colchagua Valley (Undurraga, Montgras, Santa Amelia), Valle Central (Carmen), the Rapel Valley (Andes Peaks, Concha y Toro, ConoSur, Montgras, Walnut Crest, Marques de Concha y Toro, Carmen, and Casa Lapostolle), the Valley of Curicó (Montes Alpha from Discover Wine, Canepa, Caliterra), the Casablanca Valley (Veramonte), Lontué (Viña Valdivieso and Stonelake) and from the clay-rich soils around Talca and Linares, Viña Calina, Casa Donoso, River Falls, Viña Santa Carolina, and Carta Vieja (the Maule Valley). Again this list is growing. A few more exotic varietals show promise, Malbec (or Malbecki, or Cot, one of the lesser known red wine grapes of Bordeaux), seldom produced unblended, is making some interesting varietals in Chile. The same is true for the latest releases of pinot noir (from Valdivieso), syrah (1995, from Errazuriz), and petit syrah (1995 from Carmen).

The Whites

For long, Chile has been struggling with the production of white wines. They certainly needed the strongest reorientation and the heaviest investments of the entire wine business. New computerized grape presses, stainless steel tanks in which the temperatures of the fermenting juice can be rigidly controlled, and experienced oenologists, who are concentrating on freshness and fruitiness, were required.

All too often Chilean restaurants open bottles of white wines that were stacked for far too long in the cellars, resulting in wines that taste oxidized and overpowering without any fruit flavor. The best advice I can give you is to ask for the youngest whites. The chances are good that you'll enjoy a beautiful, crisp clean white wine brimming with fruit, as the quality is improving steadily.

Sauvignon blanc grapes arrived in the nineteenth century, with the cabernet grapes, but were traditionally blended with semillon (as in Bordeaux) and aged in oak until the fruitiness disappeared. The winemakers also discovered that much of the sauvignon blanc grapes growing in Chile were of an inferior clone (known as sauvignon vert or *sauvignonasse*), which accounted for the rather dull, herbal flavors in the wine.

It was the Spanish winemaker, Miguel Torres, who introduced cold fermentation techniques in 1979. His new wines, which set the tone for the beautiful sauvignon blancs, are slowly on their way to becoming a bestselling white wine.

An interesting wine is the late-harvest sauvignon or semillon, a sweet, lush wine that tastes almost like an herb- and-fruit-infused liqueur; it makes a wonderful aperitif. The cool Casablanca Valley proved to be an ideal area where the sauvignon grapes feel right at home. But it's certainly not the only place. Look for sauvignon blancs released by Viña Casablanca, Viña Miguel Torres, Castillo del Rio, Torreon de Paredes, Viu Manent, Santa Ines, Carmen, Concha y Toro, Echeverria, Alameda, Errazuriz, Montes, Los Vascos, and Caliterra. The list continues to grow.

Chardonnay grapes, relative newcomers on the scene, caused a true revolution. The number of Chardonnay grape vineyards has increased by a surprising 1,697 percent (followed by chenin blanc at 489 percent). This increase is largely in response to increasing international demand.

Mostly thanks to the pioneering efforts in the Casablanca Valley, the Chilean chardonnay is showing a steady growth, resulting in a variety of wines offering balanced fruit and sweet oak.

Look for Bel Arbor (Central Valley), Canepa, Luis Felipe Edwards (Colchagua), Alameda, Carmen, Viña Tarapaca, Santa Carolina, and Undurraga (Maipo Valley), Caliterra and Errazuriz (Maipo Valley), Canepa, Santa Monica (Rancagua), Torreon de Paredes, Casa Lapostolle, Veramonte, Santa Rita, and Concha y Toro (Casablanca Valley) as well as new releases from other vineyards.

Other white varietals, such as riesling, fume blanc, moscatel, and gewurzstraminer, seem to be still on tentative grounds in Chile.

In Conclusion

There isn't a higher compliment paid to a marvelous meal than to pour and share a glorious wine. Wine, evoking the symbolic communion of bread and wine, is inducive to great conversation. The glorious fruits of the vine are a beautiful gift that Chile has to offer to the world. What sets these wines apart is the opulence of fruit and their mostly high quality.

I can only give you one piece of advice: Go out there, buy a few bottles of Chilean wine, invite some friends, and taste, compare, criticize, and enjoy. There is a whole price range to choose from. You will find plenty of "best values," wines rich and vibrant with fruit, at attractive prices that match beautifully with food, the ideal wine for everyday drinking.

For special occasions choose some of the more complex, sophisticated wines such as aged reds or supple and balanced whites produced by those with experience and tradition on their side. Many newly planted vineyards are maturing, and the right combination of climate and technology is slowly achieving world-class wines. Chile seems to be on the right track; it's definitely a fascinating and exiting scene.

At home, in Chile, wine connoisseurs and amateurs alike can hardly follow the culminating boom of the international market. Santiago, a city of five million people, has only two important wine shops, The Wine House and La Viñoteca, a great place to sample an interesting variety of Chilean wines, sold by the glass. Slowly, the supermarkets are expanding their wine shelves and taking wine classes seems to be the "in" thing to do.

Let's not forget that *en la Viña del Señor* as the Chileans love to call their blessed country, a lot has changed in a relatively short period of time. The better wines are entirely destined for export. Wine tourism is still rudimentary, but many wineries are opening their doors to the public. The ideal way to get your Chilean wine education started is to participate in one of the wine tours. Ruta del Viño del Valle de Colchagua in Santa Cruz offers a tour to six wineries in the Colchagua Valley. For more information call: 72-823199. Or contact Virginia Fuenzalida at Wines of Chile: 2-335-7250.

Mail-Order Sources

General Sources

Balducci's (warehouse)
11-02 Queens Plaza South
Long Island City, NY 11101-4908
800-225-3822

Balducci's (store)
424 Sixth Avenue
New York, NY 10011-8425
212-673-2600

Dean & Deluca
560 Broadway
New York, NY 10012
800-221-7714 (in New York:
212-431-1619)

Rafal Spice Company
2521 Russell Street
Detroit, MI 48207
800-228-4276 (in Michigan:
313-259-6373)

G. B. Ratto International Grocers
821 Washington Street
Oakland, CA 94607
800-325-3483 (in California:
800-228-3515)

Mexican and Latin American Ingredients

Algo Especial
2493 Bagley Street
Detroit, MI 48216
313-237-0295

La Casa del Pueblo
1810 South Blue Island
Chicago, IL 60608
312-421-4640

The Grand Central Market
317 South Broadway
Los Angeles, CA 90013
213-622-1763

Hernandez Mexican Foods
2120 Alamo Street
Dallas, TX 75202
214-742-2533

La Preferida
3400 West Thirty-fifth Street
Chicago, IL 60632
312-254-7200

Wheat Berries

Dean & Deluca
560 Broadway
New York, NY 10012
800-221-7714 (in New York:
212-431-1619)

Oak Grove Mills
266 Oak Grove Road
Pittstown, NJ 08867
908-782-9618

Chilean Dried Mushrooms

G. B. International Grocers
Oakland, CA 94607
800-325-3483 (in California:
800-228-3515)

Spanish Recipe Index

Index